FOLK ART OF RURAL PENNSYLVANIA

FRANCES LICHTEN

FOLK ART
OF
RURAL PENNSYLVANIA

CHARLES SCRIBNER'S SONS

NEW YORK

Acknowledgments for Title Page Illustrations

Slipware Plate and Handled Mug: Philadelphia Museum of Art

Saffron Box and Butter Mold: Philadelphia Museum of Art, Titus C. Geesey Collection

Photograph of Slipware Plate courtesy, National Gallery of Art, Index of American Design

PREFACE

WITH a cursory gesture, it is possible to divide the world into two classes: the "savers" and the "throwers-away." From the motivations of the "savers" results the world of "antiques." From the "throwers-away," with their steady demand for replacements and their love of the "new," comes the impetus that keeps the wheels of the business world rolling. The instinct of thrift, prime mover of the "savers," saw a possible future use for every discarded article, and filled attics, sheds, barns, and closets with the sturdy handmade articles of years long past. Such objects, made of honest materials and built for long service, survived displacement and the rudeness of time. They are now "antiques" for which collectors clamor, and subject matter for books—a possibility never imagined by the men and women who fashioned them.

But in fairness to that complex called human nature, it must be admitted that several other less worthy characteristics also brought accessions to the world of "antiques." Though shiftlessness, sentimentality, and laziness may be negative traits, the end-product of their operation is the survival of the handwork of our forebears.

This folk material, ignored for the most part until recently, has been worthy of the study given to it, for it quietly teaches the beauty inherent in sound craftsmanship and stresses the virtues that were needed for its fashioning—patience and application, two things which we of the machine world are prone to overlook. Unlike articles turned out by the machine, whose monotony and perfection are quickly satiating to the eye, handmade objects are replete with infinite subtle variations of color, form, texture, and the inimitable patinas of time and use. These elements make for a constant stimulus to æsthetic perception—a pleasure of the artist as well as of the collector.

Before I became aware that the early Pennsylvania German settlers of my own State had followed for a long period, in this new land, the traditions and crafts of the countries from which they had emigrated, I maintained a leisurely interest in the folk arts of European cultures. When it became possible to study local folk art in the collections which were being assembled here, my interest became a lively one. For the work of the early

v

Pennsylvania artisans contained in such collections did more than demonstrate the endurance of sound workmanship; it displayed a distinctive ornamentation which offered a fresh source of inspiration to contemporary craftsmen and designers. I began to collect this decorative material, often from dim and timeworn surfaces.

This book does not pretend to be an exhaustive treatise on the subject of Pennsylvania German folk art. The field is too wide for that, too replete with individual interpretations of the preferred motifs. The area of this book is voluntarily restricted by my own interest in and practice of the applied decorative arts; I hope that it is enriched by a love of the picturesqueness of the long-established Pennsylvania German countryside, and by a deep appreciation of all its ways.

With one of those ways, the thriftiness earlier mentioned, I am equally imbued. Indeed, the book was made possible only because, as a "saver," I hesitated to discard a rather well-used collection of drawings and a mass of notes which accumulated as a research by-product. They were acquired when I was acting as the State Supervisor of the Pennsylvania Index of American Design (one of the Federal Art Projects, now permanently housed in the National Gallery of Art, Washington, D. C.). Moreover, an irrepressible tendency to analyze and synthesize acted as a stronger agent for its cohesion than did a good-housekeeping instinct towards its dispersal or destruction.

Since the "antique" business is today such an important one, there is a lively traffic in the items in which it deals, and they are subject to much shifting about. Unless they are immobilized by museum ownership, they move from collector to dealer to collector, as changes in taste or as necessity and death decree. If the credit lines accompanying each object illustrated do not reflect its contemporary owner, it is because of this mobility. They serve only as an indication of the source from which the particular illustrative material was obtained.

The publishers join me in thanking the various museums, private collectors, and artists who generously furnished illustrative material. Gratitude is due Mr. J. F. Magee, Jr. for certain Pennsylvania German watermarks from his important collection; Professor William K. Prentice of Princeton, N. J., for rhymed translations of the Pennsylvania German inscriptions on the early ceramics; Mr. Elmer Anderson, Mr. Elmer Kottcamp, and Mr. George W. Schultz for photographic material; Miss Mabel Zahn of Charles Sessler, Philadelphia, for access to new fields of fractur; Miss Marjorie Lyons of the Philadelphia Museum and Miss Euretta Rank of the Philadelphia City Institute, librarians both, for perennial courtesies; The Macmillan Company for permission to quote, on page 151, from *Home Life in Colonial Days*, by Alice Morse Earle; The Primavera Press for the use of material, on pages 138-139, from *Peter Kalm's Travels in North America*, by Adolph Benson; the Yale University Press for the extract on page 169 from Margaret Van Horn Dwight's *A Journey to Ohio in* 1810, edited by Max Farrand. I wish to thank Mr. Macgill James, Assistant Director of the National Gallery of Art, who made available the collections of the Index of American Design, that invaluable record of the early arts and crafts of this country, pictured by many artists whose individuality is submerged in its vast anonymity. To them I am grateful.

Nor am I forgetful of the mostly unknown, and certainly unsung, Pennsylvania German artisans, whose devoted interest to the work at hand resulted in the folk art pictured here. Without a matching devotion on the part of the Art Director, Mr. Atkinson Dymock, who brings to his many-faceted profession an equal love of work and thoroughness, this book would not have been possible.

F. M. L.

CONTENTS

ix

LIST OF ILLUSTRATIONS

xiii

COLOR SECTION

Frontispieces to the various chapters (printed without caption or credit):

Facing page 1: Fractur drawing. Courtesy, Metropolitan Museum of Art.
Facing page 9: From sgraffito plate. Courtesy, Philadelphia Museum of Art.
Facing page 47: From fractur drawing. Courtesy, Paul M. Auman, Millheim, Pa.
Facing page 61: From sgraffito plate. Courtesy, Philadelphia Museum of Art.
Facing page 75: From fractur drawing. Courtesy, Charles Sessler, Philadelphia, Pa.
Facing page 81: From birth certificate. c. 1760. Courtesy, Archives Division, Pennsylvania Historical and Museum Commission, Harrisburg, Pa.
Facing page 123: From wood block. Birth certificate.
Facing page 135: From religious text. Courtesy, Paul M. Auman, Millheim, Pa.
Facing page 149: From sgraffito plate. Courtesy, Philadelphia Museum of Art.
Facing page 167: From painting book of Maria Heebner, c. 1840. Courtesy, Mrs. Norman A. Anders, Towamericin Township, Montgomery Co., Pa.
Facing page 183: From sgraffito plate. Courtesy, Philadelphia Museum of Art.
Facing page 191: From birth certificate. Courtesy, Archives Division, Pennsylvania Historical and Museum Commission, Harrisburg, Pa.
Facing page 225: Fractur drawing by Rev. Young. Courtesy, Paul M. Auman, Millheim, Pa.

Tailpieces:

Page 54: Tile-roofed house, called "The Weaver's House," Germantown, Pa., still standing in 1870.
Page 68: Woolen weaver's factory.
Page 129: Birthplace of David Rittenhouse, adjoining the site of the first paper mill in America.

FOLK ART OF RURAL PENNSYLVANIA

THE HISTORIC SOIL

THE study of the folk and their homely arts, an inquiry now world-wide, was at first the concern only of the ethnologically-minded. The common folk had accepted themselves and their productions unquestioningly, placidly, and incuriously. Cultures previous to the French Revolution had shown no interest whatever in the folk. The professional artist painted kings and court beauties; the professional writer recorded court scandals. After the French Revolution, a strong interest in folklore developed everywhere, spurred on as well by the Romantic Tradition. But the awareness of the artistic productions of the common man is of very recent growth.

The art of the people can flourish only in communities long settled and well established. In such localities, all over the world, the common man learned that he could satisfy his deep-seated longing for decorative interest through the medium of his objects of daily use. On demand, he or his neighbor, the craftsman, could produce them, made and decorated in traditional fashion. The patronage of the gentry was not necessary.

The great political and religious upheavals in eighteenth-century Europe, however, scattered many varying ethnic groups into other accessible parts of the world, and the folk art tradition received a blow from which it was able to recover only if the new surroundings were conducive to its survival. Even then, the transplanted folk art was somewhat altered by necessity and environmental pressure.

Southeastern Pennsylvania, a region early settled by many emigrants from various sections of Europe, presented a soil favorable for the continuance of many Old-World traditions. But Pennsylvania, showing a disposition to leave the writing of its history to its neighbors, both to the north and to the south, remained inarticulate, notably about a large section of its population, the Pennsylvania Germans. Smarting under the general indifference to the achievements of their racial group, certain historians and ethnologists among them began to record their history and their cultural contributions, matter heretofore ignored by the other historians. It was an odd state of affairs, for the Pennsylvania Germans had been here for over two hundred years. This large, successful group of transplanted Europeans had struck firm roots into the best farming soil in the State, transforming their sections into some of the most flourishing farm lands in the country.

1

The Pennsylvania German historians performed a much needed service, bringing out a quantity of valuable historical, genealogical, and ethnological material. But, like historians in general, they tended to overlook the arts and the sciences, and so they made no mention of the existence of the artistic folk objects once produced by the early farmer-craftsmen.

Among contemporaries of the historians, however, a process of discovery was now under way. A collector or two, and notably a certain museum curator, occasionally would come across an object whose provenance was not immediately identifiable. The effort to "place" these articles, and the resultant disclosures, revealed the fact that there had been a flourishing art of the common man, practiced quietly and unobtrusively over a long period of time by these strangely unknown folk and unsung craftsmen, the Pennsylvania German farmers and artisans.

In the third decade of the twentieth century, when the fever for collecting antiques attacked the layman, astute dealers saw the financial possibilities of collecting and selling "that dumb furniture" of the Pennsylvania German, a kind of merchandise hitherto without market value. The pendulum of taste had swung in its favor. To these dealers, no longer able to find good specimens of Georgian and American Colonial furniture demanded by collectors of the choice, this new field seemed a gift from heaven. Old barns and chicken-houses disgorged it. The countryside was full of the stuff.

Now that the automobile made it feasible to maintain country homes, city dwellers bought and remodelled substantial farmhouses, old dilapidated tenant houses, even abandoned old stone barns. These back-to-the-landers soon found out that a delicate Georgian or Colonial piece of furniture could not be made to harmonize with the honest, peasant-like directness and simple construction of the Pennsylvania German or English type of farmhouse. Only the sort of furnishings that once had filled it seemed at home in it.

Thus began the search for appropriate household gear, and the discovery by the general public of the folk objects produced and used by the Pennsylvania Germans. Outstanding among these objects are the decorated ceramics, the earliest, largest, and most important collection of which is owned by the Philadelphia Museum. This group was assembled in 1891-1892 by the late Dr. Edwin Atlee Barber, the museum curator referred to earlier.

As the interest in the art of the common man grew all over the world, more scholars and museums began to take a share in it. The museums set up exhibitions of historically important interiors, vying with each other in acquiring outstanding examples. From the "House of the Miller of Millbach," in Lebanon County, Pennsylvania, the Philadelphia Museum procured two rooms, the "great hall," or family living room and kitchen, and a bedroom. These are unique examples of eighteenth-century Pennsylvania German housing.

In these impressive, oak-panelled interiors are installed furniture, cooking utensils, and all the objects of daily life likely to have been used by the rooms' original occupants. One receives a sharp, æsthetic shock on entering, however, for these are peasant rooms, and

2

they are set in a long line of American and Georgian interiors full of the utmost grace and the elegant craftsmanship of their periods. When I was making a close study of the wonderful Pennsylvania German ceramic collection, a portion of which is displayed in the "great hall," I found these rooms a pleasant background for work, pervaded as they are by that dreamy stillness which fills any museum during a week-day, a hush broken only by the footsteps of an occasional visitor.

After a while, even one who is absorbed in study realizes that the breathless, waiting quiet of this room is not natural. There is no family activity in the kitchen. The table lacks the litter of garden truck, casually deposited there. There is no cheeping of small chicks, kept warm by the fireplace. The real logs in the fireplace do not splutter or crackle. Despite the patina of age, the result of generations of handling, the room needs life.

Suddenly this silence is broken. Clacking, bustling sounds echo through the long line of Georgian interiors into the quiet Pennsylvania German rooms. The noise comes nearer. A pleasant young teacher is coping with a charming group of small children, very much alive. She collects them, they disperse; she collects them again, and shoos them through one door after another, until they come to a standstill around her in the great kitchen. Immediately the room itself comes alive. It is furnished now with the bustle that had been missing.

Before the enormous fireplace, the teacher takes her stand. These rooms, and not the Georgian interiors, are what she has brought the children to see. But they are rooms utterly unlike anything within their small range of experience. She points out all the unfamiliar objects, the iron cooking pots on the crane, the strange forks and utensils hanging from the carved beam which makes the shelf over the ten-foot fireplace opening; the curious iron objects which are set around the logs and andirons. "These are all handmade," she says.

The five- and six-year-olds look at her uncomprehendingly, politely, silently.

Enthusiastically the teacher points out two decorated dower chests, an old cradle, the oaken panelled walls, the heavily moulded door trims. "These are all made by hand, children," she continues with no lessening of vibrancy in her voice. The infants still are silent. Finally a thoughtful five-year-old, after long pondering, says, "Miss Johnson, where did they get all the clay?" For the moment she looks nonplussed. I smile sympathetically, following the child's perfectly logical train of thought. In his school, clay is the only plastic raw material with which he has had any experience. Clay is what you make things out of. Ergo!

Patiently the young teacher tries to explain the difference between wood and iron and clay. But when the flicker of the electrical contrivance which simulates a low flame in the fireplace catches the children's interest, I elicit from her the admission that hardly needs to be made.

For it is obvious that it is almost impossible to make the handcraft era of America's historical development intelligible to children of the average, well-to-do families of the present day. These children have no opportunity to see any necessary trade or craft carried out in their homes. The raw materials from which life was made and out of which this great kitchen was fashioned are incomprehensible to them. A child less well situated financially has the fun and good fortune to see his father at his basement work-table, repairing a broken chair, turning out a set of shelves, making window screens. The child is given a piece of wood, some nails, and a hammer. If he has any mechanical bent, it develops early.

The production of food, our basic necessity, is entirely separated from the life of the well-to-do child of our machine age. Food comes in cans or frozen lumps; it is purchased in bags at the green-grocer's. The pre-machine-age child knew something of agricultural processes. In all Pennsylvania German towns, even those of large size, a vegetable patch occupied a portion of the back yard; it was of more importance in the family economy than unlimited play-space for a child. If a child showed any interest, however, he could have his own tiny patch, where he could poke the seeds in and watch them grow. He helped gather fruit; he picked berries, and knew something of the tedious work of preservation and storage. The home vegetable garden of the Pennsylvania German family has in fact persisted up to the present day, surviving the introduction of processed foods.

Nowadays all clothing can be purchased, with the result that the whole field of the manufacturing of textiles and their transformation into clothing, once such a necessary part of the farm or home economy, becomes only a subject for abstract study. In days not so far removed, when home sewing was general, small girls became needlewomen by imitation and precept. True, it was difficult to learn to wear a thimble, but it was worth while trying in order to be permitted to handle a pair of scissors on the scraps which were doled out as the raw material for a doll's dress. The infant needlewoman learned the lesson that the refractory tools and material taught her.

All these folk habits, once an inescapable demand of pioneer or folk living, have been practically wiped out by modern inventions and machinery. Having in consequence much leisure on our hands, we nowadays evince a pathetic and nostalgic interest in the ways of our forefathers. A large portion of educational procedures is devoted to the study of the painfully hard-working practices of our ancestors. Numerous adult groups crave and receive education in the handcraft arts. Women's magazines are filled with articles on the old-time crafts and their methods, and even with patterns for carrying them out. The present-day amateur craft worker, entranced with his discovery of the world of raw materials, is apt to be uncritical of the quality of his achievements.

The centuries-old tradition of craft work, which presupposes a long apprenticeship training, was broken about 1850, when, all over the world, folk art began to die out, killed by the invention of machinery. Any handmade dish of today represents only a kind of useful play, something entirely divorced from the stark necessity which once created the demand for a sturdy dish to hold one's food, along with the need of a chair on which to sit, and of an enduring iron tool with which to work—objects of daily use made by folk who knew no other way of life.

For over 250 years the hands of men and women and children labored successfully to make of this country, particularly the Pennsylvania German section of Pennsylvania, a land where, as a seventeenth-century Englishman expressed it, "the poor could improve their condition so much that they could live without begging or stealing." Opportunity had come to these sober, God-fearing people through the good offices of another equally God-fearing and peace-loving man, an unobtrusive Englishman named William Penn.

The world war of the seventeenth century, usually called the Thirty Years' War, had laid whole sections of Europe in ruins. This religious war between the two great confessions, the Catholic and the Protestant, had drawn in all the important European states; it was eventually settled by the Peace of Westphalia, and a state of toleration was agreed on among the major faiths, Catholic, Lutheran, Reformed, and Calvinist. Up to that time, a ruler's subjects had been forced to share his religious beliefs, at least outwardly, but for several centuries an underground river of dissatisfaction with formalized religion had flowed from country to country. The intense suffering caused by the recurring religious and political wars destroyed many men's beliefs in the established Church and in the word of princes. From the cheerlessness of dogmatic theology they turned to the ecstasies of religious emotion. Religion was brought "from the head to the heart," and the great pietistic movement in Germany was born.

In England at about the same time a new ideal sprang up in men's hearts. There too, men were weary of strife and apprehensive of the future; many of them looked to emigration as the only relief from political and religious struggle. To William Penn, the quiet Englishman, the other side of the Atlantic seemed to offer a bright future; in that far-off land he envisioned a peaceful asylum, not only for his fellow members in the Society of Friends, but for the oppressed and persecuted of every country. For this asylum he required land. King Charles II, who had neither money nor credit but plenty of territory, owed Penn's father a large sum of money which he had no means of paying. To cancel the debt, Penn accepted a great tract of land in America.

Needing colonists in addition to his Quaker associates, William Penn visited the Rhineland in 1671. The fervor of the great pietistic movement was at its height, and his talks found willing listeners among the wretched and suffering Protestant inhabitants of this once prosperous country. To those whose only hope seemed to lie in the life beyond the grave he offered a new haven on earth. Penn promised them a peaceful home, freedom of conscience and toleration of all religious denominations, good land, and fair dealing. After the first settlement of English Quakers on his new land had been made, certain Germans, imbued now with the vision of what was really "the promised land," began to collect in companies and gravely to acquire the necessary gear for the long and dangerous journey.

Encouraged by Penn and the land companies he had organized, they thus uprooted themselves from their tragic country and sailed down the Rhine to Rotterdam and thence to England, where they finally boarded what might be called the Pennsylvania German "Mayflower," with their Bibles in their hands and their hearts filled with prayer. Francis Daniel Pastorius, a scholarly man disgusted with the vanities and frivolities of European life, led this first little party to Penn's city, "The City of Brotherly Love." There they founded Germantown, a suburb of Philadelphia which, though long since incorporated in the city, still retains a certain individuality.

In contrast to the peace and contentment that these brave emigrants found in the new province of Pennsylvania was the state of the poor folk left behind in their homeland. Religious and political wars broke out again and again. Under a wise and kindly ruler, the Palatinate would be brought back to health after a period of many years' hard work, only to be burned or devastated anew at the order of some ruler or princeling. For this is the region where all the Great Wars take place, this country along the Rhine.

The dreadful, monotonous tale of misery goes on. Again all classes of citizens were plundered, fields ravaged, houses, churches, and even bake-ovens destroyed. As happens in all wars, the cattle were removed; the desperate inhabitants were reduced to hiding in the woods, degraded and despairing. But enthusiastic letters from the new country again brought hope to weary Europeans, and stimulated by Penn and his agents, a steady stream of Swiss and Germans poured into Pennsylvania. This emigration, which had begun in 1683, continued until the American Revolution.

These settlers were devout, simple, honest folk, prepared for hardship and used to work. Many of them were extremely poor. Unlike other classes of immigrants whose reasons for emigrating were often dubious, they came here with the strong purpose of establishing a permanent home. They knew good land, and saw to it that they acquired it in their purchases. So astute were they that all the best farm land in eastern Pennsylvania is now in the hands of the Pennsylvania German farmers, some of it still held by descendants of the original settlers.

In the Pennsylvania German mind, work and thrift, if not tenets of religion, were next things to it. Given this ability to labor and the knowledge of good farming practices, nothing was too much trouble, no day too long. Everyone worked, for the land and the land alone must support them. There were no dread overlords; the spiritual conditions were peaceful; the raw materials were here in abundance, and out of these raw materials they fashioned their lives, loving the earth. And the earth repaid them.

He planned for the future, this Pennsylvania German farmer. At first he lived in a simple log hut; he made a garden, built a milk-house, a spring-house, a smoke-house, and a great barn to house his ever increasing stock. When, after many years, he had enough money and the opportunity to do so, he built himself a substantial dwelling-house. Solidly established now on the land, with his churches built, his schools running, he at last found a little time for the decorative notes of life, for that love of ornamentation which had lain dormant in him.

By the middle of the eighteenth century the art of these newly rooted folk began to flourish in Pennsylvania. The potter tried out his hand and produced objects of decorative beauty; the cabinet-maker exerted himself to do his best when he received an order to make a dower chest for a maiden or a wardrobe for a couple about to be married. The smith turned out graceful hardware for the new house. All craftsmen were busy people in the latter half of the eighteenth century, creating those honest, substantial objects which we can truthfully call the Folk Art of Rural Pennsylvania.

Except for the conservatism of the folk who cherished it, this racial memory of skills and designs might have disappeared very soon from the isolated sections where it was practiced. New arrivals in the community brought new skills and fresh ideas, however, keeping it alive when otherwise it might have perished.

It is evident that after 1800 the general pressure of living must have increased somewhat, for designs became simpler, and labor was not so generally lavished on handmade things. The dying-out of the apprentice system may have contributed largely to this noticeable change in the character of the ornamentation. With easier means of transportation, the folk could move about. The machine age began to creep up on them. Increased affluence and the pressure to accept an imported or machine-made article began to undermine their inborn craftsmanship, and slowly the era of folk art passed away.

By 1850 it was dead, not only in the Pennsylvania German country, but almost all over the world.

FROM THE EARTH ITSELF—CLAY

"In the evening arrived at Brooke's Tavern, the sign of Dr. Franklin. . . . . This road is marked by a peculiar appearance in the roofs of the different buildings, which reminded us of England. Instead of shingles, the ordinary and universal covering, the barns are often roofed with thatch and the houses with tiles, fabricated in the neighborhood."
—John Penn's Journal—April 6, 1788

NOTHING was of more importance to the newly arrived immigrants in Pennsylvania than the character of the soil. Coming from a land which their ancestors had farmed, between wars, for a thousand years, the colonists, for the most part farmers and workers in the vineyards, had learned from experience that the richest soil lay beneath the thickest forests. Armed in advance with this bit of agricultural wisdom, the agents who arranged parties for colonization took large tracts of limestone soil covered with primeval forest. Confronted by the woods in this new country, woods so much denser than the ones they were used to, the colonists marvelled at the beautiful, tall, smooth trees which grew in such close ranks. At the same time they faced the task of clearing them intrepidly, knowing they would be rewarded for all their labor by a rich tilth.

The less agriculturally-minded Scotch Irish, hailing from a more pastoral country, had already chosen the low lands, the open meadows, the natural clearings, the fresh soil of which produced enormous crops with little effort. Exempt from the numbing toil of clearing the virgin forests, they were left with plenty of time for hunting and fishing in them, occupations for which they were temperamentally better fitted. Because the soil gave so generrously, these settlers assumed it would always do so and neglected to return anything to it by way of fertilizer. When the time came that the crops inevitably lessened, the Scotch Irish moved on westward, setting the restless pattern for American pioneer life. They had farmed the easiest way, and those who came after them were forced to do the chopping and grubbing.

But the harried, prayerful groups of Germanic folk who looked to Pennsylvania as a haven in which they intended to make a home, not only for themselves but for their descendants, willingly accepted the hard way, the way of chopping and digging. This new colonist, trained from childhood to all kinds of manual work, toiled from dawn to dark. Deliberately he set to work to clear the somber woodlands, tree by tree, field by field. Relentlessly he swung his axe, bringing down logs for his cabin, providing fuel with which to heat it, and eventually clearing the space in which to sow his crops. As no one farmer knew how, or could find time, to practice all trades, well-organized groups of colonists included all the indispensable artisans whose skills were essential to the maintenance of a permanent settlement. So the blacksmith, weaver, shoemaker, tinker, miller, tanner, cooper, tinsmith, gunsmith and potter found themselves laboring shoulder to shoulder, in order to make a space in which to live in Penn's lovely wooded land. After this was done, during the seasons when the demands of farm work were less insistent, each artisan practiced his craft as a side line.

If he happened to be a potter, he had a special interest in the quality of the earth, apart from its fertility. It had also to be of a nature that would furnish him with the material to carry on his trade. Distribution gave him no worries. His future customers, his neighbors, ate uncomplainingly from one dish of pewter or of wood, waiting patiently for the time when the potter could produce a few earthen pots and dishes to replace those they had left behind them—those familiar, cherished objects for which there had been no space in the tiny overcrowded vessels in which they made the long painful journey.

Fortunately for the early potter, the soil of the counties, Montgomery, Berks, and Bucks, was a clayey loam with the potter's clay lying right beneath it. When he needed clay, the craftsman located it by a simple method. Choosing a likely spot in his damp, lush meadows, he walked over it. If the ground resisted his tread, he knew that clay formed the firmly packed bed beneath his foot, for the soft, unresisting wet places consisted only of black loam. Having located a spot, the potter stripped the top layer of soil, about six inches deep, from the clay layer, over an area about five by ten feet. The clay, sometimes yellow, sometimes bluish gray, was dug out and hauled to his workshop—for by now he had built himself a place in which to work and a kiln in which to fire his product. When he exhausted the clay in one pit, he opened another, immediately contiguous, leaving only a partition of soil and clay between them. The abandoned pits acted as a drain for the newly opened ones.

Once a potter had found his source of clay, he sometimes kept his rights to it, even if he moved to a new neighborhood. In an old Berks County record there is an account of a pertinent transaction. A potter sold a section of his farm but retained the right in the deed of sale to dig clay from the land for a period of twelve years; provided that, annually, he contracted to fill up and smooth off the openings he had made. And though the land was no longer his, he insisted on the privilege of keeping open the road for the passage of carts and horses hauling potter's clay from an adjoining tract.

In addition to making all kinds of utensils for the housewife, the potter fashioned roofing tiles for the house. Though wooden shingles could have been produced in unlimited quantities, as cedar trees were so plentiful, the farmer-potter carried on the roofing traditions of his homeland, covering the strange, new dwellings in this new land with red clay tiles whose shape was exactly like that produced by any tile-bakery of mediæval Germany. Even in the mid-twentieth century, this quaint clay tile can yet be seen, in out-of-the-way corners of Berks County, still at its ancient task of providing a fireproof roof for spring-houses, milk-houses, and sheds. The Pennsylvania German tile was a flat object, 5/8″ thick, 14″ long, 6 or 7″ wide, lightly corrugated on the outside by the potter's fingers to make channels for the rain, with a nob modelled on the underside so that it could be hooked on to the cross-pieces of the rafters in overlapping rows. From early in the eighteenth century to the middle of the nineteenth, the manufacture of these tiles was kept up, despite their frangible nature.

Until the advent of machine-made dishes and pans in every country store in the 1850's, the potter found a continued demand for even his easily broken wares. Since the country housewife depended entirely on earthenware for daily use in her kitchen and spring-house, many types of this Pennsylvania redware—so called because the local clay fired a pleasant brownish-red—were turned out. All potters made nests of pots in graded sizes for apple-butter or milk, lidded earthen jars for pickles and preserves, mixing bowls, jelly molds and colanders, handled jugs for vinegar which were always stoppered with a corncob. They turned out red clay teapots, dark brown coffeepots, cups and great thick mugs of quart capacity, built to hold enough liquid to satisfy a thirsty man; many sizes of pitchers from which to pour it. To hold the traditional foods, there were enormous platters, oval, octagonal and round; casseroles with ornamented covers. These foods were prepared in cooking pots and pans so large and heavy that one wonders nowadays how the cook ever handled them when they were filled with the quantities of food the large families of the early settlers demanded.

For general use in the household, the meadow-land clay could be turned into wash-bowls, candlesticks and lampstands, hot-water bottles, soap-dishes, shaving bowls and shaving mugs, vases, flowerpots and hanging baskets. In the few instances when a letter or a will had to be written, there were inkwells and sanders at hand.

For the rare moments when the country woman's craving for something frivolous and ornamental could not be denied, the potter produced his version of the fashionable imported Staffordshire mantel ornaments. Though they were undeniably crude and quaint, they were undoubtedly cherished. In fact, it may be broadly stated that if the Pennsylvania German potter's fingers could shape it and it could be safely fired in the kiln, any article desired was attempted. The potter filled an important need in any settlement and thus was able to meet the undemanding æsthetic standards of his clients, who, used to earthenware in their homelands, were happy to have the same forms reproduced here.

But life in colonial America could change even such a sturdy traditionalist as the Pennsylvania potter. An insistent demand for a new article of food, the fruit pie, created a new utensil, the earthenware pie-dish or "poi-schissel" whose shape is unlike any other dish in the world. It is a rather flat, curved dish, minus any rim or base. Its unbroken curve, which permitted a pie baked in it to slip out easily, is its unvarying characteristic. Fruit,

11

never too plentiful in Europe, ripened in the hot sunshine of Pennsylvania in great abundance. Peaches, a dainty grown in greenhouses in Europe but never tasted by the common folk, were so plentiful here that they were fed to hogs. "Apples, cherries, pears, quinces, plumbs; apricots and nectarines; mulberries, goosberries, currans, strawberries, raspberries, grapes, hurtleberries [huckleberries], whinberries, bilberries, and crampberries"—Lewis Evans, a British surveyor, travelling here in 1753, enumerates them all, for the astonishment of Europeans. The fruit pie was invented by the English or Scotch Irish settlers, but the Pennsylvania Germans, compelled by their inborn thriftiness to make use of this enormous flood of fruit-stuff, enthusiastically took over the idea from their neighbors and developed it later into what was practically pie mass-production. As the early fireplaces were not equipped to bake pies satisfactorily, the Pennsylvania German housewife had to wait until her husband found time to build the outdoor bake-oven of stone, so like the one left behind in the far-away country along the Rhine. With the new oven, the new pie-dishes, and under the spur of the newly acquired passion for pie, she developed the skills which have earned for her a reputation for perfection in this kitchen art.

Even to this day, "Baking Day" is an institution in the Pennsylvania German country. Pies are turned out in quantity, with special cupboards in which to store them after they have filled the air with their pleasant odors. A farmer's wife took great pride in the number of varieties of pie and cake she could set before a guest, who, perhaps unused to such an opulent display of pastry, might well hesitate to choose when confronted with an awesome row of perhaps twelve uncommunicative, identical pies. But the hostess, able herself to identify them only by the cryptic furrowings she had placed on their pale, brown crusts, would enthusiastically urge him to sample all of them. Certain women were in great demand as pie bakers for funerals. In fact, the alternative name for raisin pie in eastern Pennsylvania is "funeral pie." Four meals a day, and pie at every meal, could soon dispose of fifty pies, which was the number a young girl boasted she had made in harvest time in the 1860's.

Such production demanded an enormous quantity of "poi-schissel." Every household had them in several sizes. For contemporary antique hunters they are the articles most readily found for sale in the countryside, having been pushed aside by more modern if less artistic containers. But even today not every housewife has completely discarded them, for there are still families who think that no pie baked in any other kind of dish tastes quite as good as these which slide out so easily from their quaint red-brown plates.

After the introduction of tin and other types of containers, the earthenware pie-plates were sometimes put to very humble uses. Table scraps for the fowl and farm pets were set out in them, and if they were broken it "made nothing out"—they were so plentiful. In the litter of a hen-yard I acquired my first "poi-schissel," abstracting it from under the beaks of the hens while they were still picking at its empty, glossy surface. My country hostess, seeing that I valued it, opened an old cupboard on her kitchen porch and pulled out several others, blacked on their undersides from much service. "If these are of any use to you, you are welcome to them," she said. "I'm glad to get rid of that old stuff."

During the long period the local potteries flourished, fuel, one of the few essentials needed to carry on the potter's craft, was so plentiful in "Penn's Woods" that lavish consumption of it ranked as a civic virtue. With fuel provided, the equipment necessary for making pottery, the oldest craft known, was simple and varied little all over the world. It consisted of a potter's wheel, which the potter himself constructed, a few wooden and wire tools, and some molds, which he used in order to save time and to obtain some semblance of uniformity in his product. As the potter worked at his trade only in the intervals when farm work slackened, his basic material, clay dug from his own meadows, had to be put in a workable condition in advance and stored away from the danger of freezing, in a cellar usually built below the workshop. The clay, a bluish, crumbly mass as it came from the pits, was hauled by the potter to a convenient spot near the building where he intended to work. There he had already set up a mill in which to grind it, for the clay could not be used for potting until it had been reduced to a uniform texture and the impurities in it broken up. This mill, a simple mechanism consisting of a group of knives set in an upright post revolving in a stationary tub, was operated by a long sweep or beam to which a horse was attached in lieu of a motor. The tub was filled with clay, the clay sprinkled with water, and the horse was started on his monotonous round.

A pottery, like most of the early craftsmen's workshops, was always the center of a group of onlookers, and small boys, if they could manage to evade a few farm chores, were particularly in evidence. If one of them was lucky enough to be selected as apprentice boy, he was given the task of keeping the horse in motion. There were many dull jobs around a pottery that fell to him to carry out; from his point of view, they were endless and boring, but to this job he brought the same enthusiasm as the boy of today brings to his first jalopy. Proudly he carried a switch, which he was cautioned to use with restraint; with great gusto he shooed off his envious friends when they attempted to climb on the sweep for a ride without his permission. With equal vigor he yelled "Whoa" when the boss potter decided the clay was "done," the moment reached when the clay changed from a brittle, crumbly mass into a plastic, putty-like substance. It was then molded into large blocks weighing about one hundred pounds each, and stored in the cellar until needed. When the potter was ready to work, he carried up a supply of this moist clay to his bench. Before turning any of it into pots or plates, he worked it over and over, removing every fragment of foreign matter. This procedure was very important, for a bit of root or a stray pebble would cause the object either to break in firing or would leave a hole where it burned out. After this working-over, the clay was ready for use.

To make a batch of pie plates, the potter would cut the clay with a piece of wire into lumps. These were flattened out into rough sheets and piled on each other like a stack of buckwheat cakes. They were then rolled out to the desired thinness with a wooden roller, very like the one used by the housewife in rolling out pie crust. In order to keep these disks from sticking to the workbench while being rolled, the potter, again borrowing a kitchen technique, sprinkled the bench with dust, previously gathered from the roadway or the field.

The task of collecting this dust was one of the unpleasant things expected of the apprentice boy. On the driest, most torrid, most sunshiny day, equipped with a wheel-barrow, a fine sieve made of woven horsehair, and a pot to store the dust in, he was set to work to collect the supply for the coming season; it was a hot, dirty job that he would have considered great fun if he had not been obliged to do it.

When the rolled clay disks had been cut into the desired sizes by means of a simple compass-like tool called a disk-cutter, they were laid out to dry partially before being decorated.

Unlike his Quaker neighbors, "who not only had no time for art but no place for it in their scheme of salvation,"* the Pennsylvania German never renounced his love of color and pattern. To please himself and his clients, he was apt to add some decoration on even so humble and commercial an article as a pie plate. It may have been no more than a pattern of fluidly drawn lines in an ochre-yellow which contrasted agreeably with the red-brown background, but the application required several extra operations which one might think his native thrift would have dispensed with. This type of decoration, called "slip decoration," was applied to the flattened disk. To prepare the "slip," as the material used was called, the potter mixed white New Jersey clay and water to about the thickness of cream. This he put into a "slip cup," a clay vessel which he had made himself; it was a simple tool about the size of a teacup, with depressions into which his fingers slipped to insure a firm grip, and it was fitted with several goose quills through which the liquid clay could trickle. With a few deft movements, a pattern of three or more wavy lines quickly appeared on the flat disk. When the liquid clay design dried out, it left a slight elevation on the plate, and as this was considered undesirable in objects of daily use, since this raised portion might cause the glazing subsequently to be applied to chip off, the disks were then pounded with a tool called a batter, to make the surface uniformly even.

To change these flat, decorated disks into curved pie plates, the disk, by this time about half dry, was shaped over a mold which the potter had made previously and had baked very hard. It was a clumsy, thick, heavy object resembling the pie plate in shape. With considerable force the ornamented disk was slapped onto the convex side of the mold, decorated side down; in order to make the clay disk take on the shape of the mold, the throwing operation was repeated several times. Then, after smoothing it down with his hand so that he was sure it was adhering to the entire surface, the potter, again borrowing from the technique of the housewife, took a spatula and trimmed away the clay from the edge of the mold, exactly as a pie crust is trimmed. In fact, the technique of making pie plates,

*In the words of Elizabeth Robins Pennell.

14

even to the ornamentation of the bevelled edges, seems closely related to that of making pies. The housewife sealed the edges of the pie by pressing them together with a small jagged wheel, which decorated them at the same time. The potter used a tool called a coggle, running it over the bevelled edge of the plate to make a series of notches. These probably lessened the ever-present danger of chipping, for the redware was never very hard.

Before being glazed, the plates had to be thoroughly dried out. The glaze, a mixture of red-lead and water with red clay added to thicken it, was run through a primitive machine called a glazing mill, to reduce it to a uniform consistency. In order to make the glaze adhere to them, the plates had first to be warmed. In winter the potter piled them up on a heated surface; in summer he made use of the hot sunshine. The apprentice boy, to whose lot fell all the unpleasant tasks, was ordered to spread them out on the ground until they soaked up enough sunshine to warm them thoroughly. Then the potter, seated in the shade, took the "pie dishes" one by one as the boy passed them to him, dipped a large brush in the glazing mixture and quickly painted the inner surface. The glaze, fired in the wood-burning kiln built by the potter, softened the harsh white of the slip decoration to an agreeable yellow and accentuated the tone of the rich burnt-sienna base.

The farmer folk, happy to have the potteries operating, were unaware of any threat the lead-glazed dishes might possibly hold for their health. No one had ever told them that lead was poisonous. But after the Revolution, when the newly formed United States began to think of making its own kitchen and table ware, an agitated gentleman, grinding a very obvious axe of his own for the manufacturing of salt-glazed pottery, a much harder ware, inserted this notice in the *Pennsylvania Mercury* in 1785:

"Previous to the glorious Revolution, all bulky and low priced articles were imported so exceedingly cheap as to discourage manufactures of them of any importance. Here and there were a few scattered Potteries of Earthenware, infamously bad and unwholesome, from their being glazed with a thin, cheap coating of lead. The best of Lead Glazing is esteemed unwholsome, by observing people. The mischievous effects of it fall chiefly on the country people and the poor everywhere. Even when it is firm enough, so as not to scale it is imperceptibly eaten away by every acid matter; and mixing with the drinks and meats of the people becomes a slow but sure poison." The statement was correct, so far as the claim for the superiority of salt-glazed pottery went. The time came when its tough gray and blue glazes completely supplanted the coarse red slipware. But until that day arrived, all the most conservative potters continued to turn out their "poisonous" wares, no doubt to the complete satisfaction of customers with minds equally conservative.

Before the days of the country store, the only contact maintained with the city was through the welcome visits of the peddler or the rare trips which the farmer made to Philadelphia or Reading in his Conestoga wagon, that distinctive Pennsylvania carrier. He went to barter his salable goods—butter, flour, and whiskey—for such things as salt, spices, coffee, tea, and pins, articles that the farm did not provide. Money was a scarce article; what little he had he kept locked up in his "old country" chest. The idea of dispensing it for city luxuries never entered his mind. His women folk, if they wanted something that was outside the line of the starkly useful, looked to the local potter to supply their modest demands for the æsthetic. If a woman was fortunate enough to live near Andrew Headman, Georg Hübener or David Spinner (to name a few potters who signed their choice pieces), she might barter for a plate on which she could have inscribed her own choice of sentiment, set down in her own language.

It must not be overlooked that this large, scattered group of country folk had their own dialect, known as "Pennsylvania Dutch," in which they transacted all their affairs, many of them never using a word of English. In the eighteenth century 95 per cent of the population in certain towns conversed wholly in German dialect. English was the language of law and of the State, and the Pennsylvania Germans who had dealings with the English-speaking courts were forced of necessity to learn it, but as rugged individualists they wrote it in a manner untrammelled by any rules of spelling, one in which d's and t's, b's and p's were cheerfully interchangeable. Without this knowledge of their orthographic practices, it would be difficult to detect the classic "Dorothea" lurking behind the Pennsylvania German's "Dor-de-a," and "Veronica" would be sunk forever in the curious "Fronica." Even after the introduction of the public-school system, when country dwellers were forced to study English, they still carried on their transactions with townspeople, compelled to be bi-lingual, in "Pennsylvania Dutch."

This persistent adherence of the early settlers to their own tongue explains why a dish ornamented with a homely proverb, with a bit of vulgar peasant humor or a verse from the Bible set down in the only speech familiar to a woman, had a more intimate appeal to her than the most elegant of objects imported from far-off, unknown England. The sight of one of the well-known Old-World maxims brought back to her the memory of the sententious shake of the head with which the solemn ones had been uttered, or the good-natured smile which accompanied the hundredth repetition of the familiar joke. The frequency with which the same German sayings appear on the work of the local potters shows how greatly this traditional ceramic literature was cherished in this strange new land.

In addition to familiar or original inscriptions, the potter of these show pieces had at his finger tips all manner of decorative devices, and several techniques in which to execute them. He could enrich the simplest of these, already described as decoration in white slip, with two additional colors, black and green. To manipulate the colored slips as they trickled from the single quill inserted in the slip cup required considerable skill, but if the potter deemed himself to possess it, elaborate designs of birds, flowers and lettered inscriptions were often executed in this slithery medium. Multiple quills were reserved for the scrollings used on everyday ware.

16

The potter also had at his command a much more easily controlled method of decorating these gift pieces, and one more suited to his deliberate temperament. In the nomenclature of ceramics, it is called "sgraffito," a word taken from the Italian verb, *sgraffiare*, to scratch. It describes an old Italian method of decorating, a kind of fresco painting in which a white coating is laid over a darker ground and an ornamental pattern obtained by lines scratched through to disclose the dark undertone. The majority of Pennsylvania German decorated pieces were "sgraffito." A coating of white New Jersey slip clay was laid over the concave side of an already molded red clay plate. With a sharpened stick, any desired design could be scratched through the light layer, until the red clay base showed through. This simple method gave the potter two colors, his basic reddish brown and earthy yellow, to which he frequently added areas or splotches of a rich green. As he bought nothing that he could make himself, even these green dashes were obtained by burning scraps of old copper kettles to make oxide of copper. Manganese added to a glazing of red-lead provided him with a fine dark brown tone, which was used by at least one potter as a background for ornament traced on in white, red, and green liquid slips. Blue is a color which appears only on a few late pieces. It was an oxide of cobalt and was expensive. As it fused at a much higher temperature than was needed for the ordinary redware, its use was not possible until the manufacture of salt-glazed stoneware began. That cobalt blue and salt-glaze were affinities is evidenced by the inevitable blue squiggles on the warm gray of pickle-jars and crocks.

While most of the decoration of these gift pieces was done free-hand, there were a few tricks which the potter, like any other sensible artisan, had contrived in order to save unnecessary work. A pattern cut out of paper could be traced around for the main portion of the design, embellished with free-hand details. Or a paper on which a pattern had been drawn was laid on the receptive clay, and the outlines were pricked through with a blunt tool. The dots thus impressed in the clay formed the basis for the motif, which was then drawn freehand. Sometimes designs were cut in intaglio fashion in a mold into which the clay was forced, producing a decoration in relief.

There is no reason to think that these gift or souvenir pieces were ever made in any great quantity; they were probably turned out in odd moments by the "boss" potter or by his journeyman helper who wished to display his skill or a design perhaps new to his employer. They were highly valued as objects of decorative interest in the home, and only a rare, iconoclastic housewife ventured to cook or bake in them. In the important collection of the Philadelphia Museum, the backs of most of the plates are as fresh as the day they came from the kiln. To their owners they represented more than an object of sentimental value; they served in the simple lives of the country folk as a piece of Sèvres or Meissen would in the homes of the gentry, and they were always carefully handled. They were never common, and today are very valuable.

Until about fifty years ago, however, the very existence of a locally-made peasant ware was unknown to collectors. Then Dr. Edwin Atlee Barber, curator of the Pennsylvania Museum, turned up a curious plate in a junk shop. Wishing to have the German inscription deciphered, for he assumed this to be a European piece, he found that the language was not "High German," as he had supposed it to be, but a dialect; moreover, one spoken in his own State. As supplementary information indicated that the supposed German plate had been made in a nearby pottery, he began a search for additional pieces of the ware. With a few interested cronies he drove out leisurely in the horse-and-buggy of the day through the pleasant Pennsylvania farm lands, looking for pieces which might be purchased, as he planned to acquire a collection for the Museum. He was fortunate to meet descendants of the potters of long ago who furnished him with much detailed information about their forebears and their methods of work. They also sold him certain pieces, long cherished in their families and well authenticated, at prices they must have considered astounding or they would not have parted with them. It is amusing to think that the maker of one of these gift pieces probably purchased his entire farm for less than a plate from his hand now brings at current prices on the rare occasions when a private collection is put up for sale.

But even in those days when the collection for the Pennsylvania Museum was being quietly assembled, word must have leaked out that such things were being looked for and had value, apart from family sentiment. In the possession of a lady whose husband was a desultory collector and a companion of Dr. Barber's in the 1890's, is this quaint note received by him from one who was, undoubtedly, an early scout for antiques:

"Mr I go fore this Plate and the old man Tell me 6.00 Dollars I told I give it But the girls kick Dond sell that plate Fore nothing Now I let you know I do the Best two get it"

THE WORK OF DAVID SPINNER

Bucks county, in 1800, contained a busy group of potters. One of the outstanding craftsmen among them was David Spinner. Because his ability to draw freehand exceeded that of his fellow potters, he was considered quite an artist by his neighbors. He excelled in delineating women in fashionable dress, soldiers on foot as well as on horseback, and animated hunting scenes. As evidence of the pride he took in his work, he often signed his pieces "David Spinner Potter" or "David Spinner his Make" in a large, flowing, eighteenthcentury hand. Unlike his fellow potters, he wrote his inscriptions in English.

This sgraffito plate depicting a mounted horsewoman, "Lady Okle," shows his characteristic skill in draftsmanship. To get a strong red mass, the entire body of the horse is boldly cut through the yellow ground. The lady is garbed in green. The simple border on this plate is indicative of the type Spinner generally employed.

Courtesy, National Gallery of Art, Index of American Design.

THE WORK OF GEORG HÜBENER

A potter whose products give evidence of a particular mastery of decoration and lettering; his establishment is believed to have been in Montgomery County. Authority and knowledge are shown in every boldly incised line. His pieces have great richness of texture and pattern, heightened by the free use of heavy green blotches.

Hübener's characteristics are well displayed on this plate. In the blank spaces he set his initials G. H. and the date, 1786. "Cadarina Raeder her dish" fills out the line of the couplet:

"With the clay, (such skill he brings)
The potter makes all kinds of things."

Above. The double eagle centered with a heart was a favorite device.

Left. Typical motif adapted to jar. Double bands of scallops accentuate the shoulder, on which the inscription is placed.

Arms of the City of Frankfurt. Familiar heraldic models furnished inspiration.

Courtesy, National Gallery of Art, Index of American Design.

As a central motif the peacock alternated with the eagle. The tulips with their odd, unbotanical, pinnate leaves vary little on any of the pieces. Hübener seems to have been the only local potter to use double bands of inscriptions, the outer one of which states:

"Mathalena Jung; her dish
This dish is fashioned out of clay
And when it breaks the potter's gay
So take good care of it, we pray."

The inner, excellently lettered band carries an equally familiar legend:

"Anyone can paint a flower
To give it fragrance only God has power.
1798."

Unmistakable Hübener tulips and urn in sgraffito from field of plate. In this instance only one band of inscription surrounds it.

Courtesy, Parke-Bernet Galleries, Inc., New York.

21

Bolle-Kessi or Bulb-kettle.

A cheerful sight on a farm windowsill in late winter was this odd red and yellow vase, with onion shoots sprouting out of every opening. As onions inevitably sprout, resulting in waste, this vase functioned perfectly in utilizing the habit of the vegetable. The sprouts were clipped to provide for thrifty folk a taste of the spring greens of which winter had deprived them.

Its Swiss prototype, made of metal and swung on chains from the ceiling, was called a "Bolle-Kessi," or bulb-kettle.

Courtesy, Philadelphia Museum of Art.

Courtesy, Art Institute of Chicago.

Above. Handled jar in sgraffito and colored slip, dated 1795. Tulips, hearts, and pomegranates decorate it.

Left. Handled jar with lively design of polka-dotted birds and fluently executed tulips. Glazed redware background; motifs in yellow, green and white slips. Made in 1787, perhaps by Christian Klinker, the potter who made the jar on page 29.

Courtesy, Philadelphia Museum of Art.

22

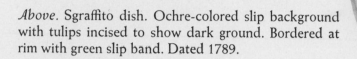

Tulips growing formally from ornamental urns were favorite motifs of the early potters.

Above. Sgraffito dish. Ochre-colored slip background with tulips incised to show dark ground. Bordered at rim with green slip band. Dated 1789.

Right. Slipware plate, made in 1778. On a dark red ground, quaint, squat, stemless tulips fill in the space left by a corpulent urn. Fat tulips are used even to space out the band of lettering.

Right. Sgraffito plate by John Monday, made in 1828. The traditional motifs continue to be used; the lines are still flowing and skillfully executed.

All examples, courtesy, Philadelphia Museum of Art.

Octagonal dishes are unusual. They were shaped over convex eight-sided molds. The plate above is executed in sgraffito on yellow slip. Although the potter, with considerable ingenuity, employed the boundaries of one of the segments of the plate as the outline for the urn, he spread his boldly conceived decoration over all the others, frankly ignoring its octagonal form.

Octagonal dish decorated in relief and glazed in a monotone dark terracotta. In the process used to obtain ornament in relief lurked the first germs of mass production, for after the mold was made, dishes complete with ornament could be turned out with no further handwork. The design was engraved in intaglio in the convex octagonal mold. Clay was then pressed into it, and when the dish was removed, it bore a pattern in relief. Made in 1794, probably by Jacob Taney, Nockamixon Township, Bucks County, Pa. An octagonal platter, decorated in colored slips, can be seen on page 41.

Courtesy, Philadelphia Museum of Art.

Above, left. Slipware plate. Rich red ground, yellow, black, and green decoration. Dated August 18, 1796.

Above, right. Slipware plate. Tulip decoration in green, blue, and white slips. Dated October 1797.

Courtesy, National Gallery of Art, Index of American Design.

Right. Central motif of sgraffito dish. Incised tulips in red and green on yellow ground. Dated November 1796. Width of dish 14".

Courtesy, National Gallery of Art, Index of American Design.

THE WORK OF JOHN LEIDY

John Leidy, a Montgomery County potter, was an outstanding craftsman, working successfully both in sgraffito and in the more difficult technique of slip painting. His pieces are large and well devised. Marginal inscriptions, borders of multiple lines, repeating ornamental forms, plus a wide choice in motifs—birds, tulips, fish, stylized flower forms—and straight lines characterize this gifted potter. When he made the pieces illustrated, he was only sixteen.

Left. Sgraffito plate by John Nase, of Montgomery County, who operated a pottery from about 1830 to 1850. Deer scratched boldly through glazed yellow background to show red clay base. Green is dashed around in the usual profuse manner. The multiple-pointed star contributes an original note.

THE ANIMAL ON SGRAFFITO WARE

Motif of leaping stag and tulips taken from the center of a plate made in 1773, one of the few subjected to really hard use, as its surface is worn, its color almost gone. Its inscription, translated, reads: "My greetings to you, Baraba (Barbara?) Mardelin. Jesus, dwell in my house and never leave it."

Jar decorated in sgraffito with horse and deer; background elaborately filled in with tulips, birds, and trees. The ground is yellow, decoration in red. The design was transferred to the vase by pinpricks through a paper pattern.

26

SOLDIERS

A desire to heighten the sales appeal of his wares may have prompted a potter, in 1786, to substitute for the traditional patterns of his homeland a pair of Revolutionary soldiers. The inscription, favored by potters in Germany, was equally liked here.

Courtesy, National Gallery of Art, Index of American Design.

Courtesy, National Gallery of Art, Index of American Design.

Johannes Neesz, Montgomery County, Pa., 1775-1867, whose work resembles that of David Spinner (on p. 19) was probably the latter's pupil. The cavalier, a favorite European motif, became, with trifling alterations, the Continental soldier featured on his plates, all the main outlines of which are so similar that it is evident that Neesz, unlike Spinner, relied on a pattern round which he traced. Neesz's steeds are drawn in simple outline on the yellow slip coating; Spinner's are silhouetted in red against light slip grounds.

COIN BANKS
AND MUGS

Left. Bank of glazed dark-brown earthenware. From Powder Valley, Lehigh County, Pa.

Courtesy, Pennsylvania State Museum, Harrisburg, Pa.

Right. Handled mug in sgraffito, 1816.

Courtesy, National Gallery of Art, Index of American Design.

Coin banks took the shape of familiar objects: houses and beehives and jugs. The birds perched on the tops were so nicely modelled that it seemed a shame the bank had eventually to be smashed to free the slowly acquired contents. In the early days few coins came a child's way, for money was scarce. Banks like these are still made today for country folk in Czecho-Slovakia. The idea may well have been brought to Pennsylvania by the early Moravian settlers.

Courtesy, National Gallery of Art, Index of American Design.

Courtesy, Philadelphia Museum of Art.

Handled mug, intricately covered with the usual motifs, 1801. Inscription, translated, reads: "I say what is true and drink what is clear." Handle terminates in modelled tulip.

Stoneware bank, jug-shaped. Cobalt decoration. Made in 1880 for Anna Jamison by R. C. Remmey, Philadelphia.

Gracefully stated tulips and other floral forms in colored slip, with borders in both slip and sgraffito decoration, are found on an earthenware jar made by one of the pioneer potters of Bucks County, Pa., Christian Klinker, who was believed to have come from Germany. On the bottom he scratched his initials C. K. and the date of making, 1773. The potters who arrived earliest in this country, saturated with the traditions of their craft and as yet untouched by the pressure of the New World, turned out the most vigorous and beautiful work.

This unknown potter's work is distinguished by his strong, sure line, with which he depicted both birds and tulips in poses of extreme vivacity. The stems of the latter curve with great animation from bases made of alternating straight and sinuous lines.

Sgraffito Plate, *c.* 1830.
The double-headed eagle, symbol of the Holy Roman Empire, was often used on inn signs, as well as on ceramics. An inn with such a sign, though officially called "The Spread Eagle," was facetiously dubbed by the neighborhood "The Split Crow."

BIRDS

Sgraffito Plate, *c.* 1830.
The potter who planned this American eagle was a deliberate worker. He first drew the design on paper, pricked its outlines through onto the plate, and then drew with assurance over the dotted guide lines he had made. A curved gouge was used to mark the tips of the feathers.

A quaint triple alliance of the *"Doppel-Adler"* (double eagle), heart, and tulips. Samuel Paul made it, he boldly states, for Maria Helbard in 1798. Paul may well have been an apprentice of Hübener's for he used the same double bands of lettering and the double eagle, somewhat less well executed.

Courtesy, Metropolitan Museum of Art.

Small Faience Bowl. Syria. Fourteenth Century.

Oriental potters, four centuries earlier, delighted in the decorative possibilities offered by the peacock.

THE PEACOCK

Readily identified among the various birds used as decorative motifs by the Pennsylvania German potters is the peacock. His crest and tail furnished them with two details easily depicted within the limits set by a line scratched in clay.

The peacock on this sgraffito plate is drawn in prideful strut, flanked by a conventionalized flower and a rather unusual feature, a cartouche, containing the date 1793 and the initials H. R.

Courtesy, Reading Public Museum and Art Gallery, Reading, Pa.

Against a greenish-gold background, this obvious peacock and floral spray are outlined in the strong orange hue of the clay base. The inscription, *"Das ist der Pfau"* (This is the peacock), offers an unnecessary explanatory note. A later, almost identical example of this unknown potter's work, dated 1806, bears an old German inscription, which translates roughly as "I am a bird in every thing. Whose bread I eat, his song I sing." Diameter 11".

Courtesy, Metropolitan Museum of Art.

THE TREE OF LIFE

Remarkably virile design distinguished by wavy, repetitive lines with unusual arrangement of tulips tangent to the rim.

Courtesy, Philadelphia Museum of Art.

Sgraffito plate made on January 17, 1794, in Bucks County, Pa. Rhythmic, undulating stems supporting tulips and pomegranates crowded together with long scalloped-edged leaves make a bold space-filling device. Violent, not too well placed dashes of green detract a little from the pleasing rhythms.

32

THE TREE OF LIFE

Between this plate and the one on the opposite page there is a close relation, both in motif and in organization. The use of the tree-like pyramidal form is infrequent compared to other more favored devices.

Courtesy, National Gallery of Art, Index of American Design.

Sgraffito Plate, signed R. G. 1812

The peacock is perched on the tip of a Tree of Life. The effect is curiously Oriental. The series of concentric arcs, suggesting loops of drapery, is faintly reminiscent of the Adam and Regency periods, the attenuated influence of which by 1812 had probably seeped even into the "interior."

Courtesy, National Gallery of Art, Index of American Design.

33

Courtesy, Reading Public Museum and Art Gallery, Reading, Pa.

Above. Sugar bowl, made by John George Buehler, who came from Würtemberg in 1842. He set up a pottery at Leesport, Berks County. Not satisfied with the simple openwork motifs on this rather irregularly shaped bowl, the potter further enlivened the surface by sticking on bits of clay, stamped with a rosette, a nineteenth-century fashion of Rhineland potters. Dark brown, glazed.

Left. Tobacco bowl. 1857. Made at Haring Pottery, Bucks Co., Pa.

Courtesy, National Gallery of Art, Index of American Design.

Courtesy, Metropolitan Museum of Art.

Covered Dish.

To make a jar in pierced work required nice judgment. Elaborate pieces like these were probably made by newly arrived potters to demonstrate to a prospective employer their proficiency in the craft. An inner lining in lid as well as jar turned them into closed containers, used as sugar bowls and tobacco jars, such as the one on the upper left. This, with its inscription *"Zum Andenken Ano 1857;"* may well have been the work of an immigrant journeyman, as the numeral 7 is written in the European fashion. Pierced work was made in various sections of Germany.

Redware tobacco jar, Somerset, Pa. From the author's notebook.

A series of borders, a detail found on the work of skilled eighteenth-century potters, enlivens this large slipware platter. A peacock outlined in yellow and green slips is sheltered beneath a gracefully drawn tulip, silhouetted on a red ground. To add to the decorative effect of the band of lettering, a familiar German proverb, each word is separated from its neighbors by green, wavy, vertical lines. Translated, it reads: "Good and bad luck are our daily breakfast fare."

Courtesy, Philadelphia Museum of Art.

Courtesy, Mrs. Lowrie, Titusville, Pa.

While not all potters displayed a mastery of the principles of design, most of them had a fine feeling for spatial arrangements. Here, on an eight-inch sgraffito plate, is a different conception of the bird and tulip, drawn with complete artlessness, an interesting contrast to the well organized conception above.

CERAMIC
TOYS

Inkwell, made in 1814 by J. Fretz. Panniers hold removable inkwells.
Courtesy, Philadelphia Museum of Art.

Below. Ceramic toy. Water-whistle in glazed earthenware with spots and lines of slip decoration in white and black.

Courtesy, Philadelphia Museum of Art.

The local potter was often the source of children's toys. Clay was so magically turned into miniature animals, birds, and dishes that the craftsman, flattered by the gaze of fascinated small boys and girls, found himself equipping all the children in the neighborhood with ceramic playthings.

Besides all manner of dolls' dishes, and whistles shaped like birds, the potter made dolls' heads and infants' rattles—clumsy hollow cats or deer with clay balls inside, planned to be shaken by adults for infant entertainment.

Dr. Henry Mercer, enumerating the objects which constituted the beginnings of the great collection belonging to the Bucks County Historical Society, makes note of a gift of dolls' dishes to that august institution, gravely giving the donor's name as "Little Girl near Cornelius Herstine's Pottery." "Little Girl" gave not only her plates and a tiny bank, but also a nest of miniature apple-butter pots, exactly like her mother's.

Courtesy, National Gallery of Art,
Index of American Design.

Ceramic wind instrument. Water was put in the body and the user applied his mouth to the beak. The European prototype of this toy is called a *"Wasserpfeife"* or water-whistle.

Courtesy, Philadelphia Museum of Art.

Pottery figures of cock and hen. Buff-colored glaze with brown decorations.

Water-whistle, shaped like a peacock. Gray and brown mottled glaze with sgraffito markings and touches of green slip.

The idea for both the inkwell and the water-whistle may well have been brought over from their homelands by the Moravians, who founded Bethlehem, Pa., in 1741. Similar articles were made in Moravia in the seventeenth and eighteenth centuries.

Courtesy, Philadelphia Museum of Art.

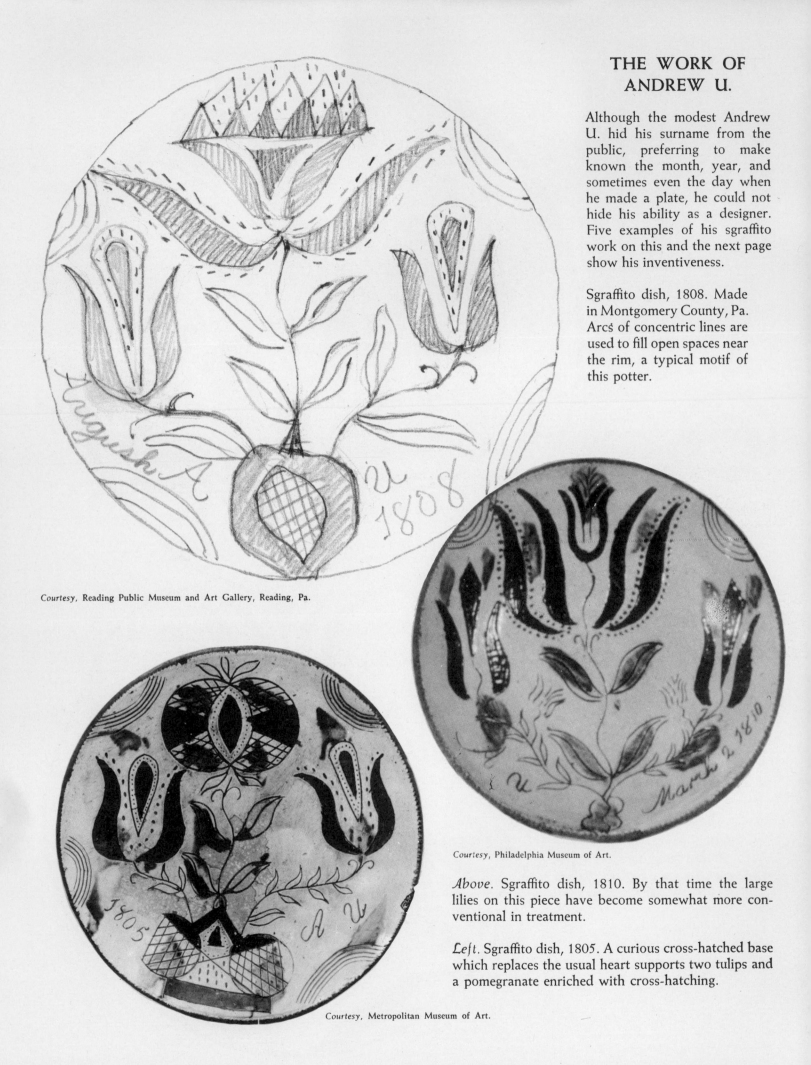

THE WORK OF ANDREW U.

Although the modest Andrew U. hid his surname from the public, preferring to make known the month, year, and sometimes even the day when he made a plate, he could not hide his ability as a designer. Five examples of his sgraffito work on this and the next page show his inventiveness.

Sgraffito dish, 1808. Made in Montgomery County, Pa. Arcs of concentric lines are used to fill open spaces near the rim, a typical motif of this potter.

Courtesy, Reading Public Museum and Art Gallery, Reading, Pa.

Courtesy, Philadelphia Museum of Art.

Above. Sgraffito dish, 1810. By that time the large lilies on this piece have become somewhat more conventional in treatment.

Left. Sgraffito dish, 1805. A curious cross-hatched base which replaces the usual heart supports two tulips and a pomegranate enriched with cross-hatching.

Courtesy, Metropolitan Museum of Art.

THE WORK OF
ANDREW U.

Two rosette forms used as flowers vary the arrangement preferred by this potter, who made this dish on Feb. 28, 1810.

Courtesy, Metropolitan Museum of Art.

This is a good example of the potter's creativeness. Twin peacocks flank the tulip which issues from the heart-shaped base. Made on "March the 1, 1801." As the earliest example in this series of illustrations, this plate may demonstrate a youthful vigor in design which lessened slightly in later years. From the author's notebook.

DECORATED HOUSEHOLD UTENSILS

Below. Red earthenware pitcher, 1827, with yellow slip decoration.

Courtesy, The New-York Historical Society.

Courtesy, National Gallery of Art, Index of American Design.

Above. Pennsylvania redware pitcher. Graceful tulip forms in relief show degenerative influences of later years.

Below. Orange-brown pitcher, with dark brown bands bordering a pleasant decoration, contrived from the owner's name, applied in cream-colored slip.

Left. Small covered jar in redware, with tulips outlined in yellow slip. Rims ornamented with border of dots.

Courtesy, National Gallery of Art, Index of American Design.

Courtesy, Bucks County Historical Society, Doylestown, Pa.

Above. Large octagonal platter. On warm orange-sienna ground is placed a conventionalized plant form, in pale cream, yellow, and green slips.

Earthenware Fat-Lamps, c. 1800.

Before the advent of kerosene, lamps had changed but little in their essentials since Roman times. In all of them, a wick was laid sidewise in lard, oil, or other fat. These are identical with Schwabian prototypes.

Below. Redware platter, made for daily use. A four-quilled slip cup produced the well-spaced scrollings. Platters like these held "schnitz and knep", a famous dish in Pennsylvania German cookery, made of dried apples, a piece of ham, and dumplings, or "knep" (German *"Knöpfe"* or "buttons").

Fruit drying was an important part of the year's work. Preparing "schnitz" (dried apples) was an occupation which permitted neighbors to get together. "Apples what blew off" were peeled, cut up, and dried, a Pennsylvania German method of salvage eventually adopted by others.

Below. Earthenware Strainer.

41

GEOMETRICAL DEVICES IN SGRAFFITO

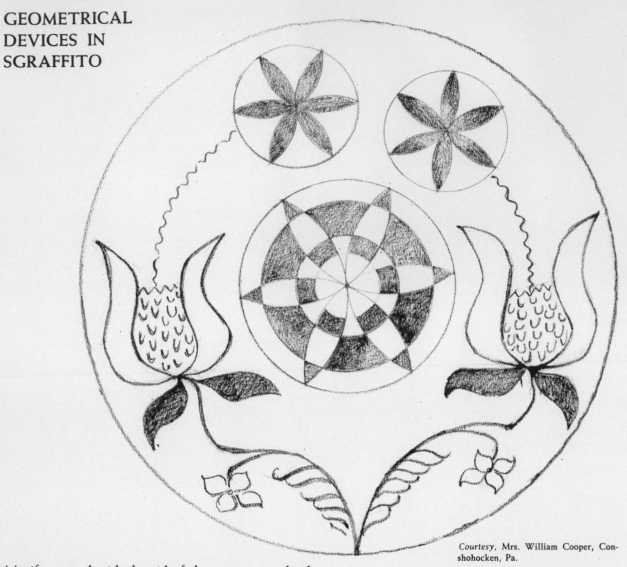

Courtesy, Mrs. William Cooper, Con-shohocken, Pa.

Motifs created with the aid of the compass and ruler. In later days, when the original inspirational sources of design were weakened, the potter whose artistic skill was perhaps not equal to developing a direct, freehand drawing on the clay resorted to mechanical devices.

Sgraffito plate, incised lines and areas disclosing orange base, beneath clay-yellow ground. Green slip fills in two small circles. Diameter 13".

Tulip motif, from plate.

Inscription, translated:

"In the dish stands a star
And the girls would willingly have the boys. H.T. I.S.T. 1823".

Left and above. Courtesy, Philadelphia Museum of Art.

Plate made by Benjamin Bergey, Montgomery County, Pa., around 1830-1840. Well-balanced design of skillfully traced-in slip, filling entire field of plate, 13″ in diameter. After applying the decoration, Bergey beat the slip, which stood up in slight relief, into the clay base to prevent its chipping off with use. This method of ornamentation, identical with that employed on the plates and platters intended for "every day" (see platter, p. 41), differed from that of the other potters whose decorative slipware, planned only for display, lacked the smooth even surface which daily use demanded.

The motif, the pelican, piercing her breast in order to feed her young, is an incomplete presentation of the ancient Christian symbol signifying atonement and piety. Three infant birds, usually depicted in their nest, gaping open-mouthed to receive the blood from her wound, are omitted.

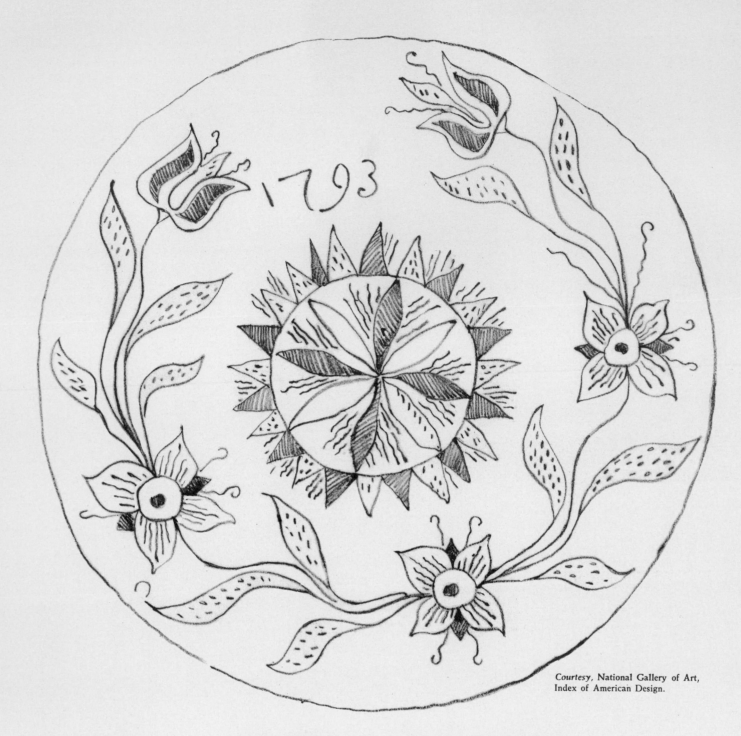

THE WORK OF ANDREW HEADMAN

Andrew Headman operated a pottery in Rock Hill Township, Bucks County, Pa., in the last decade of the eighteenth century and the first two decades of the nineteenth. This potter, who usually preferred to center his plates with a large eight-pointed star or four-petalled blossom, experimented once or twice with a parroquet in that spot. Headman's work is always in sgraffito, in the usual colors: clay red, earth yellow, and copper green.

Left. Headman's initials, a trefoil, and the date 1793 set in a cartouche, are inscribed on the bottom of a small mold used to shape octagonal saucers.

In 1808 Andrew Headman made, dated, and signed the impressive plate to the left. In 1818, while still reproducing the same design, he omitted the signature. To inscribe it without colliding with an already drawn leaf required an effort of judgment which he may no longer have felt like expending after so many years of working at his trade.

Courtesy, National Gallery of Art, Index of American Design.

Though frequently used in fractur writing, the parroquet is unusual in ceramics. It has vanished from the local scene, but when this plate was made, the parroquet was a common sight in Pennsylvania. "Near a field of maize, in the forest, I saw large flocks of parrots, of which we often shot many, with great ease. They were not shy and soon re-assembled after one shot had dispersed them." (Maximilian's "Travels," 1832-1834.)

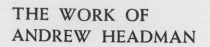

*Courtesy, National Gallery of Art,
Index of American Design.*

FROM THE SURFACE OF THE EARTH—FLAX

"The German-Town of which I spoke before
Which is at least in length one mile or more,
Where lives High German people, and Low Dutch,
Whose trade in weaving Linnen Cloth is much,
There grows the Flax, as also you may know,
That from the same they do divide the Tow;
Their trade fits well within their Habitation."
—Richard Frame—1692

IN 1834 Anna Mari Miller took a piece of the fine homespun linen stored in her dower chest, chose set little cross-stitch patterns of stars and birds and flowers, arranged them symmetrically on the long linen panel, and embroidered them in red cotton, stitch by careful stitch, counting every thread. At one end she made a net panel for further embellishment and in it darned two ladies in wide white hoopskirts. In the same tiny cross-stitches she set down her name and the date. This long towel, purely decorative, served both to show off her skill with the needle and as an outlet for the love of embroidered linen, a taste for which was latent in all Palatine women. Ornamental needlework could not be indulged in until a way of life which permitted a few graces had been firmly established. This state of well-being seems to have arrived toward the end of the eighteenth century. Then, as embroidered dated linens indicate, the beauty-starved country women were able to find a little time in which to carry on the traditions of their European great-grandmothers with equal vigor, skill and grace—though how any woman could find heart to embellish a piece of homespun linen is to be marvelled at, when one considers the amount of labor consumed in the making of the fabric itself. Only a strong, smoldering passion for decoration could have induced her again to handle a piece of homespun linen, constructed literally out of unending toil, to labor on it once more with eye-consuming stitchery.

But they loved needlework, and from that time on, as specimens from their hands indicate today, young girls such as Barbara Byberin in 1808, Susann Diller in 1832, Marea Schaffer in 1834, Kadharina Kral in 1855, and even Madelin Deiner as late as 1859, got out their finest and best linen woven at home and their colored threads, and embroidered these long linen panels to store away in their painted chests, as part of their "*Haus steier*" (*Aussteuer*, or dowry).

In the days when Pennsylvania was first settled, in all rural districts as well as in many towns the home was the center of textile production; for many early settlers it was their only source of fabric. Homespun was a descriptive word indicating the place of manufacture. Nowadays, the adjective "homespun" means coarse or plain; sometimes it is followed by the word "virtue," as if to designate a special variety. But in the days when

47

spinning was absolutely compulsory if everyone was to be garmented and protected from freezing, dire necessity was the motor which drove all the treadles on all the spinning wheels, and virtue an expected by-product. As there was no elegance in the vicinity of the early Pennsylvania German settlers with which to contrast it, even the connotation of "coarse" and "plain" had no meaning at that time. For no matter how coarse or how plain a piece of woven textile, the most unremitting labor was required to produce it, from the moment of the sowing of the flaxseed in the basic material, the fertile earth, to the time it was taken off the loom, a finished piece of fabric.

Day in, day out, spinning went on interminably, an occupation followed when other work had slackened. At such times, from Monday to Friday, every member of the family might be employed at the wheels, for no one ever had too much yarn made up in advance. Sturdy as were the fabrics woven by the early settlers, hard work wore out garments, which had then to be replaced; increases in the size of families demanded more and more materials; and when some members grew up, married and left home, as part of their dowries they took with them a share of the family weaving to start them off until they could themselves continue the relentless cycle. A Pennsylvania German farmer in the eighteenth century described his family, with what was undoubtedly a faint touch of boasting, as consisting of "three sons and eight daughters, five are able to turn the Spinning Wheel and throw the Shuttle." But his hearers felt that compulsion nudged the elbows of his pride, for they all knew how utterly dependent they were on the dainty flax plant. Until they found the time to rid the woodlands of the wild animals that made the raising of sheep almost too difficult, flax was their only textile crop, and many hands were the power that turned it into fabric.

Today it is impossible to visualize the amount of hard work necessary to reduce the flax plant to even the state of a workable fibre, which could then be spun. No modern weaver seated pensively at her loom, turning out "hand-loomed" fabrics, would produce a single inch of it if she had first to take part in any of the operations of planting, harvesting, and changing the innocent, blue-flowered plant into a thread ready for weaving. Yet Pennsylvania German women assumed their share of even the agricultural processes.

These began in the early spring when, in late April, the flaxseed was sown in an area set aside for it, from one-half to three acres. So that the flax would have long, straight, unbranching stems when it reached its full height of two or three feet, it was seeded thickly. By June it was covered with a mass of lovely blue blossoms, furnishing a handsome contrast to the ripening fields of golden grain. The blossoms turned into seeds, the seeds ripened, the stalks became woody and hollow, and by July the flax could be harvested.

This operation was done entirely by hand, a hand free of even a sickle, for it was necessary to pull the plant up by the roots so that no possible inch of the precious fibre might be wasted. At some stage or other of the harvesting, all of the family participated, but the job of uprooting the flax was handed over to the boys and girls, as it was less hard on young backs. The flax was pulled out in small bundles, which would be gathered carefully and set aside; the children had been cautioned to handle them gingerly because of the seeds, which were highly valued, for when pressed they yielded the oil known as linseed. These small bundles, tied with straw, were set up in wigwam fashion to dry, and later were hauled, with the same care for the seeds, to the barn. There the flax was spread out on the threshing floor, the root ends weighted down with a heavy plank, and the seed heads batted with a heavy wooden tool, an operation which freed the pods of their precious contents. This hard dusty job was taken over by a man, for it took both strength and skill to handle the weighty, home-made "batter," as it was called.

Next the stems were straightened out, tied in bundles, and stored in a dry place. At this stage the flax would not deteriorate if the process of turning it into linen had to be interrupted; it could be stored without danger for several years. But if the work were to be carried on without a break, the tough outer straw covering, called "boon," had to be rendered brittle so that it could be separated from the inner filaments, which are the true flax. The major part of this process, called "retting," was turned over to the sun, the rain, and the dew, with occasionally a little help from man. The farm workers spread it out thinly on a dry part of the meadow and turned it from time to time with a long pole, so that all the elements could do a thorough job of rotting the "boon." When the boon separated freely from the flax, it was "done."

For the second time it was gathered up, tied in bundles, and hauled back to the barn, to go through the process called "breaking." This, the hardest part of flax-cleaning, again required a man's strength to operate the heavy wooden machine, called the "flax-break," whose function was to knock the fibres apart and remove the already loosened outside boon. To render the flax even more brittle and thus make removal of the boon easier, it was first heated on grates set over a slow-burning fire. Two women passed the flax bundles back and forth carefully, inch by inch, while the male operator clapped the wooden break down on the fibrous bundles. For many hours on sunny autumn days one heard the sound of the clapping of the flax breaks, and the smoke of the fires drifted across the fields.

For a third time the flax was gathered up, tied in bundles, and taken to a shed or stable, to go through the process called "swingling" or "scutching," an operation which could be delegated to children, for the job, though dirty, was not one that called for great strength. The purpose was to remove the last vestiges of flaxseed and fragments of boon. With a tool called a "swingle," a sharpened wooden knife with nicely rounded edges, the flax was carefully belabored on the beveled top of a firmly set upright block of wood.

Now it began to take on its characteristic gloss, appearing as a bundle of long, clean, hair-like fibres. It was next subjected to a process called "hatchelling," the object of which was to straighten out and separate the fibres into several grades. The "hatchel," the simple tool on which the work was carried out, consisted of a trestle on which were screwed three blocks, each one set with highly polished, home-made nails arranged in rows like the teeth in a series of combs. The result of drawing the flax through these iron combs, first through the one with the widest spacing and then progressively on to the finest, was exactly like that of combing a woman's hair. The first and second combings removed the last vestiges of foreign matter and the coarser, shorter fibres, leaving great snarls of it in the hatchel. These snarls, called "tow," were carefully set aside and saved, to be later woven into various fabrics in which roughness and coarseness of texture were not considered a drawback. Nothing was ever wasted, particularly no part of a material which required so much work to transform it from a plant fibre into a piece of cloth. The "hatcheller" had to be very deft, for in unskilled hands the flax was apt to turn entirely into tow, a product which, while useful, was not the be-all and end-all of flax-growing. Hatchelling was "woman's work" to be carried on in the attic. The operator took the comparatively small mass of fibres remaining in her hand after the passage through the finest set of nails, and twisted its smooth, blond and shining strands into neat spiral hanks. These were tied with cord and hung from the attic rafters. If the fibres were long, she might give them an approving glance —allowing herself a moment of pause in the grim task of turning the flax plant into linen— this task which had begun in April and in November was far from completed.

The flax twists must now be spun into the finest of yarn, and the work of spinning would take up the freer moments of most of the family. Pennsylvania German families had a proverb which indicated the time they allotted to the annual spinning: *"Lichtmess, Spinna vergess. Un 's Fuder halwer g'fress."* They aspired to complete the yearly spinning by Candlemas Day, having begun it on Hallowe'en. Flax culture is ancient, and it is natural that superstitions should cling to it. The Pennsylvania Germans believed that in order to secure a good crop of flax, it was necessary to bake a batch of doughnuts on Shrove Tuesday. If you wanted to have a good long flax, it was important to hand out doughnuts generously to friends and neighbors.

Although the more active members of the family devoted only their evenings to the spinning, elderly women might busy themselves all day at the wheel, whose monotonous droning or squeaking was an expected part of the ordinary household sounds. Under the faint and flickering light of a fat-lamp one might see four or five spinning wheels at work: the young girls would be preparing the yarn for their dower linens, the mother would be about her perennial task of keeping her family clothed; an elderly woman would be spinning away at the tow. The coarse yarn spun from the tow would be woven into heavy bags in which to carry grain to the mill, or it became the linen warp which later, with woolen woof, was woven into the sturdy material called linsey-woolsey, a fabric in which all pioneer farm folk were clothed. Tow was used both as warp and woof to make a rough fabric for working clothes, known locally as *"werk-tuch."* At an auction of a farmer's "movables" in 1751, ten yards of it brought 13 shillings.

Flax in any state of its processing from field to loom was eagerly bought up at every "vendue" or country sale. By acquiring it the purchaser placed himself that many steps nearer the eventual textile. If he had any cash on hand, he always willingly exchanged it for the partially processed fibre. In the eighteenth-century inventories of early farmers' estates, one can find such items as "ould Spining wheal and sum yearn," "clean flax," "44 pounds of flax, swingled."

If flax had undergone its complete transformation into fabric, emerging as "check linen," "flax linen" or "sacks and cloth for a Wagon Cloth" (one of the great white covers for a Conestoga wagon), it was snatched up. In the rural districts where almost everything essential was made at home, everyone was able to calculate the hours of labor required to produce an article. If that amount of time could be saved and used to work on something else of equal importance, the investment of money, scarce as it was, was made.

Processed flax was considered an article important enough to be given as a wedding present. In the mid-eighteenth century, a well-to-do farmer gave his daughter 100 acres of land and some of his best flax, so that she could spin her own cloth, a gesture both generous and moralistic in intent. For by his gift the Pennsylvania farmer assured himself that his daughter, though removed from parental supervision, would have no idle moments while waiting for her own flax crop to be sown and harvested. He "started her out right."

As the spinning of tow was a dusty, dirty job, it was the one tackled first, in order to get it out of the way. After that, the wheels began to hum as the finest linen yarn was made. Flax spinning, a much cleaner task, was made the excuse for an occasional party. Since opportunities to meet one's neighbors socially were infrequent, the spinning party was an ingenious device of women for getting together. Word was sent around to all the women in a community, and picking up their flax and their spinning wheels, they managed, either on foot or on horseback, to get to the central meeting point. Here they spent the entire day, gossiping and spinning with equal energy. In the evening, the young farmers arrived. The women, with an enormous amount of linen yarn to their credit, and refreshed by the gossip and by the lavish meal that their hostess provided for all, were ready to join the men in the barn for hours of games and dancing. These parties kept up until daybreak. Then the tired spinsters, single and married, together with their spinning wheels, were gathered up and taken by the young men to their homes.

Lacking the excuse of a party, a wily young girl, if she would shoulder her spinning wheel, might be permitted to use a chance hour to walk to a neighboring farm for a chat with her close friend. These rare hours were much sought after and the spinning was faithfully done by the well-disciplined maiden. Not to spin in one's free moments was considered a neglect of duty, and a subject for frank comment by one's neighbors.

Even after all this toil both in the home and at parties, the spun yarn was not yet ready for work on the loom. While tow was left its natural color, the finest linen yarn had yet to be bleached, a complicated series of processes whose final result transformed it from its natural brown hue into something only a little lighter. After it was taken from the loom, it was subjected to at least twenty more bleaching operations, involving baths in a decoction of wood ashes, alternating with baths in sunlight and then in buttermilk, until it approached the standard of whiteness the housewife considered necessary for her best linens.

A loom was an essential part of all early households. The women of the family were expected to operate it until travel conditions improved sufficiently to enable itinerant weavers to move about from farm to farm, hiring out their services to help with the weaving. In a surviving account book of one such itinerant we find the scale of prices for 1726: "John Lederach's flaxen cloth is 36 yards @ sixpence per yard. The price of tow cloth which I made is 15 yards and a half at 5 pence. 30 yards of tow and 21 yards of flax for Jacob Garman."

Eventually, the time came when all this interminable work began to pile up as surplus. Women, by their own efforts, by inheritance and by the purchase of other women's weaving at country sales, now had a reserve of fabric on hand, stowed away in their dower chests. The hardest part of the life of the early settlers was behind them, and they had time to think of something besides the sternest necessities. Now the fine fields were cleared, the great stone barns built; the roads, once woodland trails, had been opened up and improved, so that it was possible to get to the city, where there was material already woven, of a quality unknown to them. If the head of the family could be wheedled into it, these wonderful, fine cloths were purchased. Though it occurred only rarely, a few women managed to get some stuffs they did not have to make themselves, and the helpless male who permitted these purchases complained in a letter to the paper of his choice, the "Philadelphische Correspondenz," in 1781, about the desire for the luxuries of life at that time.

Our correspondent's plaint might well be summarized here. In 1741, for him the "good old days," his capital had consisted of two suits of homespun clothes, four pairs of socks, four linen shirts, and two pairs of shoes. These had been given to him by the farmer for whom he had worked from the age of twelve to twenty-one. He then married, and rented a farm of forty acres. At thirty-two, he had saved enough to buy a sixty-acre farm. As he made more money, he bought more land; thus he could present his first daughter who married with a farm and the flax to do her own spinning, as already mentioned. He spent no money unnecessarily, so the wedding portion of the first daughter was one that we can be sure met with his approval. At this time, apart from taxes, his annual expenses were not more than $10, and he was putting away $150 every year in his strong box. He bought cattle, fattened them for market, made more and more money, so that he was even able to put it out at interest.

Then, he wails, a change came over his way of living, for by this time his women folk evidently took an interest in the excess profits and decided to have a share in them. When his second daughter married, his wife, instead of handing over a few surplus pots and pans to the bride so that she could begin her own collection of kitchen ware, *bought* new kitchen utensils for her! And his third daughter wore *silk dresses!*

It goes without saying that this family of rebellious females spent but little time at the spinning wheel since they had found the means to buy the materials they needed for clothing. And though our correspondent complained that all these purchases were making his expenses larger than his income, his women folk had discovered that money was the magic key that would free them forever from what was evidently needless drudgery at the flax and wool wheels.

From now on, women who were able to buy a few textiles could indulge themselves in a long suppressed love for something beautiful, something beyond the sheerly useful. From their surplus of home-woven materials, they now dared to take a length of linen and cover it with fine stitchery to make a purely ornamental towel. From their best flax they could now weave a patterned table cover, not for daily use but for "best," a term which often meant that it was too good ever to be used. In the chests in which such articles were stored the accumulation of plain and embroidered linen grew from year to year, a credit to housewifely abilities, a source of quiet pride.

The results of the invention in England of power-driven looms in 1785 were naturally felt sooner or later even in the hinterlands of the newly formed United States, although in all the rural districts the habit of using the hand-loom persisted for many years. As late as 1840, some of the Pennsylvania German women were still following their traditional toil at the wheel and the loom, though by this time the most conservative of farmers could hardly prevent their purchases of certain types of machine-loomed fabrics. But when the farmer himself was eventually convinced that cloth could be bought for less than it cost to manufacture it under his own roof, the homespun industries disappeared with almost startling speed. And no one was more delighted than the farmers' daughters when the days for home spinning finally passed, for with them vanished the dirtiest and most tedious task that had ever fallen to the lot of women.

Great improvements in transportation methods made possible the distribution of factory-made goods to even the most remote rural districts. Country stores became the willing agents for all kinds of merchandise and were the strongest influence in changing even so rigid a set of habits as the Pennsylvania German farmer cherished. After 1850, the blue of the flowering flax disappeared from the chequered layout of the summer fields; the farm women dressing flax were no longer a subject for derogatory comment by haughty foreign travellers; and spinning wheels were objects relegated to the dusty attics. And only a generation or so later, these same spinning wheels were looked upon, with what was really astounding detachment, as objects so quaint and decorative that, ornamented with satin bows, they were considered worthy of display in the parlor.

Today, as a final degradation, many spinning wheels have been moved out of doors, to be hung in front of the country shops, where they serve as the stop-sign for the motorist hunting for antiques.

Though the spinning wheels might be treated in a frivolous manner, the worthy product they once produced was not set aside with equal lightness. Thriftiness, one of the primary virtues, was closely seconded by another equally respected—viz. "taking thought for the morrow." As such things were taken very seriously, her Lancaster County neighbors found Phebe Earle Gibbons very irritating because in 1867 she could write with faint amusement: "We no longer make linen; but I have heard of one Dutch girl who had a good supply of domestic linen made into shirts and trousers for the future spouse whose 'fair Proportions' she had not yet seen."

PENNSYLVANIA GERMAN SAMPLER

As their basic course in ornamental needlework, Pennsylvania German children, like children in other sections of the country in the early days, were taught to embroider samplers. Painstakingly they counted threads and followed with tiny cross-stitches the designs in the pattern books. Little girls with a British tradition of needlework behind them went beyond these simple alphabets and borders; they learned in their schools to embroider on their samplers ladies and gentlemen, landscapes with animals, pious mottoes, and sentimental verses.

But Pennsylvania German samplers are rarely this frivolous. The planning shows a practical trend. The embroidered alphabets served as practice workouts, and, later on, as models for the names and initials with which young Barbara or Maria or Catharina would mark the articles she was preparing for her future home. In addition to the alphabets, motifs of conventionalized flowers and urns, hearts and birds, tulips and animals, were studded in more or less orderly fashion on the homespun linen surface. In time these would also be used by the maiden as the basis for cross-stitch embellishment on her best household linens—her "show" towels. See pages 56, 57, 58, 59.

Barbara Landis's sampler shows order in arrangement, whimsey in the selection of motifs and typographic nonchalance in spelling. In a Pennsylvania German accent, she sets forth, in mingled upper and lower case, an ancient sentiment:

"BarBara LaNDIS DIS WorK DoNe WheN DIS YOU see reMeMBer Me WheN I aM DeD aND GONe. 1827."

Courtesy, National Gallery of Art,
Index of American Design.

On "show" towels, (*Parade Hand-Tuch*) the finest stitchery was lavished, for these long, embroidered panels were used only for display. Here, as in Europe, they were hung as decorations on the doors, where they served not only as indisputable evidence of the housewife's deftness with the flax wheel and the needle, but also had a practical use. In the days when water had to be drawn from a well, laundering was a tedious process; so cautious housewives, when guests came, did not set aside a slightly used towel. Instead, they covered it with a "show" towel, always made with two tape loops for ease in hanging.

Red cotton was used to work out the motifs neatly distributed on the linen surface, motifs which are identical with those worked on the childhood samplers. Almost all "show" towels are initialed, but some proudly carry the full name of the owner and the year the towel was worked.

Mennonite maidens featured a curious device on their handiwork. From the central motif of a crowned heart spring six lilies interspersed with the initials O E H B D D E, these being the first letters of the words, "*O Edles Herz Bedenk' Doch Dein Ende*" (O Noble Heart Reflect on your End!). Shown above.

56

Below. The couplet used as border on English pewter plate, 1661. From the author's notebook.

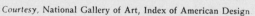

Courtesy, National Gallery of Art, Index of American Design

"Show" towel worked in brilliant wools on coarse linen. Made as an engagement gift for Jacob Stauffer by his future bride. Many towels are shyly marked with twin hearts, but few so boldly state the reason for their making. The use of an ancient English couplet on a traditional Pennsylvania German piece of needlework is indicative of the changes taking place in a once isolated culture.

After the introduction of aniline-dyed woolen yarns, towels worked from the 1840's on demonstrate the local fondness not only for the intense colors of these bright wools but for the wider decorative possibilities they offered.

Freed from the limitations imposed by the technique of cross-stitch, inventive needlewomen experimented with new stitches. Some devised new motifs for their embroideries; others adapted existing ones. One Elizabeth Buchwalter took as her inspiration the twin birds on a branch (common to practically all printed birth certificates), traced them, and worked out, in rows of closely set chain-stitch, a precise copy of their forms.

Below. Detail from towel made by Eliza Ann Brackbill, 1847. Birds and tulip surmounting a barn symbol. Height 10". In reds, yellow, blue, and faded brown wools. This towel also carries a red cow, a bird resembling a turkey, and four-leaved clover symbols.

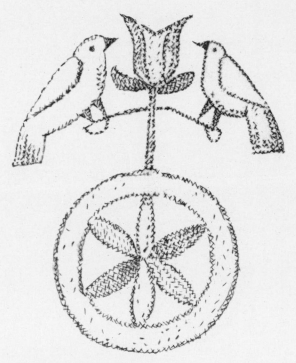

Left. "Show" towel, made by Cadarina Kuns, 1827. Finished with elaborate drawn-work panel featuring three wide-skirted ladies and two peacocks. By means of a different stitch, C. K. evolved the whirling swastika, an unusual form on "show" towels but a very common one on latter-day barn decorations.

58

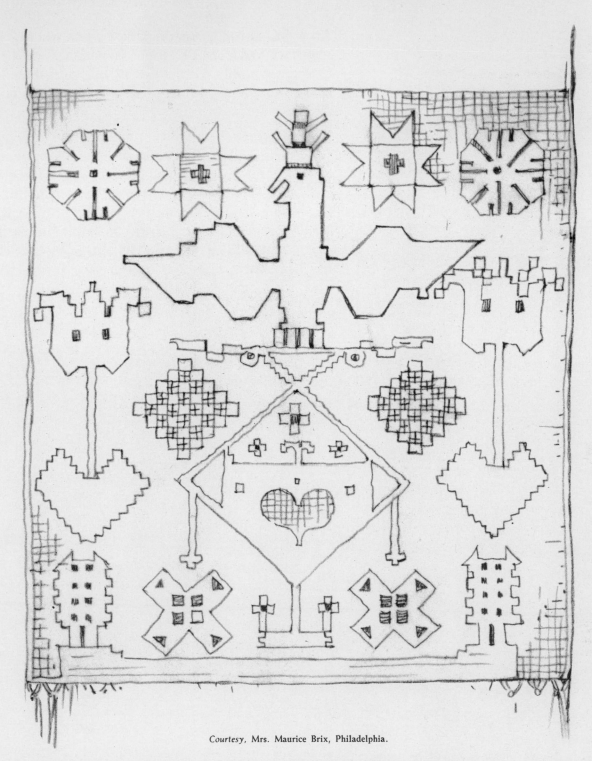

Drawnwork Panel, 12" x 13", from "Show" Towel.

"Show" towels were ornamented with cross-stitch and later with other types of stitchery, transverse borders of fringes, etc., and were often finished with a panel of darned net. To make this, threads were drawn and whipped together to form a coarse net into which characteristic patterns were darned with soft linen threads. In spite of the angularity enforced by the square mesh, it is easy to identify the crowned eagle, the tulips springing from hearts, and the usual geometrical symbols. Sometimes the darning was enhanced by the addition of color. See p. 58.

FROM THE SHEEP WHICH GRAZE
ON THE EARTH—WOOL

"Here you need not trouble the Shambles for Meat, nor Bakers and Brewers for Beer and Bread, nor run to a Linen-Draper for a supply, every one making their own Linen and a great part of their Woollen Cloth for their ordinary wearing."

—John Fenwick

TWENTY-ONE-YEAR-OLD Mr. Isaac Weld of Dublin, travelling through the rural regions of Pennsylvania at the end of the eighteenth century, missed his calm hedgerows and familiar fields, the specimen oaks of his own broad acres. He made rude comments on the queer snake fences and rough log cabins, and sneered at the colonists for their lack of appreciation of woodland vistas.

But had he ridden through the endless woods a century previous, when the settlers were making their first attempts to chop out a space in which to live, he might better have understood why the settlers thought a cabbage patch or an open treeless field ten times more beautiful than the most rounded of oaks, the most romantic of glens.

For on the extent of cleared space with which he could surround himself depended both the safety and the livelihood of the settler.

But trees were not the only things to be conquered. Bears, wolves, and panthers darting out from the shelter of the close forest ranks were always to be feared. Bears were insupportably insolent. They were known to creep out of the woods, cross a momentarily unguarded space, and spring upon a full-grown hog feeding noisily at his trough. The pig's agonized outcry carried to the farmer his first signal of trouble. If a gun was not at hand, the bear escaped unharmed and walked away, erect and impudent, his squealing dinner firmly embraced in his paws. Grey wolves, less brazen, preferred the helpless, silly sheep. Traps or gun provided a temporary relief from marauders, and provided also the skin of the beast, which was depended on for warmth. But to solve the problem of warm woolen clothing for winter without indefinite recourse to such means, it was necessary to create a world safe enough for sheep to live in; a world of sunny fields and open grassy spaces, where innocuous sheep might graze unmolested. Toward this end the work of the colonist was directed, and by the time Mr. Weld came along, this war against the trees and predatory animals was about over. Young Weld travelled through a farming country, safe not only for sheep but for himself.

As the State was settled so much later than the northern colonies, it also lagged behind them in the production of wool. As early as 1736, however, certain sections must have been made safe enough for a venture in sheep raising, for in an inventory of a farmer's will of that date, among the few household goods is listed "42 lb. of woolen yearn."

Though the settlers now had this new textile source, they used it sparingly, for there was none too much of it. To eke it out they added some of their staple textile crop, flax, and wove a fabric whose warp was made of flax and whose woof of wool. This was the famous linsey-woolsey, which all country folk wore. To our present-day eyes, this home-made cloth seems to be a strong, long wearing, workaday material which, while far too heavy for any modern wear, was well fitted to the times and the rough work for which it was worn. But something in its homespun quality provoked comment from fine city ladies cloaked in scarlet broadcloth and imported muslins. When forced by the exigencies of travel to pass through the rural sections taken over by the "peasantry," they were frequently amused by the sight of the German women, "dressed in striped linsey-woolsey petticoats and short gowns . . . They looked very strangely . . . The dress of the women grows worse and worse. We find them now with very short petticoats. No short gown and barefoot."

For years before the Revolution, Great Britain kept up a powerful campaign to squelch all infant industries, all tendencies to encourage the production of wool and the manu-facture of textiles in the colonies. While this was undoubtedly irritating to progressively inclined colonists, the Pennsylvania German farmer, having successfully raised his own wool, and with a flourishing spinning and weaving industry under his own roof, remained unperturbed by the plans of politicians and the troubles of city dwellers. In 1765 Phila-delphians might, if they wished to do so, in order to encourage the growing of wool, pledge themselves not to eat mutton or lamb for two years. The Pennsylvania German farmers found it unnecessary even to consider such a pledge, for they did not think lamb or mutton fit for food, an idea they persisted in holding even to the end of the nineteenth century. They specialized in great displays of beef and pork products, but looked on lamb scorn-fully as not worth butchering, for there was still no market for it in the Pennsylvania German towns. The identical adherence to custom kept the Pennsylvania German farmer in homespun long after other sections of the state were wearing factory-made cloth. He had no intention of wasting the surplus of wool that had been accumulating over the years, and until it had all been used, the cheapness of manufactured textiles never tempted him away from his age-old habit of making homemade stuffs.

Sheep washing and shearing took place in May and were often made into hilarious occasions. The flock was driven to a convenient stream. Certain spots must have been pre-ferred for the purpose, for in 1746 "Ye sheep's washing Place" on Tacony Creek was noted. Following the shearing of the sheep, the fleece was dried on the grass. All burs and foreign matter were removed; tangled mats were cut out and set aside to be later spun into a rough yarn. Wool was too valuable a material to be wasted, and even though the resultant cloth was coarse and full of prickles, it was worn uncomplainingly, for it was warm.

After the cleaning and sorting, it was the task of the women folk to card the wool, a tedious process that filled in every spare moment. To card wool, the housewife took a tuft and combed it between two "wool cards." These were rectangular pieces of wood, fitted with handles and set brush fashion with teeth of fine wire, slightly bent. The tuft of wool emerged, after certain deft operations of the carder with her wire tools, as a fluffy roll of neatly combed parallel fibres, ready to be spun. This tedious job of carding by hand could be circumvented if in the neighborhood grist mill the miller had installed a carding machine, run by the same power that ground the meal. In that case, the bags of wool were carried to the mill with the grain, and when the miller returned them to the housewife, they were ready for spinning.

Cloth made wholly of wool was used only for "best" and for Sundays. The material for men's clothes was woven of the finest yarn the spinner made, and then was taken by the farmer, on one of his rare trips, to a "fulling-mill" where, after being subjected to a process of washing, dyeing, and finishing, it emerged as "fulled cloth," the fabric from which his Sunday clothes were made. Women were glad to wear a simple flannel, which when treated to a pressing in the same mill acquired a pleasing gloss and was known as "pressed cloth," their Sunday-best.

To be serviceable, wool had to be dyed, for its natural color was too light. Dyeing was a process requiring skill and considerable empirical knowledge. Many women must have done much experimenting to discover which plants and which barks furnished satisfactory coloring material for wool.

For dyestuffs as for everything else, the farm was forced to depend on itself. Indigo was generally the only color purchased. It produced a permanent dark blue and was so steadily in demand that men earned their living by peddling it from farm to farm. The daily clothing of the early settlers was apt to be a practical brown, for the barks of trees, with which so much dyeing was done, furnished more satisfactory browns and yellows than any other material. "Butternut brown," the term invariably used to describe the color of the early settlers' garments, was obtained from the bark of the butternut tree. Both the warp and the woof of linsey-woolsey were dyed with it, though in later Colonial days, stripes of other colors varied its original monotony.

From black oak and hickory barks a good yellow was extracted, and the bark of white maple made a dull but durable gray. The berries of sumach furnished a rich red-brown, their own handsome color. Sassafras bark, which even in its natural state is strongly colored, dyed wool a fast orange.

Some of the frailer plants furnished brighter colors than the barks. Pokeweed, with its purple-red stems and inky-hued berries looking as if suffused with dye, invited much experiment. Some women boiled the juice with alum, from which they obtained a crimson; others found that the roots produced a rich red. The fragile jewel-weed or "touch-me-not" with its watery leaves and dangling orange flowers could be depended upon to dye woolens an excellent yellow. False indigo, still preserving in its common name its early use, gave to the housewife a blue with which she made shift when there was no genuine indigo at hand. It must have been an indifferent and unsatisfactory dyestuff, for though it cost her nothing, she never used it if she could find the money, a scarce article in early days, with which to buy the genuine. This expenditure of cash on the part of the farm wife, whose thriftiness was her pride, indicates how necessary the blue of indigo was in her coloring plans.

Long after the actual need for it was past, the process of home dyeing was persisted in by country women. In order that the scrubbed boards of the kitchen floor could be kept immaculate, the work took place outdoors, in a great brass kettle kept just for the purpose. These kettles, the pride of the housewife, were swung over small hot fires, kept up with the addition of bits of fuel taken from a stock pile which had been gathered by the children long before the day chosen for the task. With all preparations made in advance, the job of dyeing, though a messy one, was not too greatly dreaded. The dye bath was prepared, the material to be dyed was immersed in the boiling liquid, and when the desired color was obtained, it was removed and draped over the supports placed for it. Outdoors, the superfluous dye dripping from the newly colored yarns or woven goods damaged nothing. The sight of brightly dyed skeins of yarn and of yards of material hung up to dry must have given the air of a gypsy encampment to the farmstead, bright in its own autumn colorings, for fall was the chosen time for the home-dyeing of yarns, in order to have them ready for the winter weaving.

Over the irregular and varied sounds of farm life, over the cackling of hens, the honking of geese and the lower-pitched noises coming from the stock, there used to be heard resounding through the air a heavy, regular "thwack—thwack," issuing from the house. The meaning of this familiar sound, which is without significance to present-day ears, was perfectly understood by anyone in the Colonial era, for it was the noise that accompanied weaving on the handloom. Every farmhouse large enough to accommodate one had a loom as part of its household gear. Weaving on the family loom was another of the homely skills which every girl acquired, just as she learned that other textile essential, spinning. On the home loom the women of the family turned out plain fabrics for everyday use and contrived simple checks and stripes from yarns dyed for the purpose. While these may have been a change from the plain brown textiles they habitually turned out, the desire for a still livelier pattern and bolder color could not be suppressed.

In addition, women in all of the colonies knew how to weave the simpler coverlets which adorned their beds. These home-woven coverlets, usually blue and white, were woven on a flax warp, with wool, dyed a strong blue with the precious indigo, used as the woof. Because of the limitations of the weavers' technical skill and the simple loom on which they worked, home-woven coverlets from no matter what Colonial region looked pretty much alike. The patterns resulting from the interweaving of blue and white were always geometrical. When a woman more inventive than her neighbors devised a variation on a familiar pattern, there were always friends eager to try the exciting novelty on their looms. Patterns for weaving were exchanged just as were new designs for quilting, so that any regional variation eventually acquired a far greater distribution than was originally intended or thought possible. Before the days of magazines, this hand-to-hand method was the only means by which ideas filtered through a region. It is edifying to see how a decorative idea will be followed by a whole district, varying only where another idea, equally popular in another area, impinges on it.

But textile production, even in the earliest days, was not entirely dependent on the free time and the skill of women in the home. Professional weavers were essential members of all the early groups of German colonists, outnumbered only by farmers and carpenters in the first settlements. Germantown, now part of Philadelphia, was the first place in the State to be settled by a group of Palatine immigrants, most of whom were weavers. Not long after their arrival, the quality of their work, in both linen and woolen textiles, was already being recognized. So outstanding was their early production in stocking manufacturing that to this day "Germantown" is the descriptive name for a kind of yarn used in knitting.

When roads were opened up so that travel to the back country became easier, some professional weavers became itinerants. Well-to-do farms looked forward to their coming, for their labor was always welcomed to help weave the year's accumulation of spun yarns— and in addition to their skills, they were the transmitters of local gossip. Sometimes this member of a highly respected craft loaded his own loom on a cart, setting it up in temporary headquarters wherever there was a demand for his skills. With him undoubtedly went his "pattern" book, not only for his own guidance but to enable his customers to pick out the designs that pleased them.

These early weavers prepared all their "drafts" very carefully. They were drawn in manuscript books, which today are of great interest to modern workers on the hand-loom. There are two of these books in possession of the Philadelphia Museum, the earliest bearing the date 1723, and the name Johann Ludwig Speck; the other belonged to John Landes, who probably worked at his trade in the latter half of the eighteenth century. It is more reasonable to suppose that he kept up the general habit of itinerant craftsmanship, together with the tailor and the shoemaker, than to imagine that his clients made their way to a permanently established workshop. For the weaver to move himself and his pattern book was far easier than for his clients to transport themselves and great bulky masses of yarns to his shop. over the rough roads existing at that time.

Little is known about either of these early weavers. John Landes left a few notations as to his prices: 12½ cents a yard for what he called "fancy," 10 cents a yard for weaving plain linen or flannel, and all of 20 cents for "diaper" (a patterned fabric).

Rural women always looked forward to the coming of the weaver and his pattern book, for it presented them with a high moment, the rare opportunity to make a choice. As the roughness and harshness of early living made simplicity the basic pattern for everything, the pleasure of choosing anything could not be indulged in until the first faint glimmer of modern trade practices was visible. Every woman in the family must have taken her part in the lively discussion over the designs offered in the pattern book, evidence of the weaver's taste and artistic ingenuity.

Necessity compelled the feminine head of every household to see that she had enough material to clothe her family adequately, and ample reserves of raw material stored in advance of the family's textile needs. But long after this pressure was eased, she continued to accumulate spun yarns in her attic and to store up household linens in her chests. Pride spurred her on, a pride with all the weight of European tradition behind it, for according to her standards no one could have too much linen or bedding. Eventually, when a great store of plain textiles under her roof had given her a feeling of security, she might take a moment in which to plan a little added beauty for her everyday, serviceable, dun-colored fabrics. The memory of the handsome, figured textiles of her native land had never left her. Next to the chest, beds presented one of the few large spaces on which patterns could be displayed. In her mind's eye she saw every bed covered with colorful spreads, either of her own weaving or a pattern of her own choosing. With her modest decorative schemes in mind, she had always plenty of work planned ahead for the looms. In addition, custom of long standing dictated the number of quilts and coverlets, the "*Haus steier*" allotted to each marriageable son and daughter, all of which had to be prepared in advance, for no one dared to deviate from so rigid a social pattern.

Eighteenth-century folk, and all continental European stock in particular, had great concern for the appearance of the bed. This tradition they brought with them unchanged. The beds of the Pennsylvania Germans were of impressive bulk, a matter of inevitable comment from persons unfamiliar with their traditions. In the make-up of beds as in everything else, they held to the fashion of their ancestors. With clean straw brought from the barn, they filled a homespun blue-and-white checked linen bedtick until it stood up about a foot in thickness. On this foundation they piled other linen tickings filled to equal thickness with carefully hoarded goosefeathers. The Pennsylvania Germans, like most Europeans, preferred to remain comfortably warm between their great feather ticks than to shiver, though in a more sanitary fashion, between sheets and quilts as did the sophisticated city folk of British origin. To restrain this unwieldly mound of feathers and make it smooth and presentable, a closely woven heavy coverlet was necessary—the reason for the weight of certain bed-coverings which today seem extraordinarily cumbrous.

After the invention of the Jacquard loom in the early nineteenth century, the Pennsylvania German weavers produced their most notable work. Since improved roads made it possible for their clients to come to them, the weavers set up their little shops in many small towns and villages located in well established sections of the State. Here they turned out their splendid products, making them both for stock and to order. When the weaver accumulated a stock of these coverlets, made at times when he had none on order and marked with his name and the date, he piled them into a capacious chest built especially for the purpose, put the chest into a wagon, and peddled its contents around his neighborhood, for he was both manufacturer and distributor. When he made coverlets to order, he proudly wove the owner's name and date as well as his own, for he and his clients were alike in their respect for possessions. No woman who was in driving distance of the weaver's shop could resist ordering one of his coverlets, so much handsomer than those woven at home.

The weavers added to the too familiar color scheme of blue and white many new and striking colors, delightful to the eyes of color-starved women. Fearlessly they mingled reds, the new magentas, strong blues and greens in coverlets, always beautiful in their owner's eyes and quite acceptable to modern tastes accustomed to peasant color schemes. To the simple farm women the patterns, as well as the colors, must have been equally entrancing. They were so much more elaborate than the monotonous geometrical figures they produced on their own looms. Here were new motifs of peacocks, and, for the first time, unmistakable roses; gracefully curving blossoms of many types; great suns with many radiating points; patriotic symbols of which the young, proud country was so fond; mediæval houses, and contemporary Independence Hall—the choice was overwhelming. For those who disliked such innovations, all the old familiar motifs were also available; those used by the decorators of chests and the carvers of buttermolds: the traditional cock, the pair of doves, the tulip, both in profile and in front aspect, the heart, the star and its many variations, and for really restrained tastes, the geometrical field.

The 1840's seem to have been the heyday of the coverlet weavers. By that period the resources of most folk, even those whose immediate forebears had been indentured servants, had so increased that they not only lived in comfort but had ready cash to expend on "nice" things. The local artisan operating a hand loom must have found it a worthwhile business for at least half a century, as indicated by the many coverlets bearing dates ranging from 1820 to 1870. But after a change in fashion, when the rule of quiet or pastel color schemes began, the bold and even violent color schemes of the country weavers became outmoded. Cotton became much cheaper, and white machine-woven coverlets displayed in the country stores tempted women with cash on hand. The hand-woven coverlets were tucked away in the familiar chests, for by this time their odd color combinations set the teeth of Victorian women on edge. Others were debased from their once showy positions on the plump beds to very lowly uses. Folded, they became comfortable cushioning on the seats of wooden settles or wagons; some women found them particularly suitable padding for ironing boards; others dyed them to reduce the color, and thriftily used them for curtains or couch covers.

Although coverlets were produced in other regions, those made by the Pennsylvania German weavers were the most individual, both in color and conception. Once, as pieces of skilled handcraft, they were considered worthy of exhibit at the earliest county fairs. Today, a century later, in their time-softened reds and eggplant purples, their olive greens and indigos, they again compete for recognition at the same fairs, this time as cherished family pieces and a telling record of a bygone craft.

Left. Handwoven Coverlet. In little shops in village or countryside, the nineteenth-century coverlet maker turned out his products, weaving his name and address in the corner, to which he often added the customer's name, if he were executing it to order. Henry Keener, of Womelsdorf, Berks County, Pa., made this coverlet for S. Divert in 1843. Its field shows a pleasant combination of rigid and curving forms. The scalloped border is unusually restrained.

Courtesy, Landis Valley Museum, Landis Valley, Pa.

Jacquard coverlets were reversible, one side with a light background, the other dark. In 1843, C. Wiand, of Allentown, Lehigh County, Pa., relieved the severity of a field filled with octagons by adding a border of graceful rosebuds on two sides, and one of trees on the other two. Such diversity in borders is common on woolen coverlets made by local weavers. Red, blue, green, and white are a favorite combination.

Courtesy, National Gallery of Art, Index of American Design.

69

Right. The motifs used here are familiar ones: tulips, hearts, great and little stars. The rose-tree must have been a much favored border; so many weavers used it. Woven by J. N. Schultz, Mercersburg, Pa., for Adam W. Ryder in 1850.

Flaunting peacocks, perched on curving trees, spread their tails over rather meek turkeys. Large rosettes and eight-pointed stars fill in the remaining spaces. One of the handsomer types of coverlet turned out by professional weavers.

Coverlet in Blue and White.

Spaced with characteristic motifs, tulips and many pointed suns, and featuring three types of birds: the cock, the pair of doves and two of an unidentified species, decorated with hearts on their breasts. Width 79". Length 94". A coverlet with a definite folk quality, said to be a piece of home weaving; made, however, in a family which included many skilled weavers.

Courtesy, National Gallery of Art, Index of American Design.

Coverlet with unusual color scheme of orange-russet and indigo wool on ivory cotton warp. Made for Elizabeth Rawlings by J. G. Weaver, 1837. From the author's collection.

The 1840's seem to have been the heyday of the weavers of woolen coverlets, the peak of the half-century period during which the business flourished. Jane Woolverton owned this coverlet, of graceful flower forms, nicely disposed. The border of doves and rose-trees, more in harmony with the field than is usual, was employed by many weavers. Its popularity was probably based on the sentimental appeal doves and roses held for a feminine clientele bored by a too long period of geometrical forms. Made by A. Zelner, Plumstead Township, Bucks County, Pa. 1840.

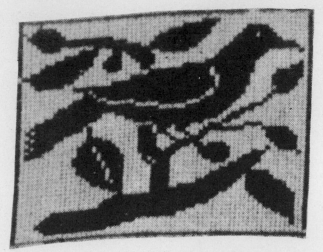

Bird on branch. Detail from corner of coverlet.

Turkey and Rooster. Pennsylvania German motif.

The urn with flowers, preferred motif for the decoration of dower chests, was employed as a unit in a coverlet border. Detail of coverlet shown on page 71.

Detail of border of coverlet. Architecture combined with rose-trees. Pennsylvania German weavers were fond of breaking up the wool background with stripes of different colors.

FROM THE SURFACE OF THE EARTH—STRAW

"To me, at least, it is a novelty to see most of the buildings, whether of wood, brick or stone, thatched or covered with straw instead of shingles or slate. I am told a well thatched roof will last at least twenty years. . . ."

—From a journal of Governor Steel, Manchester, N. H.

THE Pennsylvania colonist depended on his own soil to furnish him with every necessity of life. From the clay itself, after a few slight processes conducted by the potter and assisted by fire, he obtained all manner of utensils, and, in addition, a fireproof roof. If in the same earth he sowed flax, after many processes and much work on the part of everyone he obtained his household textiles. And from the self-same soil he procured not only his expected food, but also a second satisfactory roofing contrived from what was a mere byproduct, the straw of his staple breadstuff, rye (for the early German settlers ate no wheat bread).

Rye straw was a most adaptable material, for which he found many uses, all sanctioned by long tradition. But the primary use was to furnish both him and his stock with a roof over their heads, for the Pennsylvania German settler, though surrounded with unlimited wood from which to make shingles, preferred to follow the accustomed fashion of his homeland and cover the roofs of his barn and sheds with rye thatch. This picturesque habit he kept up long after other sections of the colonies had given it up. At first the early settlers in New England also used thatched roofs, but as theirs were made of reed, which had to be especially cut and hauled to the building site, sometimes over long distances, they discarded this method as soon as possible.

The use of rye thatch appealed to the German settler's sense of thrift. Straw from his fields was always at hand and cost him nothing. It needed no preliminary processing except careful handling. In order that the straw, in view of the several purposes for which it was destined, might remain long, smooth, and unbroken, it was always cut with a sickle. With these long, golden strands the Palatine settler thatched deep, sloping roofs for his barns, exactly like those he had made in his homeland. Tiny mediæval dormer windows were contrived of the same straw, allowing light to enter the upper part of the barns and giving an indescribably foreign look to these buildings. Such roofs were in striking contrast to those of later date, which, covered with shingle or slate, invariably presented a flat plane, unbroken by any type of dormer.

To thatch a barn, the farmer took bundles of straw and laid them in overlapping rows like shingles. A row of untied straw bundles laid crosswise of the peak, fastened down with a long pole and held down with wooden hooks, finished off the thatching. Since there was economical justification as well as folk custom behind the practice, it is not surprising that, in out-of-the-way districts the use of thatched roofs persisted until the mid-nineteenth century. Passing travellers considered them very quaint and always noted them in their diaries.

The settler found many other uses for rye straw. It bedded down his cattle; it was a material which could quickly be worked into all kinds of sturdy containers in which to store the things he had grown, the things he carried around, the things he wanted to keep. His infants slept just as well in a basket-shaped cradle made of rye straw as in one of wood. Beehives were made of it, and the lids of casks. With a framework of young hickory strips and heavy spiral twists of rye straw, all of the many types of basket he needed could be rapidly constructed: great oval shapes used as hampers or as carriers for grapes, enormous lidded containers in which dried fruit was stored, and, above all, "bread-baskets." These were shallow, long, or round coiled baskets of rye straw in which the rye bread itself was set to raise.

After the making of other types of containers ceased, the making of bread-baskets of rye straw was kept up by itinerants until the time came when the great wave of manufactured products carried metal bread-pans and iron cooking-stoves into all the farm kitchens. Then, as there was no longer any need for them, the artistic Old-World baskets, in which the risen bread had formerly been carried out to be so excellently baked in the old stone bake-ovens, also went into the discard.

This flood of new metal equipment wiped out another of the homely arts of our forefathers. After this time, the few remaining itinerant basket-makers, who had been taught their craft by their grandfathers, made a pretty thin living. Most of them gave up, but an occasional one stubbornly persisted at his dwindling trade because it was the only one he knew. Making up a stock of all kinds of baskets, he took to the road, practically invisible under the mass of his handiwork. Now that they had very little need for his product, however, his former customers were apt to look upon him as a kind of tramp. Some of these old craftsmen did indeed live a vagabond existence, spending the last years of their once useful lives in such masculine time-killing occupations as hunting and fishing, occupations which at least provided them with the food that their by-passed crafts no longer could furnish. This was the tragedy that eventually overtook all handcraft workers in the nineteenth century.

Eighteenth-Century Pennsylvania German Farm Buildings.

Drawing made from an engraving originally published in 1757, entitled "A View of Bethlehem in Pennsylvania."

Despite the great amount of wood available for shingles, familiar Old-World roofing materials such as rye thatch and clay tiles were at first preferred in this new land, as this well-established farmhouse and its picturesque group of outbuildings give evidence.

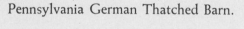

Pennsylvania German Thatched Barn.

Since rye straw from which thatched roofs were fashioned furnished an inexpensive and quite adequate roofing for outbuildings, conservative farmers persisted in its use until about 1850. And in out-of-the-way places, traces of this quaint practice could be noted up to the last decade of the past century.

But even in the environs of Philadelphia, a thatched barn was to be seen until almost 1840. This ancient structure, built in 1686, stood on the farm of one of Germantown's earliest settlers, Jacob Schumacher. The drawing above is taken from a note made in a sketchbook by Edward W. Mumford, a former New England bank cashier, who worked for Philadelphia publishers between 1835-1840. At that time, the old barn was looked upon as an anachronism, being so near a great city, and as such it appeared in a local history of the day as a woodcut made from the same sketchbook drawing.

Rye Straw Baskets.

Rye straw was employed in the making of various kinds of hampers and baskets. The straw was fashioned into heavy spiral twists, which were woven together with narrow strips of hickory. In the vernacular, these baskets were called "shtrow-karab." They were used to store many kinds of things, but above all, dried fruit. Dehydrating was once the only method of preserving the many varieties of fruit and berries for winter use. After drying in the sun, fruit was placed in cotton or linen bags, which were then stored in these great lidded hampers, whose vertical and horizontal dimensions sometimes exceeded three to three-and-one-half feet.

Eggs were carried to market in similar artistic containers, constructed with a narrow top and a broad base, so as to rest firmly in the wagon. In earlier days, two of the same type, tied together, balanced each other when horseback was the most practicable method of carrying produce to the semi-weekly markets.

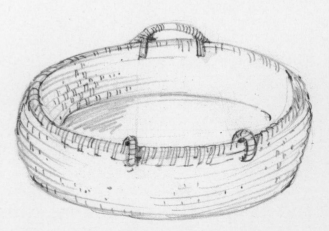

Splint basket, 24" long. In its local name, based on its suggestive form, there is a rough humor. From the author's notebook.

Basket Used by Sowers.

Outdoor Bake Oven. From a drawing made in 1800 by Lewis Miller, York, Pa.

Lewis Miller made many drawings of the life about him. Here he depicts a woman baking bread. With a long-handled shovel she inserts a loaf while two other baskets, set casually on the ground, wait to be emptied of their contents.

For some generations large, dark, crusty loaves of rye bread were the regular breadstuff of the Pennsylvania Germans. As wheat was a commodity, exchangeable for goods, bread made from it appeared only on high occasions—a funeral, a marriage, or a holiday. As a crop, rye furnished not only flour for daily bread, but also straw. This by-product, remaining after the grain had been threshed, was employed in making the basket containers in which the dough itself was shaped and raised. From these baskets of coiled straw, the loaves were turned out onto a long-handled wooden paddle called a "peel." This was used to set them on the pre-heated floor of the outdoor bake oven.

At Christmas time, instead of hanging up their stockings, the country children used to set straw bread baskets in the chimney corners, hoping that Santa Claus, whom they called Kris Kingle (Kringle) would place their gifts in them.

Bread Baskets made of rye straw.

FROM THE WOODLAND—WOOD

"The fact of the matter is, that from the face of the country being entirely overspread with trees, the eyes of the people become satiated with the sight of them. The ground cannot be tilled nor can the inhabitants support themselves till they are removed; they are looked upon as a nuisance and the man that can cut down the largest number and have the fields about the house most clear of them, is looked upon as the most industrious citizen and the one that is making the greatest improvements in the country."

—Isaac Weld: *Travels through the States of North America* 1795-97

IN his book published in 1799, Mr. Weld, the brash young member of the Irish gentry previously mentioned, expressed himself freely after a grand tour of America. His work on this country, which was issued in several languages and various editions, was regarded for a long time as authoritative. Affected by the romanticism of the time when it was *chic* to admire the beauties of nature, he wrote: "He beholds in the depths of the woods some little creek or rivulet rushing over the rock ledges in a beautiful cascade. The generality of Americans stare with astonishment at a person who can find any delight in passing through such a country as this. To them the sight of a wheat field or a cabbage garden would convey pleasure far greater than that of the most romantic woodland views. They have an unconquerable aversion to trees . . ."

These statements upset no one among the Pennsylvania German farmers; they were quite oblivious of Mr. Weld as he travelled through their section of the State, and they certainly did not read his book—for their literature, if they read at all, was limited to the German Bible, the prayer-book, and the almanac. English-speaking Americans asked him too many questions for his comfort, and when they later read his book they did not relish it. Word of their dislike must have trickled through to him, for in 1808 he said to an American visitor: "You may say to the people of America that I am sorry I wrote the book. I was out of humor when I wrote and sent it to the press . . . At different periods of life we see things in different points of view."

No doubt Weld's apology was necessary, for his statements show a remarkable lack of comprehension of the hardships of pioneering. But he was a cultivated young man used to a countryside whose fields and woodlands were tame things, subdued and ordered through generations of use, and to such a man, just barely come of age, the wildness and the extent of the forests the early settlers had conquered were completely beyond understanding. A century or so previously, another Britisher, Sir William Markham, cousin of William Penn and his deputy-governor, with more reason could write to his wife: "It is a very fine country if it were not so overgrown with woods, and very healthy."

Warned in advance of the misery of their journey and of the conditions they must

81

cope with on arrival, sober colonists came to Pennsylvania equipped with their mattocks and mauls, their axes, hatchets, and saws, prepared to attack this long-entrenched woodland. And what a wooded land it was, this great hardwood forest! Here were oak trees, red, white, and black; ash, beech, chestnut, and sassafras; hickory, walnut, cedar, and poplar —a varied collection, containing some timber entirely new to the settlers.

At first the newcomers had no time to evaluate this timber; they regarded all trees impartially. They were the elemental material from which their first shelters were to be hacked out, and the stuff by which they would be warmed. Later on they would appraise them, each as to its special value. But for a long time a tree continued to be just an annoyance which, when removed, provided one more spot to hoe in some more seeds. So they chopped and hacked and hewed at their enemies, the trees, becoming such experts with the axe that a century later the American's way with that implement was noted by William Cobbett, English farmer and politician, who said: "An axe is their tool; at cutting down trees or cutting them up, they will do ten times as much work as any other men I ever saw."

To put up a log cabin from the logs they cut they needed no bricklayer, carpenter, or smith. If two men worked on a cabin they could finish it in four or five days—a rude, honest structure which never failed to draw the attention of every European traveller. Though extremely primitive, these dwellings were frequently the only places that offered a roof and food to the rare stranger, who was grateful for the shelter and the warmth furnished by the enormous logs glowing in the fireplace. This lavish consumption of wood, while it startled the visitor, was, in the eyes of the settler, not only efficient but compulsory. The more he burned, the less there was on hand to inconvenience him. The Swedish naturalist, Peter Kalm, travelling here in 1746, was horrified at the general waste of heat, which could have been corrected, he said, by putting a damper in the chimney. It is true that a damper would have saved much of the heat, but Kalm forgot that all the early settlers had infinitely more wood to burn than they had iron for dampers, smiths to make them, or time to insert them when the log cabin was hurriedly constructed. One of the very early Swedish settlers told Kalm that, because of the absence of a damper, he was forced when a boy to climb on the roof each night before going to bed, in order to lay a flat stone over the chimney to conserve whatever heat might be left in the hot stones. By the time Kalm travelled here, he found the German settlers using a far better method to heat their houses, which will be described in the chapter on iron.

After establishing a foothold on the land they had chosen, the newcomers continued to push back the dark green forests. Each year they enlarged their bright clearings on the slopes of the valleys, chopping and grubbing out the stumps on a few more acres, so that they could plough more efficiently. Unlike other pioneering stock, who moved from place to place, the Pennsylvania Germans planned for permanency, as they were sound believers in patrimony. In order that their sons might inherit fine, well-cleared acres, the entire family worked in the fields if they were needed. Each year the sunny, well-cultivated clearings spread farther over the rolling hills, every new field adding its bit to the patchwork of light and dark green which surrounded each log cabin. Even the most casual beholder of the day knew when he saw this pattern that it indicated a Pennsylvania German settlement.

If fences were in evidence, it was an additional signpost, as the German colonists were the first to enclose their fields. These fences were made from the cedar trees which dotted the slopes. Cedar was a long-lasting wood; by making the rails as well as the posts of it, the farmers not only cleared the fields but used up that much more of the rather stubborn material with which they were eternally coping. Behind these fences went their cattle, in itself a revolutionary idea. The English and Swedes allowed their cattle to roam about freely. Unless there was a small boy or girl available to be detailed as cowherd, unsupervised cattle destroyed precious crops and undergrowth. Such cattle were a sad, scrawny lot, producing little milk or meat.

Knowing from Old-World experience the improvement which would result in their livestock if they were warmly housed in winter instead of being allowed to range the woods and perhaps freeze to death, the Germans built great log barns to shelter them. The cattle and stock grew fat and increased, ate less fodder than stock less kindly treated, were much more valuable as milk and butter producers—and above all, provided fertilizer which could now be collected, an impossibility when cattle wander about at will. All this care for the stock and evidence of good farming practices impressed the visiting foreigners, who could not fail to observe, since the main roads which they were obliged to travel ran right through the most thoroughly established German settlements. Whether the tour was made on horseback or in a luxurious private coach, every European who came over after the Revolution to report on the new country commented on the pastoral scene.

The huge wooden barns spotting the landscape were a striking architectural novelty, particularly in the eyes of the English. A frequently quoted but still apt comment made in 1753 by Lewis Evans is: "It is pretty to behold our back settlements, where the barns are large as pallaces, while the owners live in log huts; a sign of thriving farmers."

The farmers continued to live in their log cabins for a long period, but by the end of the eighteenth century even these rude dwellings had undergone certain architectural improvements. By then settlements of rough log houses, clay-chinked, had completely disappeared. In their stead were two-story houses, built of nicely-squared logs, with smooth mortar filling in the spaces between the logs. Sometimes these were covered with boards, painted; if the love for neatness and color was dominant these boarded exteriors were lined off and painted quaintly to look like bricks, in the beloved red and white of the present-day country dweller. Or this same tidiness might move the settler to keep his unboarded log house furbished up by whitewashing the mortar each season, leaving the logs their weathered brown. Having gratified his own sense of neatness and pattern, the owner paid no heed to the comments of the passing English-speaking stranger on the odd appearance of his dull, brown and white zebra-striped house, for he neither spoke nor understood English.

Eventually, if he were well-to-do, he built himself a substantial three-story stone or brick house. This new dwelling he set up next to the original log cabin, which, if it was not kept as part of the new house, sensibly became a detached kitchen, called the "summer kitchen." This is a outbuilding characteristic of eastern Pennsylvania, used to this day in warm weather in order to keep the heat of the cookstove from the main dwelling.

With the profits resulting from the combined labor of the whole family, and with easier access to the workshops of the craft workers established in the villages, the farmer might now call for finer gear with which to furnish his new home. The heyday of the folk arts of the Pennsylvania German arrived. For many years his family had made shift with rough, backwoods types of furniture. With the coming of a little actual cash and the advent of a more comfortable style of living, memories of European customs latent in this traditionalist sprang up again. Like all well-to-do parents in the Old World, who supplied the bride-to-be with certain customary pieces of decorative furniture, he, too, could now give an order to the cabinet-maker in the village for a walnut chest, a great wardrobe, a corner cupboard, or a kitchen dresser for the dowry of his daughter. The cabinet-maker, his neighbor and friend, prided himself on the quality of his work and never skimped any of the tedious processes connected with it. The Pennsylvania German was a thorough workman; he could not be hurried, but once a job was done, it did not have to be done over again. When the dower furniture was completed, the farmer as well as the cabinet-maker looked upon it with respect, knowing it was good work. Both took pleasure in the knowledge that the bride-to-be, departing for her new home, went proudly and properly equipped.

If the farmer himself happened to be a skilled cabinet-maker—and most of them had a trade they followed when farm work slackened—he might plan to make the furniture for the dowry of the son or daughter about to be married. One of the favorite gifts was an enormous wardrobe or "*schrank*," made of soft wood, painted, or of walnut finished with a high polish. Black walnut, beautiful and coffee-brown, was the best and handsomest wood for household furniture. It was the country cabinet-maker's substitute for the elegant, imported mahogany used in the parlors of city folk. If walnut was his choice, the lumber was on hand, ready to use, for long before this day he had sawed up one of his own walnut trees and laid it away to season.

Of course, if young Cadarina or Barbara or Maria were herself consulted, she might possibly prefer a brilliantly painted and decorated dower chest. In this case a softer wood, such as tulip-poplar or pine, could be employed, as its less durable surface could be given a protective covering of paint. Use and not sentiment may have dictated her choice of a chest, for the chest was a most important piece of furniture in our ancestors' days. It is the earliest piece of furniture known. From mediæval days on, it served in place of non-existent drawers and closets. Being portable, it could be used as a trunk, lifted by its iron handles, and hauled to the new home, even in an ox-cart and over the roughest of roads. It could be made by anyone who knew how to make a dovetailed box, for its essential form, except for a few changes rung on the type of support, was unvarying. The neighborhood smith could be relied on to furnish the strap hinges, handles, and lock.

The gift of a chest had the sanction of long tradition behind it. In essentials, the painted chests of the Pennsylvania Germans vary little from most European eighteenth-century painted peasant furniture, which was made cheaply of pine and lent itself well to decoration in color.

As the farmer-joiner was not apt to be also a decorator, the chest was held for ornamentation until the itinerant decorator made his rounds. Because of economic conditions in the eighteenth century, like many other artisans he took to the roads to seek his customers. We can assume that local gossip kept him informed of all the families in which there were marriageable daughters. While he may have consulted with the maiden about the color of the body of the chest, it is evident that he pleased himself in the decoration of it. There is so great a likeness in pieces of work obviously from the same hand that we can be sure that for no client's opinions would he change a single form or color in his particular version of the traditional motifs. One concession was made to pride of ownership: on pieces decorated to order, the painter always planned a space (often an ornamental cartouche) in which were lettered the owner's name, the year, and sometimes even the month and day.

But it was not necessary to depend entirely on the home workshop for a chest, for certain village carpenters not only built them but also decorated them and signed their works. Although the dressers, cupboards, water-benches, and other gear made of the softer woods were usually given only a coat of paint and left undecorated, on the dower chest, with its simple aspect and inviting flat surfaces, was lavished all the long-suppressed love of color and pattern innate in the Palatine settlers; it is on the chests that the characteristic tulips, unicorns, doves, vases, hearts and other symbols are spread out, unstintingly.

Towards the very end of the eighteenth century, when the influence of the great British cabinet-makers began to filter through from the towns even to the country cabinet-maker, a change took place in the style of the dower chest. In lieu of mahogany, the village woodworker used the native black walnut and finished it with the high gloss which this fine, hard wood took so well. No painted ornament was ever used on these elegantly finished chests. Decoration was limited to inlays of lighter woods. But at this point the influence of Mr. Hepplewhite and Mr. Adam and the whole British tradition fades away. Their classic inlay motifs go by the board, and in place of their laurel leaves, their delicate festoons, their classic urns, appear the whole battery of familiar Pennsylvania German motifs—the heart, the tulip, the birds and the stars.

The Colonial era in America might well be called the wooden age of our civilization. Every settler had to be adept in the use of woods. Several generations of working with the strange new American woods had acquainted him with their qualities. He knew which to use for pliability, for stiffness, or for durability; which took a fine polish in cabinet work; which stood up under strain. As he knew that cedar wood resisted moisture, he made his pails, tubs, and cisterns of it, and his fence posts as well. Out of hard, tough hickory, he fashioned chairs and axles. Butternut or white walnut was another wood he liked for furniture, as it could be given a surface almost as pleasing as that of black walnut. Since the equipment and tools used in his work in the fields were made almost entirely of wood the colonist developed much skill in searching out forest growths shaped by nature to the exact line fitted to his purpose. Having prowled through his woodland until he found the desired curve in a sapling, with a little whittling and some work with the draw-knife he turned it into the farm implement or sled runner or handle he needed.

The craft of whittling and carving with a pocket knife is one familiar to most European peasantry, the Swiss above all. With the skill inherent in him and the love of decoration as well, it was natural for the Pennsylvania German also to use his gift in making other articles that were needed in the house. A strong, sharp knife was in every farmer's pocket; with it he shaped all manner of necessary household articles—egg-beaters, ladles and measures, spoon racks, and buttermolds.

The well-tended stock of the Pennsylvania farmer produced quantities of butter, an always marketable product. As butter and pastry were the two plastic substances available on the farm with which to gratify the love of form, the opportunity to transform them by wooden molds into decorative reliefs was not overlooked. Tradition was always behind the practice, though the molds made in this country differ both in shape and detail from their European prototypes. The buttermold is the most commonly encountered household article carved of wood. Every farmer, against the time when he might feel an urge to whittle, had laid away a bit of walnut or a small chunk of pale, smooth, seasoned wood saved from an ancient apple tree. From it the wielder of the penknife cut the mold and its handle in one satisfying piece, shaping it skillfully so that it fit the hand comfortably. Into its flat face, with sharp, unerring strokes, he cut in intaglio the invariable tulip, star, heart, and all the motifs so familiar to him. On the wholly hand-whittled molds the variations rung on these few motifs seem unlimited. Later on, when molds were turned out in quantities on a lathe, though still ornamented with hand carving they became a much less individualistic expression of the carver's traditional, artistic instincts.

Every farm kitchen had a wooden box to hold salt, hung by the fireplace to keep the contents dry. The back, which was also the support, was usually whittled into a graceful outline. In addition these boxes were sometimes carved, sometimes decorated with designs in color. On other types of wall boxes, used to hold kitchen cutlery and tableware, a little thought was always given to the shaping of the general contour. Even the shapes of the openings by which they were suspended contributed their bit to the decorative whole.

Once the household was well equipped, when the powerful urge for whittling overcame him the farmer occasionally carved objects for pure love of the craft. These carved birds, animals, and figures were often primitively conceived, but when painted in bright colors they provided some of the few ornaments the country folk had.

Weathervanes, though ordinarily the work of the smith, were also carved out of wood and then well protected by paint. Some are quaintly shaped humans, their movable arms whirled around by every passing breeze.

After the general disappearance of the skilled craftsman in the middle of the nineteenth century, the artisan who once earned a simple livelihood by working in wood could no longer find enough work to keep him busy. Some took to the road as itinerants, rambling the eastern section of the State, leaving behind them a trail of crudely carved eagles, roosters, and peafowl—ornaments which they often exchanged for board or for liquid refreshment at the country taverns. Schimmel, a picturesque, irascible old-country German, is the best publicized of the woodcarvers, but there were other quiet citizens who carved entirely for their own amusement, for this love of working in wood ran so strongly in the blood of certain Pennsylvania Germans that, when there was no longer any utilitarian need for it, they kept it up as a hobby.

An odd example of this persistent urge, this survival of a mediæval craft, is seen in the work of Noah Weis, 1842-1907, the lifetime proprietor of a tidy country inn located in a Lehigh County village. As a boy working on his father's farm in Hosensack, in the same county, he showed a definite artistic bent. The local doctor urged him to develop it, and was willing to back his judgment with financial help. But the boy's father "had work for him to do on the farm"; so this typically Pennsylvania German attitude of early days put a blunt stop to any plans for education considered non-essential. After Noah Weis became an inn-keeper (for it was evident his father could not keep him on the farm), and in his turn became a father, he took out his jack-knife one day and carved some toys to amuse a sick child. From that time on, he began to satisfy his need to work out his artistic impulses, suppressed for so many years. The walls of Weis's Inn became his exhibition galleries, and after they had been completely covered with his carvings, he used the walls of another building near at hand. Like many another simple, uneducated person, he was never deterred by the difficulty of a subject. He tried his hand at anything. To appeal to the secular tastes of his patrons he placed round the walls of the reading room a complete hunting scene. There is the life-sized hunter and his spotted hound-dog, a covey of quail, his old home, and a stage-coach drawn by six horses.

All of these familiar objects were carved as large as possible and with all the realism Weis could achieve. As the folk sculpture current in his day, the cigar-store Indians and merry-go-round figures, were as gaudy as fresh paint could make them, he too colored his carving as realistically as possible. In some of these carvings he achieved a highly personal style, which can only be described as a double-faced bas-relief. Panel after panel of Bible subjects, translated from engravings in a Bible history, covered the walls of the outbuilding. These huge wooden decorations, executed with only one tool, the pocket-knife, were done with great gusto, even if they lacked the artistic finesse which would have resulted from academic training. For many years Weis found the time to work at his beloved carving only in the very early morning hours, before even the first of the tavern patrons arrived.

Weis left no workable piece of wood untouched if it was possible to embellish it. He made himself a gaudy, elaborately carved sleigh, in which he drove the winter roads. The neighborhood used to be greatly diverted by the sight of "Pop Weis," as the dignified inn-keeper was known, in this Old-World outfit. Unlike artists who were often at a loss for a public, he never lacked admirers, for he found them among the patrons who were always at hand in the inn, ready to behold reverentially the sacred sculptures, to admire without reserve the hunting scene, and to give honor to the great George Washington, who, seated on a horse, dominated the office of "mine host." Probably one of the last craftsmen to work for the sheer love of it, Noah Weis in his intense absorption in a bygone craft may have been an anachronism in the prosaic era in which he found himself, but he was a happy one, for he was unaware of that fact. Like his forebears, he found his pleasure in work.

Detail of Carved Panel under Cornice. Height 5½". Width 42".

Courtesy. Philadelphia Museum of Art.

EUROPEAN WARDROBE. DATED 1737. CARVED CHESTNUT.

Memories of such carved pieces influenced the work of artisans newly come to Pennsylvania. Lacking the leisurely viewpoint needed to use the carving chisels, the decorators made a speedy translation in paint of the familiar tulips, urns, hearts and many-pointed stars. Even the carved spandril fans appeared in a painted version, done in red, yellow, and black. See page 104, lower left.

Courtesy, National Gallery of Art, Index of American Design.

Miniature chests and small boxes with sliding lids gave early decorators occasion for some of their most delightful flourishes. Both the candle-box above and the excellently designed diminutive chest are the work of the same hand, a hand which also decorated chests of normal scale. On both, the same colors are used: red, blue, black, and green, on a ground of antique white.

On the candle-box, the background is indigo; on the chest, bandings and mouldings are red; feet are black.

Candle-box, 1777. 14½″ long, 6½″ high.
Chest, 1787. 17″ long, 8″ high.

The parrot on the chest is closely related to the ones used on birth certificates of the period.

Courtesy, Paul M. Auman, Millheim, Pa.

Left. Suggestive of early wallpapers is the decoration found on certain small caskets made with domed lids. Sprigs and small floral forms added to the polka-dotted, interlaced rosettes combine to form a quite uncharacteristic style of decoration.

Below. Candle-box. Dark red ground, panel decorated in blue, yellow, black, and brown on parchment. 1783.

Lower right. Grapes used on the top of an oaken footstool. Yellow, black, and red on a dark green painted ground.

Below. Grapes form an unusual choice for a motif in red, green, and blue on a yellow box. 12″ long, 5½″ high.

Unicorn Chests, so called because of the unicorns featured in the central panel, are the most intricately decorated of Pennsylvania chests. Flanking panels often display a mounted soldier, brandishing a sword, but sometimes the ornamenter rearranged the units of his design and substituted the horseman for the unicorns. In such cases, the side panels sported an urn and tulips. When the horseman occupies the side panels, a curious device is used above him: the upper half of a crowned human figure, with tulips held in its extended arms.

Though there are many variations in unicorn chests, a basic resemblance was achieved by using a set of patterns to establish the outlines of the major details; the minor ones were painted freehand. The construction of unicorn chests is typical of most Pennsylvania German chests. Some are supported on bracket feet; some rest on trestles; and bun feet are not unknown. Some have a plain front; others have drawers set in their bases. Backgrounds are either stippled in a rhythmic manner or painted in plain blue or green or red, in which case every inch of the space surrounding the panels is filled with additional decoration.

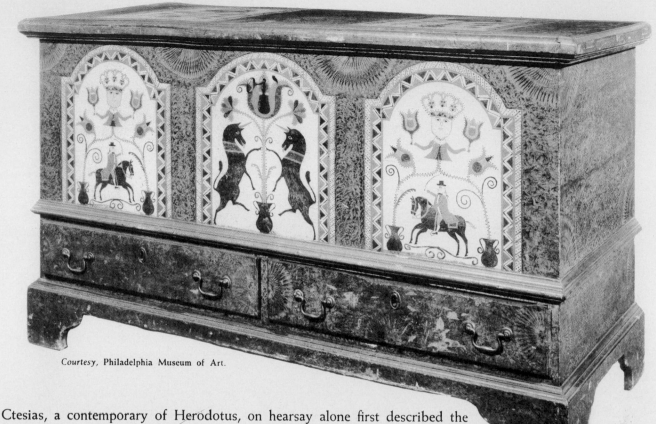

Ctesias, a contemporary of Herodotus, on hearsay alone first described the fabulous unicorn as a wild ass, native to India, colored red, white, and black, with a long horn on its forehead. By mediæval times, it had become the symbol for virtue and piety. So skittish was the unicorn that its capture could be effected only by setting a young virgin as a lure. The entranced unicorn, seeing her, put his head in her lap and fell asleep, a tale quite acceptable to a world which knew not the symbolism of Freud. The unicorn was a favorite heraldic figure; on the British coat-of-arms it is the left-hand supporter. That it actually existed, even in this country, was still believed in the eighteenth century. Mittelberger in 1750 reports a conversation with an English fur dealer, returned from the West: "They [Indians] had also met an animal which had a smooth and pointed horn an ell and a half long on its head; said horn pointed straight ahead. This animal was as large as a middle-sized horse, but swifter than a stag in running. The Europeans of Philadelphia had taken the animal for the unicorn."

Unicorn Chest, naïve work of an imitator, whose digest of the original motifs has its own charm. Inscription, translated: "Mariechen Grim, in the year 1796 —the 10th of February."

93

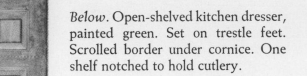

Below. Open-shelved kitchen dresser, painted green. Set on trestle feet. Scrolled border under cornice. One shelf notched to hold cutlery.

Courtesy, Philadelphia Museum of Art.

The huge wardrobe (*Schrank*) was used for the storage of clothes in Pennsylvania German housekeeping, as clothes closets were non-existent in early days. It was made in sections, so that it could be taken apart if necessary. This bracket-footed, heavy-corniced "*Schrank*" was probably part of the dowry of Martin Wisenhauer. Made in 1794, it was originally a very gay piece, every inch of it covered with painting, striping, and stippling. The stilings in greenish-blue, with panels in ivory, their flat surfaces covered with sponge stippling in red, defining twin hearts; bevels in ivory. Panels without hearts stippled in blue on ivory, their bevels stippled in red. Striping in black. To create the stylized hearts, the painter used a brush rigged in a compass.

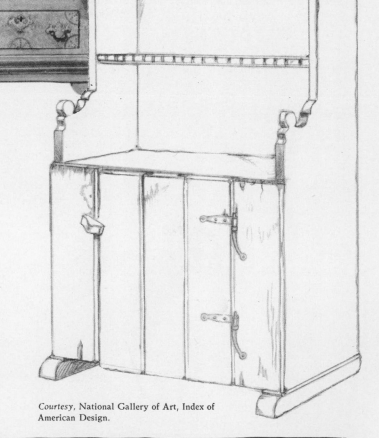

Below. The decorator , undaunted though he was, demonstrated more skill at stippling than at lettering. Owner's name painted on frieze of cornice.

Courtesy, National Gallery of Art, Index of American Design.

Courtesy, New-York Historical Society.

Angel (wood-cut) from birth certificate, printed by Dan. Phil. Lange, Hanover, York County, Pa. 1822.

Courtesy, National Gallery of Art, Index of American Design.

Courtesy, Paul M. Auman, Millheim, Pa.

Decorated kitchen cupboard, made in 1828 for "Rebeca" Braun in the Mahantongo Valley, Schuylkill County, a locale which turned out an individual type of furniture in the early nineteenth century. Once painted a light salmon vermilion. Door frames in ivory, with strong green-blue border which also outlines other panels. Symbols on drawers in yellow, black, and red. Base moulding and feet, olive brown. On chests of drawers and cupboards, this group of decorators liked to paint angels traced from contemporary birth certicates. Other pieces on page 104.

Left. Corner cupboard. Intense color covers this unusual piece. Main body buff, stippled with reds. Cornice and upper door yellow. Lower door yellow, framed in green-stippled white. Feet and finial border vermilion. Horizontal mouldings yellow, glazed with thin green.

95

It took a skilled cabinet-maker to construct a chest with sunken arched panels set between moulded pilasters in a style closely related to the carved Renaissance chests of seventeenth-century Germany. But the carved rectangular bosses on the pilasters of the originals are here quaintly memorialized in paint, a labor-saving device.

The chest of Hannes Tommes, 1774, is an excellent example of this type. The introduction of a tiny house and tree is a bit of local whimsey. In red and blue on white.

Chest of unpainted wood. Decoration in red and green, outlined in white. Owner's name, Margret Schumacher, lettered modestly on arch.

Courtesy, M. L. Blumenthal, Elkins Park, Pa.

Arched recessed panels in white on a green-blue chest. Decorated in red, yellow and brown. Unusual scalloping under arch, painted in dark brown. Mouldings picked out in red. Turned feet are a novelty. For detail in color, see page 275.

Below. Bracket-footed chest with background of panels and field of the same color. Field is stippled to set off panels. Decorations in red, white, yellow, and brown on brownish-toned ground. Crudely inscribed: "L. W. 1798 D.30 Novembr".

Two panels, each featuring a large, swirling-petalled blossom set in a simulated architectural frame, were a favorite decorative arrangement. The corners of the chest were covered with hearts, ranged vertically, sometimes alternated with tulips. Occasionally a half pilaster replaced them. See opposite page, below.

Courtesy, National Gallery of Art, Index of American Design.

THE HUMAN FIGURE

Figures of men and women made appropriate decorations for bride-boxes, quaint gifts from the bridegroom to the bride. Almost all of these flat-sided, oval-ended splint boxes found in Pennsylvania are of European origin. In Germany they were known as Berchtesgaden boxes, because that now infamous region was, in the eighteenth century, the great manufacturing centre for light-weight wooden articles.

Since bride-boxes are found in Pennsylvania German regions, they probably arrived here in the luggage of female colonists, as containers for their few trinkets. However, the one illustrated is of local make; the red-coated gentleman is, obviously, American. The crude floral decorations follow the Bavarian models. Length 15″. Width 11″. Height 5½″.

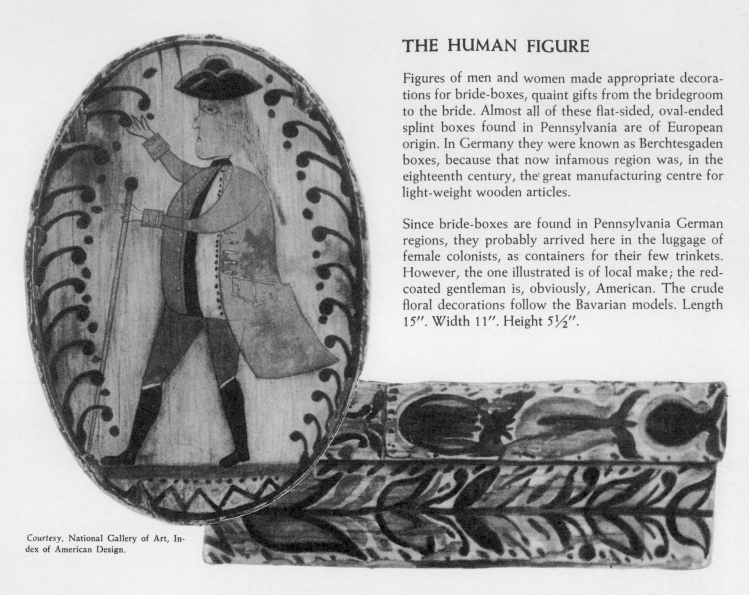

Courtesy, National Gallery of Art, Index of American Design.

Below. The human figure appears rarely on chests; the gentleman depicted, a traditional figure in European folk art, is a close relative of the one on the bride-box.

Courtesy, Metropolitan Museum of Art.

The decorator from whose work these details are taken had a passion for embellishment. The panel above, from a chest dated 1792, is very similar in conception and organization to the work shown on page 90.

Right. Central feature of a chest which displays an ingenious method of introducing the name of the owner, Stoffel (short for Christoph) Lebo, 1794. This central construction is flanked by a pair of panels similar to the one shown above. The background of the upper panel is the usual ivory, once white; the one on the right has been painted on the natural wood, the surrounding areas stippled to set it off.

The arched panel and its supporting painted columns are a very common motif on Pennsylvania German chests. Country decorators, untrammeled by architectural canons, in addition never hesitated to plant an idle pilaster in any space that needed filling. These stylized columns represent their interpretation in paint of the carved pilasters typical of the seventeenth-century chests of their homeland.

DETAILS FROM DOWER CHESTS

A striking arrangement of ancient motifs. The lion, heart, doves, urn, peacock, the tulips, and the dominant crown, are spotted about on this chest of deep gold color. Base olive-green. Decorations in olive, deeper gold, bluish white, and a red-brown. Mottled in a thin brown to set off the decorated area.

Right. Detail from chest. From the earliest times, the mermaid myth took hold of the popular fancy. In mediæval days, it symbolized the divine and human facets of man's nature. The mermaid was credited with the gift of prophecy; force or bribery were the means used to compel her to reveal the future.

Anne Beer's chest, both in construction and decoration, represents a departure from the usual type. The use of the recessed panel as support was common practice in seventeenth-century Bavaria but ranks as an oddity among the profusion of bracket-footed chests made locally. The owner's name, in script capitals, shows how outside influences were altering, by 1790, decorative traditions of centuries.

In the late eighteenth century, Pennsylvania German cabinet-makers married their own decorative traditions to those of the great British workers in fine woods. Taking their fine black walnut, they inlaid in lighter woods their favored motifs. A maiden receiving an inlaid chest could pride herself that it was in the latest mode and in smart contrast to every-day painted ones.

Right. In inlaid chests, the owner's names became an important decorative feature. From the author's notebook.

The walnut chest of Maria Kutz amusingly combines inlays of obviously French inspiration with equally obvious native grasshoppers.

Minor accessories offered a chance for colorful display. Kitchen salt-boxes were often decorated, following a familiar Old-World fashion. Anne Leterman's salt-box, the evident pride of "John Drissell his hand May 22nd 1797," is covered with barn red, then embellished in white and other colors.

Courtesy, National Gallery of Art, Index of American Design.

Below. Artisans fond of the lathe made turned and decorated wooden urns as containers for saffron and spice. In the local cuisine saffron was a favored flavoring and coloring matter. Spicebox decorated with tulips and festoons; the presence of the latter indicates outside influence of a type noticeable in the early 1800's.

Below. Egg cup in turned wood made by G. Lehn, a retired farmer of Lancaster County, in late nineteenth century. On yellow or on dull pink grounds, Lehn used red, green and white to ornament the products of his lathe, such as spiceboxes and lidded pails to hold sugar.

Courtesy, National Gallery of Art, Index of American Design.

Courtesy, Landis Valley Museum, Landis Valley, Pa.

102

Wall box, desk-shaped, in walnut with ornaments of wood inlay. Used to hold cutlery. Compartments in drawer for spices.

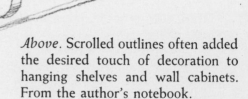

Above. Scrolled outlines often added the desired touch of decoration to hanging shelves and wall cabinets. From the author's notebook.

Below. Hanging wall cabinet with wrought iron hinges; a simplified form of carved cabinet common in the Palatinate in the eighteenth century.

Panel from Wall Cabinet.

Though created with gouge and line chisels instead of brush and color, this unusual panel of birds and arcs is nevertheless representative of local artistic traditions. Instead of being carved as an integral part of the door of the eighteenth-century wall cabinet it ornaments, for convenience the panel was made elsewhere and then nailed on. That it was no decorative afterthought, however, is evidenced by borders of matching gouge marks on other portions of the cabinet.

Panel 8″ x 10″. Cabinet 28″ high.

CHESTS AND MOTIFS

Upper right. Chest by unknown decorator, who, after planning an outstanding design, used it for many years. The motif on the left is taken from a chest made by him for Jacob Jutzae in 1781. Like the dark green chest made for Margaret Lisbet Schmitt, in 1798, it has two baskets flanking a circular ornament, the same band of ornamental lettering, and hearts neatly bordering the corners. Flowers are red and white.

Right. Decoration from painted chest (Mahantongo Valley). Body a dark green, base moulding and turned feet in black. Birds and flowers in red and yellow interspersed with black stems and leaves.

Above. Chest of drawers decorated by Jacob Mazer, a Mahantongo Valley worker. Background of pleasing green, ornament in red, yellow, rose, black and white.

Right. Chest of drawers, from Mahantongo Valley, or- namented with characteristic rows of stencilled rosettes.

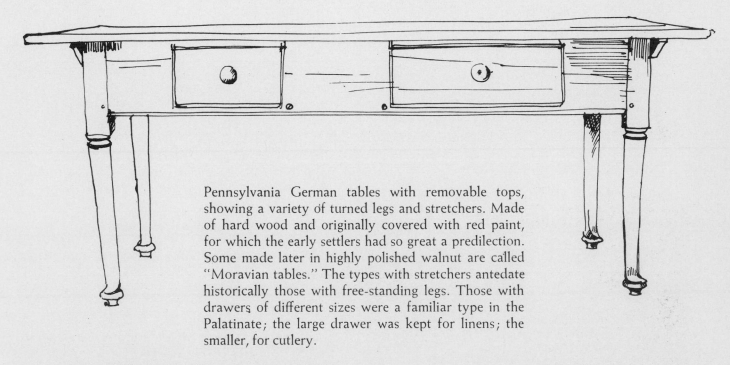

Pennsylvania German tables with removable tops, showing a variety of turned legs and stretchers. Made of hard wood and originally covered with red paint, for which the early settlers had so great a predilection. Some made later in highly polished walnut are called "Moravian tables." The types with stretchers antedate historically those with free-standing legs. Those with drawers of different sizes were a familiar type in the Palatinate; the large drawer was kept for linens; the smaller, for cutlery.

Courtesy, H. Louis Duhring, Philadelphia.

Elaborate heart and tulip decorations at the corners as well as the applied fret-work moulding distinguish this chest. It is covered in barn red, on which the decorations are worked in blue, red, white, and black. For another example of the same decorator's work, see page 249.

Rectangular panels filled with straggling tulips constitute an unusual feature of Christina Heger's dower chest. The name and date, 1775, are well integrated in the design. A heart and a six-pointed star crowd the panels, none too happily. Background is blue, with panels and mouldings bordered in red. Panels decorated in red and blue on an ivory ground.

A large, heart-shaped cartouche frames the name Maria Stohler, 1788, lettered in such a superior fashion that it points to the work of a fractur-decorator turned chest-ornamenter. Oddly arranged tulips and pomegranates cover the field of the strangely subdivided flanking panels. Ten geometric figures whirling inharmoniously add a note of restlessness to a well-proportioned chest.

A handsomely constructed chest of the type shown on page 98. Both its pilasters and the spaces around the drawers are fluted. The ogee arch of the central panel characterizes this type of chest. The decoration is executed with subtlety and refinement, the elements well contrasted and well arranged. Dated 1785. The owner's name is set down in a cryptic manner, a fashion occasionally adopted in those days. Height 26". Length 52".

Above. Chest by John Selzer.

Typical Chest by Christian Selzer.

The decorators of chests were modest craftsmen, for the most part letting their work speak for them. But Christian Selzer, 1749-1831, of Jonestown, Lebanon County, Pa., boldly signed his pieces, scratching his name on the painted vases. Though certain members of his family followed in his footsteps, they lacked the originality, the skill of the born decorator, which Christian displayed on all his chests. For his painted panels, he favored leaves of dark brown, tulips in dull red, blue and gold on ivory fields. His son, John, used green for leaves. Backgrounds of chests usually stippled brown.

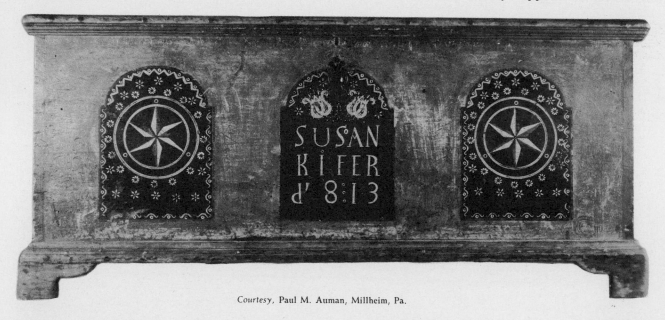

The chest of Susan Kifer. 1813. Forthright decoration, achieved by simple means: a compass, short scrollings, and rhythmic groupings of dots. Evidently a stock design of a professional decorator who planned, by omitting essential border from central panel, to accommodate purchasers' names, no matter what length. The brevity of Susan Kifer's name left him with too much blank space.

Centre County, a district far removed from the original Palatine settlements, by 1816 had produced a decorator who ingeniously united the new, patriotic American symbols with those of the Old World. To create a variety in textures, he added sand to certain areas. The black eagle carries a vermilion banderole, lettered "Wilhelm Wagoner," in yellow. Green, ivory, and vermilion border the arched panel, set on an ochre field, stippled in brown.

Dough trays, used in bread mixing. The lid, when inverted, served as a kneading table. When mounted on legs, they were called "dough troughs." Undecorated except for a coat of red paint.

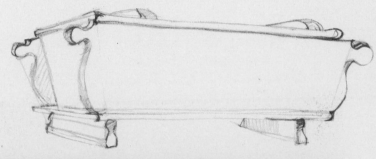

The blue-green chest of Sarah Schupp was made by a meticulous man, who not only signed it "N.S." but marked it "Num. 8" in his series. The barn symbols, often a feature of the more modest type of chest, are well scaled and well placed. Vague tulips serve as space fillers around the excellent lettering.

WOODCARVING
COCKS
AND
HENS

Above. Figurine. Cock, nineteenth century. Carved in the round. Polychrome. Height 10½″. Length 11¾″.

Left. Weathervane. Cock. c. 1785. Pine. Height 25″. Width 21″.

Both, courtesy, National Gallery of Art, Index of American Design.

Ever since the ninth century, by Papal decree, a cock has adorned the church steeple. Originally a pagan symbol dedicated to Apollo, the sun-god, for his unfailing services in heralding the rising of the sun, the cock became a Christian symbol after his crowing became associated with the repentance of Peter. The early Pennsylvania German settlers followed European ecclesiastical tradition when building their Lutheran and Reformed churches. No steeple was without its weather-cock.

In France, only the nobility were permitted to sport weathervanes. After the Revolution, when their prerogatives were taken away, the custom was adopted by the bourgeoisie, and even the peasants took on the fad. For the first time, the once proud vane appeared over barns and humble cottages.

WOODCARVING
COCKS
AND
HENS

Above, to left and right, are wooden buttermolds. Cock and Hen, nineteenth century.

For certain types of artisans, the cock furnished an excellent motif. His sharp, unmistakable silhouette and the variety of details which compose his form worked out well in wood or metal. In wood, long decorative sweeps of the chisel easily defined tail feathers; short strokes, the details of breast, wings, comb, and spurs.

Left. Wooden cake mold. Handsome cock, carved in intaglio, with cutting edge hammered into the wood. An ingenious idea which shaped an unusual cookie, one provided not only with the usual well-defined outline, but also with a highly ornamented form in relief. Width 4½". Length 5¼".

All examples, courtesy, National Gallery of Art, Index of American Design.

More elaborate than weathervanes carved as silhouettes were the whirligig type, primitive and engaging bits of sculpture. The arms, which terminate in opposed vanes, are mounted on a rod which runs through the body. The feet are mounted on another rod which permits the body to revolve.

Oaken whirligig British soldier. Polychromed. From Berks County, Pa.

Whirligig. Polychrome. *c.* 1840. Height 30".

Pennsylvania German wood carving. Figure of Justice. Height 21½". Attributed to John Fisher, a native of York, Pa.

Polychromed originally in brilliant colors. The blue blouse was bordered with green-gold. Over a blue skirt hung a red over-drapery, with delicately incised border. Justice was blindfolded with an actual ribbon of orange-red silk, and in her left hand she held a tiny pair of scales of real metal.

From her eminent position to the rear of the Judge's bench in the Court House at York, Pa., she witnessed the deliberations of the Continental Congress when it met there in 1777.

Mennonite Couple, homeward bound. Wood sculpture, early nineteenth century. Carved from one piece of wood; coated with gesso and polychromed in oil color. Height 5¼".

The pietistic sects, the Amish, the Mennonites, and the Dunkards, deliberately set themselves apart from "the world" by their habits and their distinctive costumes, known as "plain" clothes. These quaint garments, seen in a few sections of a few counties in Pennsylvania, result from no invention on the part of the sects. They represent, rather, the fossilization of styles once common in the seventeenth and eighteenth centuries; styles stripped of all non-essentials, and persistently adhered to, in spite of fashions changing around them. The wearing of "plain" clothes today demonstrates a remarkable fealty to an ideal set several centuries ago.

Both, courtesy, National Gallery of Art, Index of American Design.

BIRDS—ORNAMENTAL WOOD CARVINGS

Above, Carved bird, painted brown, with yellow markings. Head of black glass pin is inserted for eye.

Upper right. Carved bird, stained and varnished. Late nineteenth century.

Left. Decorative carving, painted in red, green, yellow, black. The bird's body is red, with black and yellow wings. Height 9", Depth 2".

The work of a woodcarver in Berks County, these carved birds served as gay bits of decoration. Their maker, knowing that legs of wood were too frail to support the weight of the body, ingeniously substituted legs of wire. The bases in which the wire is inserted were made with little effort; sawed-off finials from discarded wooden bedposts served admirably for his purpose.

BIRDS—ORNAMENTAL
WOOD CARVINGS

Right. Squirrel, by Schimmel, *c.* 1865. Polychromed.

Left. Owl, by Aaron Mounts. In unfinished wood.

After the Civil War, Schimmel, a picturesque, irascible German immigrant fond of whittling, took to the roads. From 1860 to 1890 he could be seen in the Cumberland Valley, sitting along the roadside or in wagon shops, carving rough animals and birds out of blocks of wood picked up here and there. These *objets d'art* he exchanged for food and lodging on the farms of the "Pennsylvania Dutch." Eagles three feet across were his specialty. These he painted in red, brown, black, and ochre, colors said to have been furnished by the wagon-shops in which he stopped.

Below. Poodle, by Aaron Mounts, *c.* 1865. Length 17½". Height 10½". Mounts was a companion of Schimmel, whose work is said to have inspired him to try his own hand at carving.

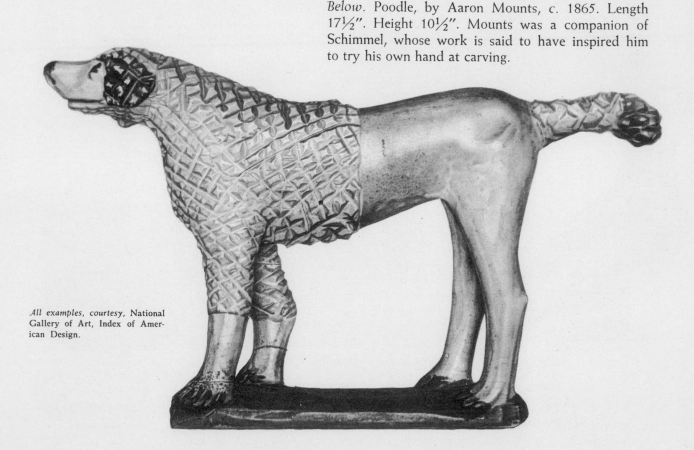

All examples, courtesy, National Gallery of Art, Index of American Design.

115

Above. Carved Wood Door Lintel. Length 3'. Height 9". From the Huttenstein property, East Petersburg, Lancaster County, Pa.

To place a blessing or prayer on the door lintel of the new house was an ancient Rhenish and Swiss custom. The new settlers did not depart from tradition. The motto carved here is one familiar to them in their homelands. Translation: "Whether I go out or in, Death stands and waits for me. Better a dry morsel to enjoy than a house full of fresh meat with strife."

Pennsylvania German powder horn, 1790. Incised with geometric symbols.

Animals incised on powder horn. From Snyder County, Pa. Undoubtedly inspired by the woodcuts in an early A B C book. Eleven animals and five symbols cover the surface.

Carved Wood Door Lintel from Middletown, Pa.

Marked with householders' initials, G. M. and A. M. 12th of April, 1764. Translation: "Whether I go in or out, Death awaits me at the door."

116

Buttermolds, prints, or stamps were used, even in early days, to impress designs on butter. The early settlers, arriving from Switzerland, that country of butter and woodcarvers, probably brought the idea with them. "Printing" butter in designs was laborious but worth the trouble, for "print" butter (so called to distinguish it from that packed in crocks or tubs) brought higher prices at market.

The care of milk and its transformation into butter devolved on the farm women. Daily they strained fresh milk into earthenware pans, which they placed in their cool spring-houses. Daily, after the cream had risen, they skimmed it off and set it aside to await churning. This took place once or twice a week. After churning about one-half hour, the butter began to form. If it took too long to "come," it was said to be bewitched. A horseshoe over the spring-house door or a cross mark was believed to dispel the evil.

Before a buttermold was used, it was first scalded, then dipped into cold water. A ball of butter was pressed into the pattern of one of the handled circular type, the sides trimmed along the edge of the mold, then inverted against a marble slab, depositing a flattened cake with the impression uppermost.

Right. Buttermold, dated 1793.

Courtesy, Metropolitan Museum of Art.

Below. Unusual oaken mold, for printing one-pound rectangle. With rugged tulip, two hearts, and the initials L. B.
Butter rolling-pin, used to work unwanted buttermilk out of butter.

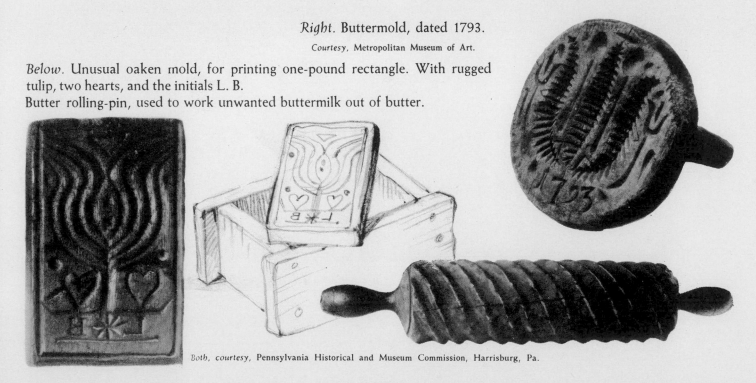

Both, courtesy, Pennsylvania Historical and Museum Commission, Harrisburg, Pa.

Courtesy, Chester County Historical Society, West Chester, Pa.

Below Not a buttermold or printing block, but a block used to smooth out linen after laundering, in Old-World fashion.

Courtesy, National Gallery of Art, Index of American Design.

Courtesy, Chester County Historical Society, West Chester, Pa.

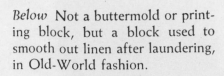

BUTTERMOLDS
TULIPS

Although buttermolds were both made and used later in other sections of the country, those made by the Pennsylvania German whittler were the most individual. He understood perfectly the limitations of his technique and the purpose for which the mold was to be used. Working even under these restrictions and with only a few traditional motifs, he achieved a great variety of designs. When he departed from tradition, the results were unpredictable. On one such departure, an enterprising farmer, long in advance of modern advertising, printed butter for market with a mold marked "Good Butter. Taste It."

Examples above and below, right and left, courtesy, National Gallery of Art, Index of American Design.

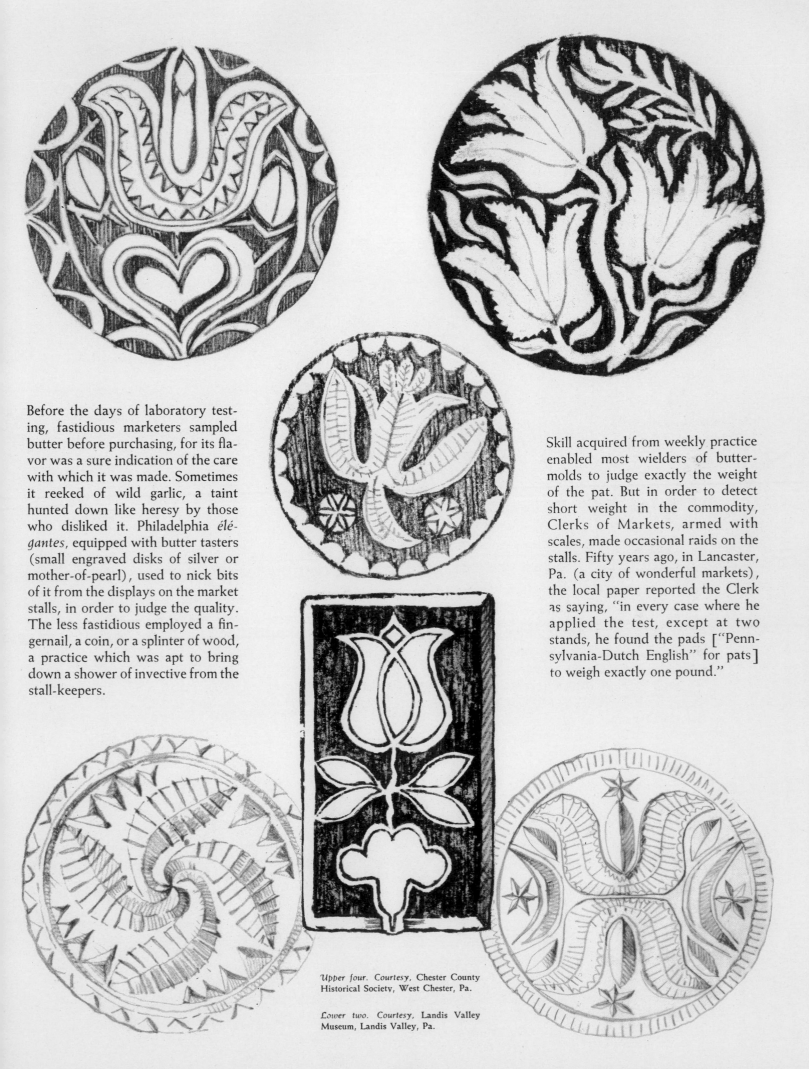

Before the days of laboratory testing, fastidious marketers sampled butter before purchasing, for its flavor was a sure indication of the care with which it was made. Sometimes it reeked of wild garlic, a taint hunted down like heresy by those who disliked it. Philadelphia *élégantes*, equipped with butter tasters (small engraved disks of silver or mother-of-pearl), used to nick bits of it from the displays on the market stalls, in order to judge the quality. The less fastidious employed a fingernail, a coin, or a splinter of wood, a practice which was apt to bring down a shower of invective from the stall-keepers.

Skill acquired from weekly practice enabled most wielders of buttermolds to judge exactly the weight of the pat. But in order to detect short weight in the commodity, Clerks of Markets, armed with scales, made occasional raids on the stalls. Fifty years ago, in Lancaster, Pa. (a city of wonderful markets), the local paper reported the Clerk as saying, "in every case where he applied the test, except at two stands, he found the pads ["Pennsylvania-Dutch English" for pats] to weigh exactly one pound."

Upper four. Courtesy, Chester County Historical Society, West Chester, Pa.

Lower two. Courtesy, Landis Valley Museum, Landis Valley, Pa.

119

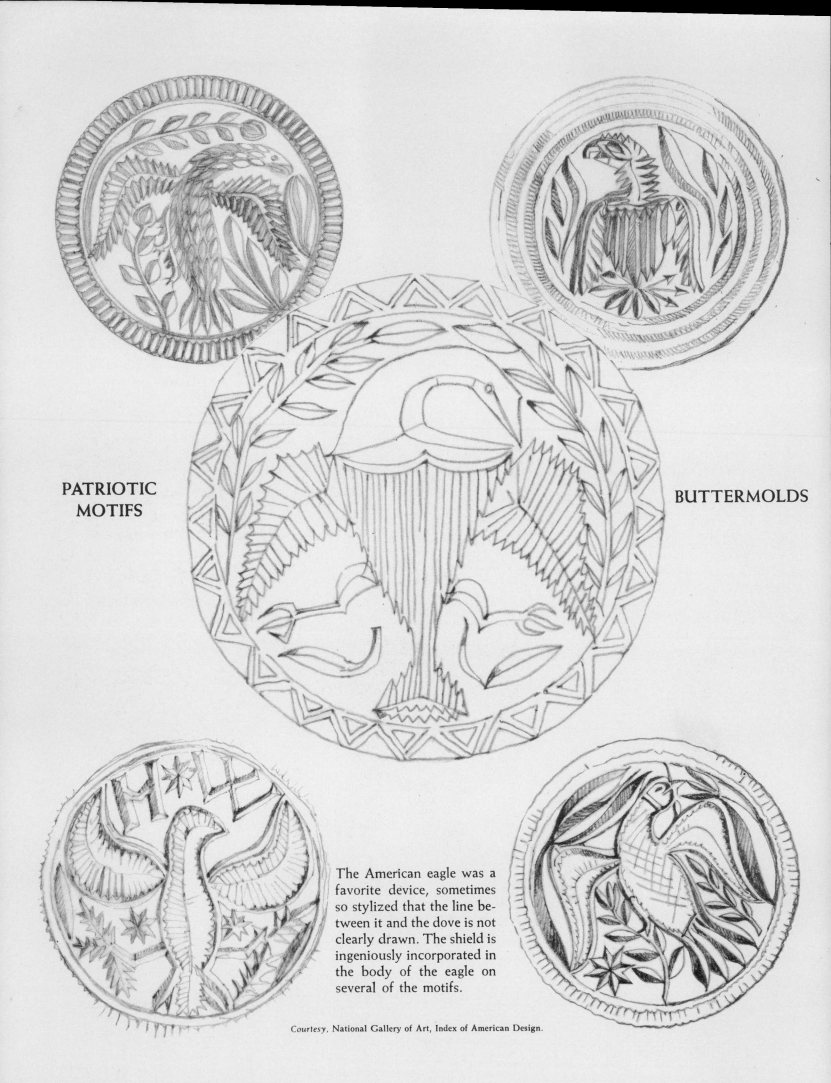

**PATRIOTIC
MOTIFS**

BUTTERMOLDS

The American eagle was a favorite device, sometimes so stylized that the line between it and the dove is not clearly drawn. The shield is ingeniously incorporated in the body of the eagle on several of the motifs.

Courtesy, National Gallery of Art, Index of American Design.

Carved wood buttermold (*left*), and impression taken from it (*right*).

BUTTER
AND
BAG STAMPS

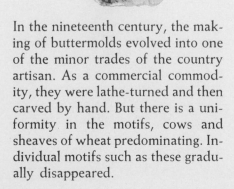

In the nineteenth century, the making of buttermolds evolved into one of the minor trades of the country artisan. As a commercial commodity, they were lathe-turned and then carved by hand. But there is a uniformity in the motifs, cows and sheaves of wheat predominating. Individual motifs such as these gradually disappeared.

Molds were sometimes devised to provide two sizes of pats, and two different designs.

All buttermolds, courtesy, National Gallery of Art, Index of American Design.

Above. Bag Stamp. Not a mold for butter, but a woodblock, which, when imprinted on the homespun bags used to carry grain to the mill, identified the owner. Most farmers were content to use only their names or initials, but the carver of this stamp surrounded the bold initials "E.B." with a well-balanced pattern. The use of bag stamps was common practice in Switzerland.

FROM BENEATH THE SURFACE OF THE EARTH
—STONE

"There is curious building-stone and paving stone, also tile-stone . . . also very good limestone in great plenty, and cheap, of great use in buildings, and also in manuring land, (if there were occasion) but nature hath made that of itself sufficiently fruitful. . . ."
>—Gabriel Thomas' Account of Philadelphia and the Province to the Year 1696.

AN excellent publicity man, this Gabriel Thomas, whose engaging description of the richness of Pennsylvania (written—and he avows truthfully—after living in the new settlements for fifteen years) is a forerunner of all land prospectuses. Although in the seventeenth century it was probably a matter of years before an advertisement came in contact with the public at which it was aimed, the various published accounts of the wealth of Pennsylvania eventually reached a passionately receptive audience, and England lived to regret such appeals. The time arrived when she was actually swamped with so great an influx of destitute Palatine refugees that to provide even makeshift housing for them became a problem of utmost concern for the Government. London and Bristol were the ports from which the ships sailed for America. There, in 1709, began to gather the great movement of the Palatines toward that "promised land," the largest mass emigration ever made from any European country to Colonial America.

All of Europe had just passed through the utterly dreadful "Cold Winter" of 1708-1709, the intensity of which was felt most painfully in the war-desolated Rhineland. Even wild animals perished in the woods, and the starving, persecuted inhabitants froze to death by the hundreds. With the mecca of America in their hearts, thousands of tragic, miserable, lowly folk made their slow way down the Rhine to Holland and thence to worried England. Nothing stemmed this tide; no threats or appeals turned them back. Everything these pious home-loving people owned had been destroyed. Hope lay only in movement elsewhere. Most of them were humble souls—farmers and workers in the vineyards, common mechanics and artisans. In a census taken of the members of a certain group patiently waiting until they could be crowded on to a tiny ship which would take them to Penn's "promised land," agriculturalists constituted by far the largest proportion, followed in numerical importance by the workers in wood, the carpenters. These were the trades of primary importance in any new colony, for they provided the vital necessities: food, and rough, quick housing. Clothing, equally important, was provided for by the inclusion of weavers and tailors, the next largest group. The workers for permanency, the stone masons, found themselves in fifth place, for no matter how much stone underlay Penn's "wooden country," things built of it could be dispensed with until primary needs were cared for. Nevertheless, when the Germanic masons were given the opportunity to practise their deliberate and long-enduring craft, they created so distinctive a pattern in their houses and farm buildings that to this day the many existing examples of their work give to the fertile Pennsylvania countryside an appearance unlike that of any other section of the country.

Though this mass emigration of the early eighteenth century was the real beginning of the great and permanent farm settlements in the eastern counties, many thousands of their fellow countrymen had preceded them to America, for compelling religious as well as economic reasons. Led by Francis Daniel Pastorius, a lawyer and a scholar, the first Germanic organized community in this country came here in 1683, one year after the establishment of Philadelphia, to found Germantown, originally an outlying village but now a section of that formerly Quaker town. Its absorption is today so complete that all traces of the Continental origins of its early settlers are obliterated. Only the craftsmanship of the masons, as demonstrated in some of its quaint houses, remains to show the strength and sturdiness of its first founders.

English-speaking Philadelphia was only five miles away, but the compact little community of Germantown resisted its influence and remained a purely Germanic settlement for a surprisingly long time. For over a century or so, the country people who came in to Germantown bartered in "Pennsylvania Dutch" with the local storekeepers and merchants, who, even if it was not their native tongue, were compelled by business exigencies to acquaint themselves with it. The streets were noisy with the shouts of the village children playing their games in the only speech they knew, much to the amazement of the Philadelphians who happened to pass by and hear them. Pastorius' first settlement of thirteen families had taken firm root.

The group which established Germantown consisted mostly of weavers of linen—German and Dutch Mennonites coming from Crefeld, a little village in Germany, situated near the Dutch border. In order to make a fair distribution of the sections into which he had divided the 5000-acre grant he received from William Penn, Pastorius had the new colonists draw lots for the choice of location. A year after the community was established, he wrote in a letter home that the most important need of the new settlement was more and more farmers and laborers, for it took very strong men to cut down the massive oaks which almost overwhelmed the new colonists, there were so many of them in the forest. He also needed a "tile bakery," so that the settlers could live under a tiled roof in less dread of fire. Until they should have space in which to grow food, and places to live, Pastorius saw no urgent need for other types of artisans. The new settlement had plenty to do to establish itself and could therefore wait several years before it required the services of the less vitally important craftsmen.

With remarkable good will the farmers, the laborers, and the carpenters commenced the struggle with the forest. Soon the cleared space appeared, and then the log houses. These, built according to a very detailed description of William Penn's in a tract called "Information and Direction to such Persons as are inclined to America," he estimated would cost, for both house and barn, fifteen pounds, ten shillings, and would last about ten years without needed repairs. The first log houses of the German colonists were built close to both sides of the long, wandering Indian trail on which their farm plots fronted, fixing the architectural pattern for a street, a pattern still adhered to, even after 250 years, and which, in memory of the compact little village through which it led, is still called "Germantown Road."

After much hard and painful work to establish the community, the call went overseas for more artisans, particularly for those in the building trades. The need for masons was urgent. The strange log cabins did well enough for a few years, but the Rhineland settlers had not forgotten the enduring stone dwellings of their homeland, and longed to reproduce them here. Stone lay around them in great abundance, right in the earth of their own community, waiting only to be quarried out. A curious stone this was, of a dark gray sombreness and glimmering with bits of mica. When the stone masons finally arrived, they and their clients were in complete accord as to what constituted a proper house. It had to be of stone and as much like the mediæval village houses they had relinquished as the differing conditions in the new land would permit. The English colonists, only five miles distant in Quaker Philadelphia, might build their neat houses of red brick, as soon as it was possible to do so. The masons in Germantown would have none of brick; they wrought in stone. It was a long time before these adjacent living patterns affected and eventually worked changes in each other, so tenaciously did both groups of settlers adhere to their own customs.

As time went on, neat, little, rugged stone houses, all very much alike, began to appear in place of the log cabins, which were either pulled down or used in the rear of the new house as the kitchen. From the front which paralleled the road, the house appeared to be only one story high, overhung by a very high peaked or hipped roof. This roof, which came so low that a tall man could easily touch the eaves, was sometimes broken by two long, sloping dormer windows, mediæval in style. Frequently the heavy expanse of shingle or red tile was unbroken. The gable end of the house, at right angles to the road, disclosed a tiny window in the space formed by the peak of the roof, which gave light and air to sleeping quarters, usually assigned to the boys in the family. A single chimney was centered on the roof. In this position it became, for eighteenth-century travellers, almost the signpost of a German householder, one who used stoves, whose flues all led into this one chimney. The English, addicted to open fires, placed their several chimneys at the ends of the roof to accommodate the necessary fireplaces.

The front door of the house was divided horizontally, a practical idea, for the closed lower section kept out investigating livestock, while the upper, when open, allowed the busy housewife a clear glimpse of the road and the infrequent passerby. During those rare moments of leisure when the eternally active housewife was occupied with nothing more urgent than the knitting of the family stockings, she was able to survey her neighbors from the excellent vantage point offered by the neat little pair of benches which flanked the door outside. As a protection against thieves, solid wooden shutters were closed over the windows every night, a custom followed to the present day by the few ultra-conservatives left in the neighborhood.

Fire was dreaded by everyone, and to lessen the danger every settler left considerable space between his house and his neighbor's. Kitchen gardens, in which grew a large variety of vegetables, flourished behind every dwelling. The loaded market stalls of today's America owe much to them. These continental Europeans, craving familiar foods, planted in their vegetable plots the green stuffs of their homelands. The Huguenots introduced okra, tomatoes, and artichokes; others grew rhubarb, eggplant, oyster-plant, leeks, and novel salad plants. Had the matter been left to British tastes, faithful here as in England to their diet of cabbage, its relatives, and the potato, the American diet would be much more restricted. It took a long time to develop a taste for these vegetables generally, so sturdily did the English hold out against the strange foods of the "foreigners"!

The pioneering English never had much patience with gardening; they preferred the broader sweeps of the plough to the tedious niggling with the hoe and spade. For many years the only kitchen gardeners available were European immigrants, who, being patient and industrious, were used to the hard work and the eternal kneeling requisite to the raising of vegetables.

As Germantown began to grow and the wave of immigration brought in more and more settlers, those who had a desire to farm broader fields moved onward, after the children had received some schooling and had grown up. Artisans, such as the original settlers, the linen weavers, and the ones who liked mercantile ventures, stayed on where they had begun. Some years later, when their industry and special skills had brought them a certain amount of affluence, they began to build more impressive stone houses, many of them three stories high, of fine proportions and sturdy construction. A famous characteristic of early Pennsylvania architecture, the "water table," is one of the features of these houses. It is a narrow, slanting, shingled roof, sometimes carried all around the house over the windows, sometimes restricted to the front of the building, where it often serves as a tiny front porch roof; an architectural feature brought in from the Palatinate where it can still be seen on a few eighteenth-century houses if the war did not obliterate them.

The work of the German stone masons has never been surpassed. They built with a passion for permanency, a passion with which their clients were equally imbued. In their houses even the interior partitions were sometimes made of stone. Though wood was abundant and made for easier building, these craftsmen worked in the harder way. Many

126

of their buildings in Germantown have lasted to this day, impressive monuments to their builders, set close to the pavements of a modern business street then undreamed of. A few of the garden spaces so essential to the early settlers still exist in this melange of houses and shops, though there are no longer any traces of "the mile of blossoming fruit trees" that once edged the roads of the ancient village. Long ago, too, the demands of pedestrian traffic shaved off the porches that once stood before each house and did away with the equally quaint, sloping cellar doors, which, in the days when far fewer people travelled the old road, casually jutted out into the pavement.

An equally impressive memorial to themselves was left by the farmer settlers who, forsaking the comparative security of Germantown, pushed on into the surrounding wilderness. Their impress is all over adjacent counties, an impress which to this day gives these counties their distinctive character. The first outgrowth of the Germantown settlement was to the northwest, some twenty miles away, where a group of Mennonites settled on the Skippack Creek in 1702.

Though one brave soul, Johannes Keim, in 1698 had taken himself at least fifty miles away, this was unusual. Common sense demanded that the Germans, like the English and the Welsh, form communities of their own, for they were ignorant of one another's languages, customs, and habits of thought. At first the demands of pioneer living were too insistent to leave settlers any time to cope with the barriers set up by differing languages. All these country dwellers were simple folk, used to a village life, with no need for any tongue but their own. For mutual protection and for immediate aid, they turned to their own kind. After the great influx of Palatines began in 1709, the immigrants spread out in radiating lines from Philadelphia to set up the beginnings of their distinctive communities in the nearby counties of Montgomery, Lancaster, Berks, Lehigh, Lebanon, and York. In these counties, known as the "Pennsylvania Dutch" counties, their descendants are still the predominating element. Here, in their fertile limestone valleys, they developed and have maintained to this day a culture and a folk pattern of their own.

When the German settler went to the land, he went with the avowed intention of staying there, for he meant to make good on the spot he had chosen. Solid, substantial, deliberate, he waited a long time before he planned for himself a permanent home. In this he could not be hurried. When he finally built it, it was as substantial as himself. Set in the midst of gently rounded, cultivated hills and smooth fields of many sizes, the Pennsylvania stone farmhouse today adds its note of solidity to the angled patterns of farm buildings which accent the rich landscape of fertile slopes and valleys, centered with their inevitable, tree-bordered streams.

Nothing points more strongly to the fact that he planned for permanency than the evidence afforded by date and namestones, for only a man who expected his descendants to live on in the house he had built would mark it with the names of both himself and his wife, a quaint and ancient Rhenish custom which can be seen to this day in the Kur-Pfalz.

Such inscriptions stood as visible demonstrations to the world in general that this man had achieved the primary aim of every peasant settler: *This is the family estate.* Sometimes a religious sentiment was also carved on the date-stone to perpetuate a tradition of equally long standing. Eventually, local forces at work in the new country had their way; later generations modified their folkways into something more like those of their neighbors', and these distinctive fashions finally disappeared.

The settlers found the limestone with which they built, first their great stone-ended barns and later the farmhouse and outbuildings, right on their own farms, in their own hillsides. The same limestone, burned in the kilns which were once to be seen everywhere in the Pennsylvania German counties, gave them the lime for the mortar which held the stones together. The masonry was varied; sometimes the stone was cut to uniform shapes; frequently it was set in random sizes, and as much of the local stone weathered in rich color, the effect was both pleasing and artistic.

In certain sections where red sandstone was plentiful, it was used as a trim on limestone buildings as well as for the entire construction of the farmstead. Gray stone houses with red sandstone quoins, a striking combination, are the result of an inspiration coming from the German Renaissance, brought over by South German masons from their homeland, where the combination was a usual one.

On these severe stone houses there was little opportunity to indulge in any display of ornament, except for a few symbols and tulips cut in the date-stones, or a panel of lettering which was placed over the door or carved on the lintel. Nevertheless the stone carvers had a place sanctified by tradition on which they could indulge themselves in the more flamboyant phases of their craft. Gravestones presented unlimited scope, and it is on their time-stained surfaces that we note a lavish use of the same motifs that were employed by their fellow craftsmen in other fields. In the old cemeteries we find again, sculptured in whatever local stone would withstand the weather, the familar folk motifs—the inevitable tulip, the heart, the crown, and the star, symbols very like those used on the barns. These country gravestones of red sandstone or granite or slate often feature fine panels of lettering, in old German or Latin characters.

In the earliest days, the stone-cutter probably dug out his own stone from the quarry and then hauled it himself to the open shed where he worked. With a toothless saw and the abrasive effects of sand and water, he trimmed it roughly to the desired size. Then with mallet and chisels he laboriously chipped away until he achieved the scrolled outline he had planned for it, the shaping of which not only demonstrated his skill but was customary in all early tombstones. There was little of the rectangle left in the top outline of any colonial gravestone.

To level the surface of the stone evenly, he applied sand and water which he rubbed back and forth with another stone. For working in softer stone, there was a hammer with a chisel-shaped edge which he used effectively. Varied textures were sometimes introduced to set off the decoration from its background. Eighteenth-century gravestones are often ornamented on both faces, the front taking the inscription and an ornamental heading, the rear being devoted to purely decorative features.

The stone-cutter, like other Pennsylvania German craftsmen, was an independent artisan who carried out his own ideas which the client was forced to accept. If something appealed to his sense of the practical the matter was settled; any further consideration of the client's wishes was superfluous. The late governor of Pennsylvania, Samuel Penny-packer, tells in his *Autobiography of a Pennsylvanian* a delightful story of this characteristic. A farmer said, referring to a neighbor:

"Dat name, TRUCKENMILLER, is so long dat ve just calls them T-MILLER and ven dey gets buried up in Keeley's crave-yard, dat is vat goes on to the cravestone."

Detail of Tombstone.
Belonging to Maria Catharina Stahl-
necker, 1760-1797.

Pennsylvania German churches and their graveyards often perch on breezy hilltops. On one of the hilliest of these in Lehigh County is the Chestnut Ridge Union Church, and in its attendant graveyard is this slate tombstone, probably the finest extant.

These ancient stones are never gruesome; the skull and crossbones, so common in New England, is rare. In its place one finds the same motifs as are employed on other forms of local decoration.

Both the reverse as well as the obverse of this tall, thin, slate slab are elaborately incised in a firm, sure line, preserving to this day the curious intricate design.

Right. The gravestone of "Andereas Herb" at Hill Church, Berks County, Pa., a union congregation founded in 1731.

Center row. Tulips from Muddy Creek Lutheran and Reformed Church, founded 1732. East Cocalico Township, Lancaster County, Pa.

Above and below, left. From Bergstrasse Lutheran Church, Lancaster County, Pa.

From Emmanuel Church, Brickerville, Lancaster Co., Pa., a Lutheran congregation founded in 1730.

Baroque seventeenth-century gravestone at Langwieden, in the Palatinate. An obvious model for the humbler local decorative attempts.

The country artisan, in emulation of the stone-cutter's art of his homeland, used the same symbolic heart with its springing tulips or lilies, the heavenly crown, the stars, the whirling swastika, as well as other geometric symbols.

All examples from the author's notebook.

Early gravestones are often simple lumps of incised red sandstone, hugging the ground. From the first Lutheran Church in America, at Trappe, Pa.

Cherub, presenting a foretaste of "fruits of Paradise." 1772. An unusual stone in Hill Church graveyard, Berks County, Pa.

From Muddy Creek Church, Lancaster County, Pa.

Courtesy, Landis Valley Museum, Landis Valley, Pa.

On the earliest tombstones, inscriptions were chiselled in quaintly spelled German, set down in Roman characters. Later on, lettering appears in German Gothic, a type requiring more skill to incise.

Left. A crescent moon, with human profile, is featured on many of these humble sandstone markers. From the hilltop cemetery, Bergstrasse Church, Lancaster County, Pa.

Courtesy, Historical Society of Pennsylvania, Philadelphia.

DATE STONES

The use of date stones stems from an ancient Palatinate custom; a commemoration of the important event of house building. When the Pennsylvania Germans finally built themselves substantial dwellings, they transplanted the custom here. Date stones included not only the owner's name and the date but often a blessing on the house.

Above. Date stone with house blessing. Johannes and Susan Kauffmann, 1771. Maidencreek Township, Berks County, Pa.

Inscription, translated, reads: "To thy care, O Lord, are commended all in this household going in or out."

Right. In 1798 Christian and Maria Huber required a pair of stones to share the honors of ownership, Christian taking the "17," Maria the "98." The stone-cutting reflects the fashionable Anglo-Classic tradition.

Courtesy, Landis Valley Museum, Landis Valley, Pa.

Courtesy, Landis Valley Museum, Landis Valley, Pa.

Courtesy, State Library, Harrisburg, Pa.

Above. The date stone for the house Peter Muhselman built in 1790 was the work of a skilled stonecutter, inspired by European eighteenth-century motifs favored by the gentry.

Above. Engaging date stone of 1765, with the folk motifs of tulip and barn symbols boldly executed. Found in a field in Lancaster County.

FROM BENEATH THE SURFACE OF THE EARTH
—IRON

"This last summer, one Thomas Rutter, a smith who lives not far from Germantown, hath removed further up in the country, and of his own strength hath set upon making iron. Such as it proves to be, as is highly set by, by all the smiths here, who say that the best of Sweed's iron doth not exceed it; and we have accounts of others that are going on with iron works."
— Jonathan Dickinson's Letters—1717

THE simple German agriculturist of the eighteenth century, forced by war and privation to leave his vineyards and familiar Rhineland fields and to transplant himself to the new world, remained a simple agriculturist, absorbed here as there in the difficulties of gaining his own living. While circumstances compelled him to be a jack-of-all-trades, there were still many occupations, the work of specialists, which lay outside his knowledge. The mining of ore was one of them. To him the fertility of his soil was all-important and any variation in its color a matter of unconcern. If the fields, after every rain, were streaked with brownish red stains, he was unperturbed, for to his agricultural mind they carried no significance.

But to a few early travellers, educated and observant men who passed through the regions, the rusty brown streaks were indications of industrial possibilities, for they marked the presence of iron ore lying just below the surface. This evidence of potential wealth appeared in the published accounts of their travels, eagerly read by venturesome men anxious to make their fortunes in the new land. Not many years after the settlement of eastern Pennsylvania, a few Englishmen made preparations to carry out the manufacture of iron in this country. It seemed a promising venture. Everything necessary for the changing of ore found in the earth into iron was available in the region: streams for waterpower, unlimited supplies of wood to be turned into charcoal (the essential fuel), and limestone. The market too was within easy reach, for the colonists, their neighbors, had nothing made of iron except the few pieces they brought with them.

Even in the eighteenth century the manufacture of iron was still conducted along mediæval lines. The early ironmasters located their furnaces where the supply of ore and wood was adequate, and ignored the problems of transportation by adhering to a feudal pattern of life. After raising the capital, the first adventurous Englishmen took up thousands of acres on which they set up their iron works on the plantation system. These iron plantations, great woodland estates, were planned to be entirely self-supporting, for it was obligatory in the earliest days to develop a way of life which could sustain the various types of workers. The houses of the laborers, the fields in which crops were raised to feed them, the grist mills and the saw mills, the furnaces, the charcoal houses, the blacksmith shop,

135

even the community "store" on which the plantation workers depended for the few things they could not make or grow themselves, all had to be planned for and built in order that iron could be mined and smelted.

Dominating this busy settlement was the mansion of the ironmaster, built on a hill from which the owner could survey the furnace and the life of the plantation. Today, of this interesting Colonial industrial set-up only ruins are left, slight traces of the mills and the workers' houses, the furnaces, barns, and offices. Of the mansion houses only a few remain as evidences of a way of life long past. These still bear the names of the original furnaces, which recall the English origins of their first owners: Coventry, Abington, Reading, Windsor, and Warwick. Some ironmasters named their furnaces or forges after the women in their families. In the eighteenth century, four plantations in various sections of the state were called Mary Ann. Elizabeth, the name of the furnace operated by the famous Henry William Stiegel, was named for his wife. Others were named after bygone Rebeccas, Joannas, Julianas, and Marias.

On the plantations there was work for many types of laborers. In addition to the skilled labor needed at the furnace or forge, woodcutters, teamsters, and charcoal burners were equally essential. Charcoal, the fuel used to smelt the ore, resulted from a process by which wood was charred. The furnaces consumed the growth of hundreds of acres yearly; so the work of cutting down the trees kept many men busy during the winter months. Turning wood into charcoal was the work of the colliers or charcoal burners. Their picturesque and essential but unpleasant profession was one very familiar to Colonial America, which was dependent on it for the fuel used in many trades and crafts of daily life.

The women of the ironworkers' families not only did the spinning and the weaving but helped greatly with the farm labor. The haying, the harvesting, the gathering of fruit in the orchards and of vegetables in the fields, were all allotted to them. This work for the community was carried on in addition to their own housekeeping, a dreary task in those primitive days, for the workers' cabins lacked everything but the barest necessities; a striking contrast to the mansion houses, whose elegant furnishings came from overseas.

Though it was in 1716, thirty years after the first Quaker settlement of the State, that a blacksmith, Thomas Rutter, established the first iron works in Berks County, the business began timidly, for the real future of the iron industry depended on the development of the country and the demands of new customers. Despite this slow beginning, several furnaces were already in operation by the time the great wave of Palatine immigration was in full swing, bringing with it a mass of potential customers eager for these articles they could not produce themselves. The arrival of the smiths, a vital part of every immigrating group, kept the forges busy supplying them with bar iron, from which they made their fine, artistic objects used in daily life.

In his community the German blacksmith commanded great respect, for he was extremely proficient in his craft. Unless the colonist could make shift with a homemade wooden tool, he was absolutely dependent on the smith for all articles which had to be made both strong and enduring. The smith forged the axes for clearing the endless forests, the nails and hardware for dwellings, the metal tools with which the earth was worked, and the iron rims for the wheels of carts and wagons. From his skilled hand came bolts and hinges for the house, knives and forks for the housewife, shovels and hoes for work in the field, even sharp fish-hooks and slim knitting-needles. All the permanent equipment for the fireplace was the work of this important craftsman; the pothooks and trammels on which the kettles hung; the crane itself which supported the hooks; the frying-pans with extremely long handles, so strange to our eyes, so necessary in the early days. Long-handled cooking utensils enabled a woman to keep her distance while cooking before the great fireplace. Without them she ran the risk of being cremated.

When the first furnaces began operating, they were the sources of supply not only for the bar iron used by the smiths but for cast-iron cooking utensils, for which there was also a great demand. As the immigrant settlers were able to bring only a minimum of household articles with them, the housewife who failed to bring a great iron pot waited for the day when she would again be the proud possessor of one to swing from the crane. Until she acquired others this one pot served every purpose.

Because of the constant demand for fuel, farming and ironmaking were closely connected. In fact, they were often practised together. Although the earliest ironmasters were English, later on an occasional Pennsylvania German who had accumulated some money in farming set up a furnace if he found ore on his own farm and could raise additional capital by taking in partners. Some of the smaller furnaces bought their fuel from the farmers, who cut it from their own extensive woodlands, and this steady contact with the iron plantations tended to give a farmer an idea of the business.

As the ore lay just beneath the surface of the earth, to get it out required no special technical knowledge and only the simplest of tools. With pickaxes and crowbars the workmen dug it out of wide trenches or pits, which they never carried to any great depth. After they had dug down about twenty feet, they abandoned one "mine-hole" and started another.

Ore was smelted in a blast furnace, a truncated stone stack about twenty feet high, built into the side of a hill so that the ore, the necessary charcoal, and limestone could be hauled to the top and dumped in continuously. This process of feeding the furnace continued with monotonous regularity day and night for about nine months of the year, for the furnace ran uninterruptedly unless stopped by accidents. The draft for the furnace was furnished by enormous bellows operated by waterpower. The purified ore ran down to the hearth, the sandstone base of the stack. In front of the furnace was the casting shed, the floor of which was of blackened sand, the material in which castings were formed. With a spade and a mold of hickory, a workman made an impression in the sand on the floor of the shed. This impression consisted of a main concave channel called the "sow," from which at right angles extended smaller ones called "pig" molds. These old-time imaginative names are still used, even in the great industry that iron-making has become today. Twice each day and night, the iron founder let the molten metal flow from the hearth where it had been accumulating, into this patterned bed of sand. When somewhat cooled, the "pigs" were knocked away from the "sow" and the old "sow" herself broken into smaller pieces. Being brittle, "pig" iron is used only for castings.

In making iron pots, pans, and kettles, the molten metal was not run directly into the molds. Small ladles which dipped it from the hearth poured it into impressions which had been made in the sand by molds having the exact shape of the desired article.

The Palatine settlers, accustomed even in the seventeenth century to cast-iron warming stoves in their homeland, introduced them into this country. As early as 1728 they were being made at Coventry Forge. German artisans perfectly familiar with the requirements made the patterns as nearly like the European ones as memory allowed. The English ironmasters cast them to meet the odd local German demand for stoves, but the British settler continued to depend on the familiar fireplace for heat. This "German" stove, or "carved" stove, as it was called, was the simplest kind of a rectangular box, with one side omitted. To install it, an opening was made through the wall of a fireplace into the adjoining room, in which the stove was to be placed. The open side was pushed against the aperture, and the stove was built into the wall by means of flanges. Supported on legs, it became the receptacle for hot embers shovelled into it from the fireplace in the room adjoining. While it lacked any means of ventilating, and the embers had constantly to be replenished, such a stove made it possible for the German colonists to work at sedentary tasks elsewhere than in the immediate vicinity of the fireplace, where space was always at a premium.

It is amusing to note how heated certain eighteenth-century minds became when the question concerned methods of keeping the body warm. Judging by the indoor temperatures maintained for the pampered women of today, no one then could possibly have been comfortable at all times in winter. Women were forced to invent ingenious devices for fighting off the cold, somewhat like those still used by European peasants in localities were fuel is scarce. Peter Kalm, the Swedish botanist, travelling here in 1753-1761, sets down his shocked impressions in his journal: In Albany, from October on, he narrates, mistresses, maids, servants and even little girls put live coals into small iron pans with perforated covers, which were placed beneath their skirts. At first he found it "positively painful to watch" and was sure they spoiled themselves. But familiarity with the sight must have lessened his moralistic attitude, for he returns to the subject again later on, this time diverted by the practice: "But nothing amused me more than to observe how occupied they were with the placing of the warming pans (braziers) beneath their skirts. In a house where there were four women present it was well nigh impossible to glance in the direction of the fire without seeing at least one of them busily engaged in replacing the coals in her warming pan. Even their negro women had acquired this habit, and if time allowed, they also kept warming pans under their skirts." No doubt the sight of Pennsylvania German women spinning demurely by their warm iron boxes was less agitating to the rather strait-laced botanist.

It was not very long before the Germans improved the five-plate stove, which had no means of ventilation. By adding the missing side, and equipping it with a stovepipe and fuel door, they now had a stove freed from the wall. This must have been considered a great step forward. The plates from which it was made were beautifully decorated with motifs in the Germanic tradition.

But when Benjamin Franklin, in 1744, invented a detached, movable fireplace and had it cast by his friend Robert Grace at Warwick Furnace, the eighteenth century really got a jolt. The invention, a simple sort of iron affair, "half stove, half fireplace," was important only because it was the first of many experiments which eventually resulted in the famous "Franklin Stove." It is edifying to read Kalm's account of the colonists' attitude towards this iron novelty, which offered but a bit more comfort in those bleak winters:

"Despite their usefulness, they have been criticized. If the chimney could not be swept, there was danger of fire. Some thought the stoves gave too much heat, and since the Englishmen were not accustomed to this, they liked open fires better, and the Germans preferred their small oblong square iron stoves . . . because they give more heat and cost less."

Despite their economy of operation, the German box stoves had only a short life, for the English furnaces which cast them were not particularly interested in creating a market for them. In 1761, the first cooking stove made on American soil was cast at Hereford Furnace by Thomas Maybury. This is always referred to as the "ten-plate stove." Though equipped with a smoke-pipe, it bore little resemblance to later cooking stoves, for the top lacked the usual removable stove lids. Nevertheless, its manufacture was an event, for it was the first stove that could be used for both cooking and heating purposes. The patterns of the castings were probably designed by English pattern makers, with motifs distinctly eighteenth century in flavor. Stoves continued to be improved, and eventually the happy day arrived when every woman was able to say goodbye to the fireplace, to its litter and its battery of long-handled forks, spoons, and ladles, and its equally long-handled three-legged pans.

But until that time came, there was always plenty of work for the smith, who was the supply centre for these utensils. As pig-iron used in casting was too brittle for his purposes, the furnaces sold him bar iron, which could be both forged and welded. This they produced either from pig-iron or from the ore itself. In the first method the pig-iron was remelted, and, when a pasty mass, was hammered under an enormous hammer operated by waterpower. This heavy "tilt-hammer," falling by gravity on an anvil, extended the mass of iron, which was then cut up into several pieces. By successive reheatings and rebeatings under the great hammers, the forgemen, amid showers of sparks, drew the iron out into bars of the required sizes. When they made bar iron directly from the ore, they put it into the heated hearths of small forges, which were somewhat larger editions of the ordinary blacksmith's forge, having deeper firepots in which the charcoal and raw ore were mingled. The forgeman worked the semi-molten ore with a long iron bar until it gathered into a lump. This blazing mass was then placed under the "tilt-hammer," which worked out some of the foreign matter. Repetition of the processes finally produced bars of a tough, malleable, ductile material, the raw material of the blacksmith's art. From bar iron the local smith produced an enormous variety of articles, for he was artist-creator as well as manufacturer.

The early smith who was the settler's main source of all tools could not possibly have envisioned for himself the minor position of horse-shoer, and, finally, mere repair man, which was the eventual fate of his craft. In Pennsylvania, this important personage held undisputed sway in a picturesque, stone building, filled with noise, sparks, and masculinity. The litter of the craft was everywhere and no amount of sweeping by the apprentice boy could keep it really tidy. Its busyness and bustle were a powerful magnet which drew small boys who stood at a safe distance to watch the blacksmith and his helper go at a piece "hammer and tongs." And this distance they kept, for his trade gave the smith a powerful weapon of defense against small boys who approached too close for his comfort. Adroitly but with apparent innocence he could always aim a shower of sparks in their direction to compel the desired retreat.

Despite the seeming disorder elsewhere, the tools of the trade, hammers and punches, tongs and chisels, were racked in order, convenient to the anvil. The anvil stood on a tough block of wood before the forge, in which the smith heated the bar of metal. An apprentice boy operated the bellows which furnished the draft for the forge.

Owing to the nature of the material in which he worked, for red-hot iron did not permit of any fumbling, the smith was of necessity a man of decision. Before he began a piece of work, he not only had to have in mind a definite picture of what he intended to make, but he had also to plan the succession of operations necessary to execute his idea. With a clearly outlined conception, and the tools necessary to execute it within his reach, the smith forced the iron into the shape he planned for it, turning it into the graceful hinge or delicately wrought fork we value today.

The blacksmith was a busy man until he was overtaken by the great wave of mechanical invention which swept over the world in the early nineteenth century. Machines began to turn out, at much less cost, the innumerable articles which his skill formerly furnished. One hundred years of cutting down forests that had, at the beginning of the charcoal iron industry, appeared endless, had so reduced the wood supply that the ironmasters were forced to turn to coke, a fuel used in England for many years. The iron industry moved to the locale where the new fuel was abundant, and its abandoned forest clearings were transformed into the fertile farm country of eastern Pennsylvania. The furnace stack no longer lit up the unbroken blackness of the forest night with its frightening glow; the forges and the furnaces gradually fell into ruins; the mills, the great water-wheels and bellows disappeared. And present-day country boys swim and dive in water-filled, woodland "mine-holes" whose original use and economic importance are completely forgotten.

For a long time the blacksmith managed to survive; his shop could be found at the crossroads of villages and in all small towns. Though the country store now supplied the articles he once made on his anvil, horses still had to be shod. And at horse-shoeing, a respected trade, he earned his living up to the end of the nineteenth century. But Mr. Henry Ford's contraption and the use of gasoline did away with his most important clients, the horses, and gave the craft its death blow. Today the blacksmith shop is a rarity and a curiosity. Hearing the sound of an anvil a few years ago, I peered into an inconspicuous dark shop, where a blacksmith was working.

"You better take your last look at this, lady, for this here's an old antique," said the anachronism, cheerfully accepting the fate which had overtaken his once vital craft.

CAST-IRON STOVE PLATES

Above. Side plate of six-plate stove. Cast at Pennsylvania's first ironworks set up in 1720 by Thomas Rutter.

The first heating stoves used in this country were cast-iron five-sided boxes, protruding through the wall into the room, decorated with texts and human figures picturing Bible stories. The Pennsylvania German settlers, used to them at home, created the demand for them here. The demand lasted half a century.

After 1753 illustrative themes were dropped in favor of innumerable variations of the above pattern, with its hitherto unknown stylizations.

Well-designed variant of the usual motifs. Since many furnaces cast stove plates, the opportunity for advertisement was not overlooked. Henry Wilhelm ("Baron") Stiegel, who once operated Elizabeth Furnace, named it after his wife.

Although a Biblical quotation still creates a decorative panel of lettering, almost archaic horticultural and agricultural symbols replace the human figure as decorative motifs. Stove plate cast in 1747, probably by Thomas Maybury, Hereford Furnace, Berks County, Pa.

The symbolic vine and fig tree, together with name, date, and well-lettered panel, combine to make a simple, dignified arrangement.

Tulip motif from cast iron "cannon" stove, made in 1759 by "Baron" Stiegel, who won renown as an ironmaster before he made the well-known Stiegel glass.

Right. Stove plate, by "H. Whelym Stigghels" (the "Baron").

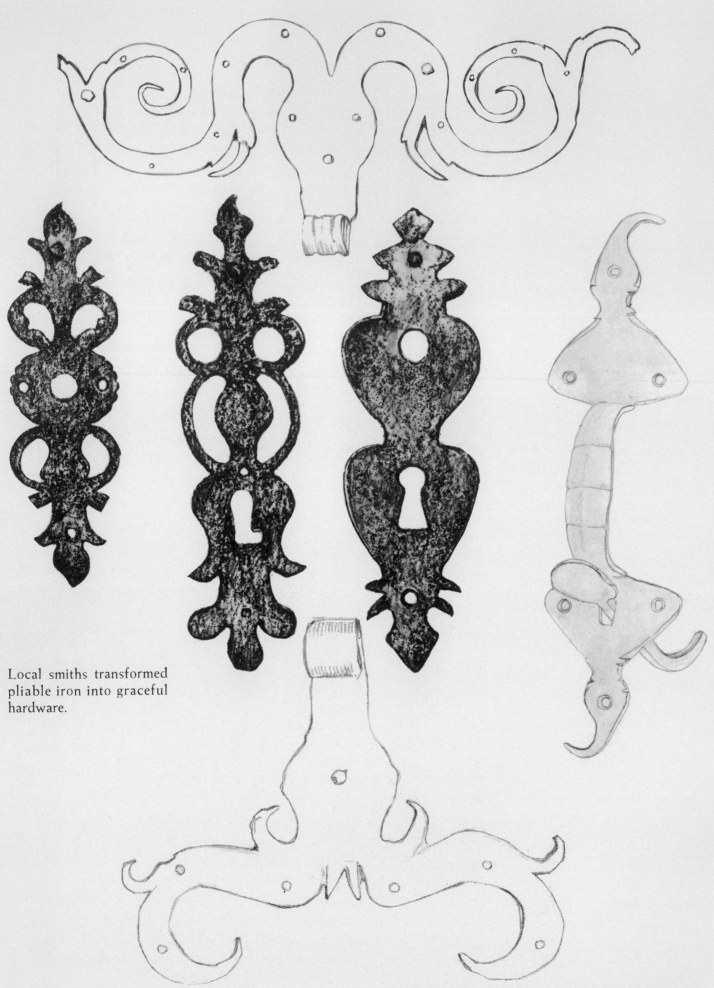

Local smiths transformed
pliable iron into graceful
hardware.

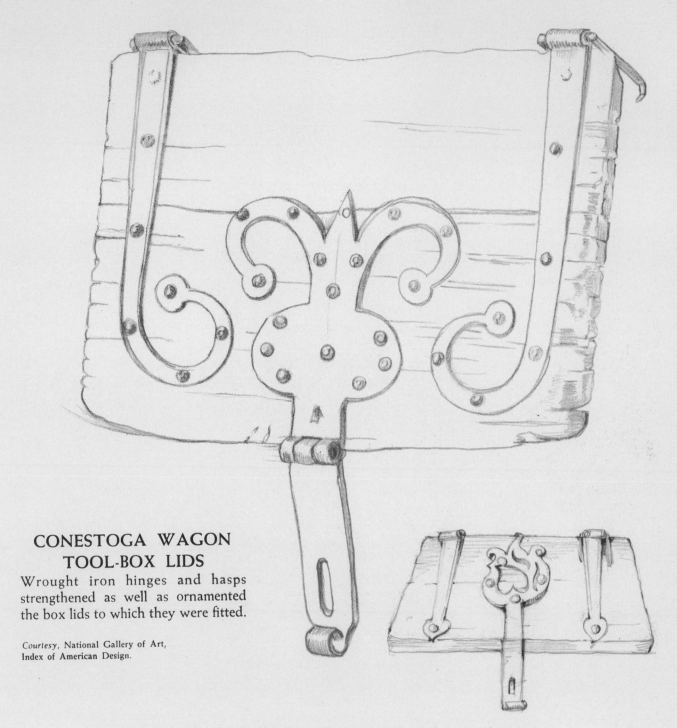

CONESTOGA WAGON
TOOL-BOX LIDS
Wrought iron hinges and hasps
strengthened as well as ornamented
the box lids to which they were fitted.

*Courtesy, National Gallery of Art,
Index of American Design.*

Before the days of railroads, freight and passengers moved across the country
in Conestoga farm wagons, so called because the best of them were made in
the Conestoga Valley, Lancaster County, Pa. They were painted in vermilion
and soft blue, with white linen covers. Local smiths made the necessary handsome iron fittings.

A contemporary observer says: "8th mo. 14, 1806. In walking out this evening, I met with
two German families on their way to the Ohio . . . They were a company of fine, healthy
looking people and travelled along with apparent chearfulness. The older females and the
little ones were upon beds in their covered waggons, whilst the young women and their
husbands, fathers and brothers went on foot. Parties of this sort I have often seen travelling
along, seeking a country where they hoped to meet with more tranquillity—than they had
witnessed in the old principalities of Germany. Considering the stability and industry which
characterize most of the German emigrants, I am inclined to believe that things must be
very much out of order, in their native land, before men like them would come to the reso-
lution of taking a final farewell of their near connexions and friends."

From *Travels in some parts of North
America*, 1804-05-06, by Robert Sutcliff.

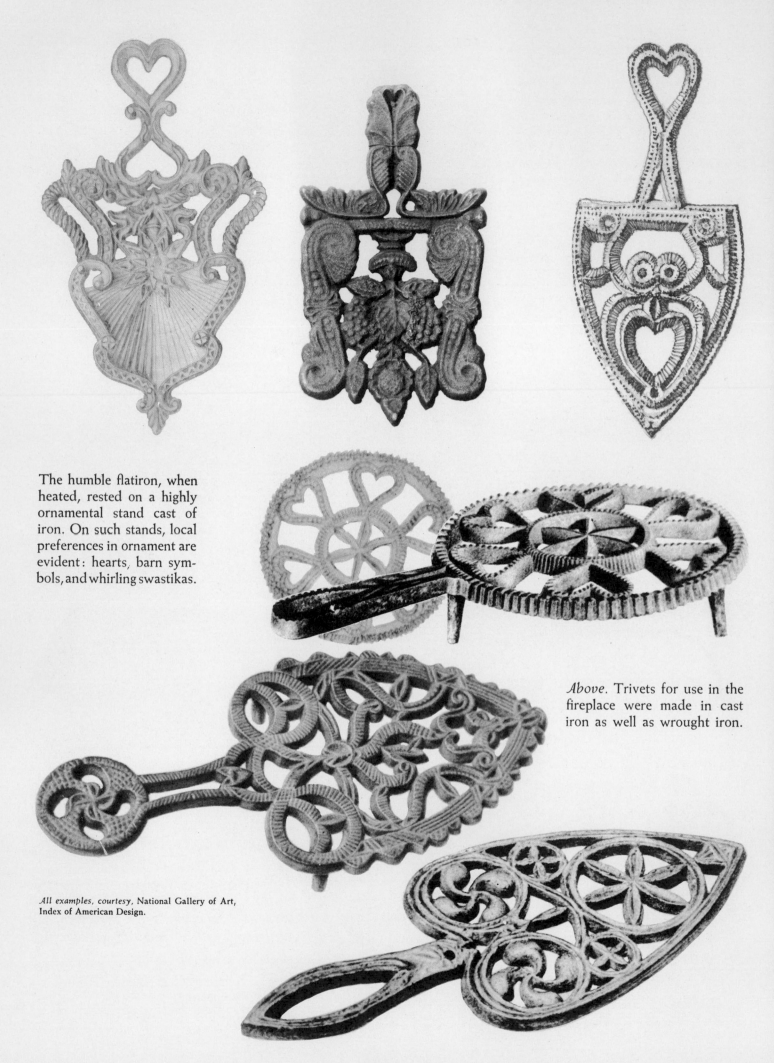

The humble flatiron, when heated, rested on a highly ornamental stand cast of iron. On such stands, local preferences in ornament are evident: hearts, barn symbols, and whirling swastikas.

Above. Trivets for use in the fireplace were made in cast iron as well as wrought iron.

All examples, courtesy, National Gallery of Art, Index of American Design.

146

Hanger for Kitchen Tools.

The blacksmith created quaint and ingenious forms of kitchen equipment in which decoration and use were intelligently united. This ornamental hanger has five cleverly turned hooks from which to suspend tools. Others can be hooked into the pierced openings.

Courtesy, Chester County Historical Society, West Chester, Pa.

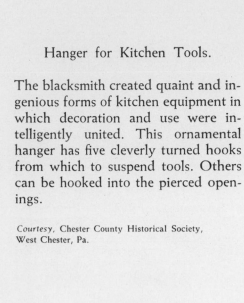

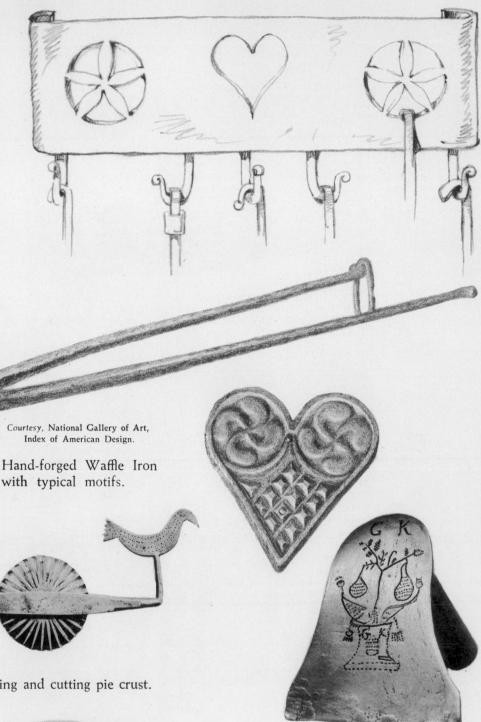

Courtesy, National Gallery of Art, Index of American Design.

Hand-forged Waffle Iron with typical motifs.

Courtesy, Metropolitan Museum of Art.

Wrought-iron device for marking and cutting pie crust.

Courtesy, Metropolitan Museum of Art.

Finely chased scraper, used to remove bread dough from tray.

Cast-Iron Waffle Baker.

Left. Pennsylvania German utensils were designed to accomplish a great deal at once. To save the housewife's time, the waffle recipe, of lavish proportions, is cast, in "Pennsylvania Dutch," on its surface. Translated:

2 pounds flour   ¾ pound butter
3 pints milk   1 spoonful salt
6-8 eggs

Courtesy, Philadelphia Museum of Art.

RAW MATERIAL FROM THE CITY—TIN

" 'I am a weaver, a shoemaker, farrier, wheelwright, farmer, gardener, and when it can't be helped, a soldier. I bake my bread, brew my beer, kill my pigs; I grind my axe and knives; I built those stalls and that shed there: I am barber, leech, and doctor.' . . . The man (a tavern keeper) was everything, at no expense for license and could do anything, as indeed the countryman in America generally can, himself supplying his own wants in great part or wholly."
—Johann David Schoepf, *Travels in the Confederation* 1783-1784

IN 1749 England passed an Act of Parliament prohibiting the setting up of any rolling or plating mills in the colonies, as part of a definite policy to discourage any American competition which might plan to turn out manufactured articles in metal. Although the act was only one of many grievances held by townspeople anxious to set up manufacturing ventures, it gave little concern to the Pennsylvania German farmer, who was obliged to be, and fully expected to be, a many-sided, one-man manufacturing plant. He himself noted no falling-off in the metals needed for his mode of life. The smiths still turned out the objects he ordered, and the foundries the stoves and kettles. Great Britain not only graciously permitted the Colonial foundries to smelt ore; she even urged the colonies to export the pig- and bar-iron to her so that she could manufacture more of it into sheet iron and tinplate. In selling back to them the articles fabricated from it, there was a fine profit to be made. So for a long time she saw to it that it was cheaper for the colonies to import manufactured articles than to try to produce them.

Before the eyes of town dwellers, England set forth many enticing articles, particularly of tinware, that shiny new metal so appealing to Colonial housewives because of its lightness. But the country wife had not yet glimpsed this new world of lightweight metal objects. Indoors and out, she still hauled about her heavy iron or earthenware utensils, taking their weight for granted. Her life was built on hard physical work, and it had not yet dawned on her that the weight of an article might be a legitimate basis for complaint. No glimmer of modern advertising practice had filtered through to the simple world in which she lived. As she never left her farm, she remained unaware of the commercial blandishments of England. Her lord and master, busy with all the trades he was compelled to follow, had little reason to leave the spot on which he settled and in which his interest was completely centered. This isolationistic attitude was kept up by certain rural people long after the economic reasons for it were no longer valid. It was sometimes bolstered by the religious beliefs of certain of the pietistic sects, who felt that by staying away from the world they could more easily avoid its enticements. In the latter half of the nineteenth century there were still families within less than a score of miles of a big town who went to it only once a year and then only to make the most necessary purchases.

But even the most isolated farmer was sometimes forced to make a trip to the nearest town in order to obtain the few things that were beyond his manufacturing skill or for which the land produced no substitute. Into his Conestoga wagon went his surplus of flour or flax, whiskey and the tanned skins of animals, and off he rumbled, his bed and board with him, for he used the wagon as his inn. Such trips took patience and endurance of a high grade. Sometimes, after the roads became slightly better, a father more indulgent than usual might take one or two of his daughters with him, at a time of the year when farm work had slackened and they could be spared at home. To see the sights and buy a few things they willingly underwent a jolting, bumping and thumping that no one today could either imagine or endure. On the trip back the girls formed a bruised but happy part of the promiscuous load of salt, plaster, dried fish, oil, calico, spices, pins, and weaving fixtures that the farmer's wife had asked for. We may be sure her shopping list had only modest requests for the things she absolutely needed, since she was as thrifty as her husband, asking for nothing which she herself could produce. But the girls, if Father could be wheedled into it, occasionally returned home with something not on the list of needfuls.

In the mass of articles manufactured for Colonial trade, England aimed to catch the eye of that reluctant buyer, the Pennsylvania German countryman. Artful splashes of red, green and yellow were a bid for the attention of the women, starved as they were for color. No woman who saw them could resist the charm of lacquered tinware, or of the dishes the Staffordshire potters made and sent across the ocean—they were so gay, so different from the brown and yellow earthenware and dull pewter and iron she was accustomed to.

If the supply of farm products left too small a balance with which to barter for a Staffordshire tea-set after the necessary purchases had been made, there may have been enough to buy another article the housewife craved, a scarlet tin coffee-pot or a shiny tin canister covered with brilliant flowers. To hands used to the weight of iron and earthenware, it seemed a marvel that anything could be so light and strong as the new tea-caddy, shiny in its vermilion lacquer, with its gay yellow borders and flowers bright as they could be painted. On her return, after it had been generally admired, she tucked it away with her few treasures and textiles in her dower chest.

In planning both Staffordshire china (nowadays dubbed "Gaudy Dutch" by the dealers) and lacquered tinware for rural trade in the colonies, England was very shrewd. So much of the latter has been unearthed in Pennsylvania that it is widely believed that local craftsmen manufactured and decorated it, together with other decorated objects of which they were so fond. But for a long time it was definitely an imported product; the manufacture of tinplate was not attempted here until many years after the Revolution, and England permitted no export of it so long as she could profit by manufacturing articles from it. By the time tinplate was being produced here, the teapots and household articles the Pennsylvania German tinsmith fashioned from it bore slight resemblance to the gay, lacquered pieces of the eighteenth century. Whether he worked in tin or in any other material, the artisan was ever a traditionalist, and Pennsylvania-made pieces bear all the earmarks of his traditions. Since the Pennsylvania German liked to see his name on his possessions, the tinsmith's pieces are marked, often with his own name as manufacturer, and quite as frequently with the name of the person for whom they were destined. This was feasible, for his market was small, one in which he often executed individual orders. Locally made, signed and dated pieces, almost always coffeepots, are never lacquered, but are left in the natural tin finish, decorated in a repoussé formed by tiny punch marks resembling pin-pricks. In this simple technique he worked out his familiar motifs. Here, as on the chests, one finds the stiffly centered tulips, the urns from which they spring, the stars, the birds, and the peacocks.

On examining the motifs on the English "tole-ware," as decorated lacquered tin is often called, one can see that they as well as their treatment spring from an entirely different tradition. The decorations on the japanned ware are the result of mass production, which demands that the same operation, the painting of a petal, let us say, be produced thousands of times. The facile brush-work resulting from repetition constitutes the outstanding difference between the work of the decorators of the japanned ware and the labored work of the local country craftsman. Whether the latter decorated a coffeepot or a chest, his was an unswerving peasant attack on his motif. Never once did his punch or paint-brush attain the airy, speedy curves or frivolous dashes which are an integral feature of the decorations on the lacquered articles. The coffeepots that he embellished with punched designs are marked with a stiff symmetry, whereas the gay, lacquered, imported pieces, whose flowers and fruit differ so considerably from anything he might have painted, are graceful and asymmetrical.

Aside from the differences between the two types of work in tinplate, really incontrovertible evidence of the English origin of the one type can be found in Alice Morse Earle's *Home Life in Colonial Days*, published in 1898, many years before any general interest was shown in Pennsylvania folk art. Under the heading, "Old Tinware," the author presents an illustration of a half dozen articles, exact duplicates of which can be seen in any tole-ware collection. But if this visual demonstration is not enough, her caption beneath the illustration is the type of evidence hoped for but rarely attained by one who finds it necessary to upset a pet belief of antique dealers and collectors. Mrs. Earle states: "This is a collection of century-old *English* tin-ware found in a country warehouse in a packing box, just as it was delivered from an *English* ship at the close of the Revolution. The pulling down of the warehouse disclosed the box *with its dated labels.*"*

Although England had once had a monopoly of the tin trade, for the best and richest tin mines were in Cornwall, the art of tinning thin sheets of iron was first invented in

* The italics are mine. F. L.

Bohemia. It was taken into Saxony around 1620, and until England learned how to process its native product, all the tinplate used in Europe was furnished by Germany. About 1670 an English company sent one Andrew Yarranton to Saxony to learn the process of tinning. On his return, he set up a successful manufacturing plant, but someone else obtained a patent on the process. This discouraged Mr. Yarranton and he failed to carry on. As the English found in the application of tin to iron, however, a new scheme for investment which turned out to be successful, they acquired a monopoly on it. In addition to their own ancient mines in Cornwall, they also imported tin from Siam and Malacca. By 1730 tinplate was being successfully manufactured in Pontypool.

This early tinplate consisted of a sheet of charcoal-forged iron, which received a thick coat of tin by being dipped into a vat of that metal. Another form, called terne plate, is a sheet of iron or steel coated with an alloy of lead and tin. In England, both coke and charcoal were used to smelt iron ore, but the tinplate made of charcoal-smelted iron was considered a better grade and was often given a second tinning, making a superior product. All early tinplate was considerably heavier than the flimsy tin of the present day and much less likely to succumb to the ravages of rust.

Until late in the eighteenth century very little tinware was used in the colonies, and what there was of it was very expensive and highly regarded. "Tinn quarts, fonnel & other things," articles that would not be considered worthy of mention today, are carefully itemized in 1757 in the inventory of a Pennsylvania German farmer's estate. The range of metals used by the Pennsylvania German settler is pretty well indicated by this inventory, obviously taken by a Pennsylvania German, as his struggles with English spelling indicate. Silver and copper are lacking, but he seemed well equipped with "Brass Cettels [kettles], Iron Potts, and all the Beuter [pewter] plats, dishis, spoons."

In the first half of the nineteenth century the demand for tin articles increased. The local whitesmiths (for that is what workers in tin were called, to distinguish them from workers in iron) attempted to meet it. To please their country clientele, they devised, besides the coffeepots and teapots, brightly colored stencilled trays and other quaintly decorated objects in the pale metal which have a distinctly peasant quality. Among these are sconces, cut into unusual shapes or left severely rectangular, decorated with pin-pricked ornament. Since tin was an easy metal to manipulate, the edges are frequently scalloped or fluted, adding an extra decorative note.

The whitesmith required a comparatively small amount of equipment—a special anvil called a "stock" on which he turned the edges of the tin before soldering them together, a small furnace with a charcoal fire in which he heated the soldering iron, the solder itself (a composition of tin and lead), some tools shaped for special purposes, and hammers and mallets. Before producing any object, he made careful patterns for the several pieces comprising its construction; these patterns, after being marked out on it, were cut out of the sheet of tin plate with a huge pair of shears and brought to the proposed form with various tools adapted to the purpose. If he planned to decorate the piece, the ornamentation had to be completed on the metal sections before they were soldered together. Punched or pinprick work was wrought with a tool blunted just enough so that a tap on it with a hammer would be unlikely to pierce the metal. The design was drawn on and worked from the surface of the tin that he planned to use as the inside—in order that each indentation made would eventually appear as repoussé. To guard against a possible perforation resulting from a too powerful rap of the hammer, the indentations were protected with a thin film of solder before the piece was assembled. If certain areas required more strength than the tin possessed, iron wire was used as a reinforcement. All edges and handles were given this extra bracing.

The lantern was one of the important articles made by the tinsmith. There was a continuing demand for lanterns, as they were subject to hard, daily wear. At seasons of the year when artificial light was necessary, all outdoor operations, such as milking and caring for the stock, depended for light on the feeble glimmer of a candle filtering through the perforations of a pierced-metal "lanthorn" of the type commonly called "Paul Revere." This lantern, in use throughout the colonies, was built on a pattern long familiar to the settlers in their homeland. It was constructed from a simple cylinder of perforated tin, with a conical top to which was attached a circular handle made of a band of the same metal. Since glass was too expensive to be used generally, it was necessary to make many openings in the tin in order that as much as possible of the one-candlepower illumination could flicker through the punctures. The local whitesmiths, as usual showing their preference for certain traditional motifs, managed to arrange the many necessary perforations in their favorite patterns of stars and hearts as well as in the usual circles and whorls. Though as a source of light it was unbelievably poor, the use of the perforated tin lantern persisted for a surprisingly long time, since there was nothing in it to get out of order. When glass became cheaper in the first few decades of the nineteenth century, the "lanthorn's" perforated tin walls were supplanted by a type in which glass panels were inserted, carefully protected by wire strips.

The need for a concentrated source of light was supplied by multiple-branched chandeliers executed in this same modest metal. Used in country churches and meeting places, tin chandeliers were a rural substitute for elegant, imported ones of brass or crystal. Their many arms were shaped in graceful curves, with the bases of the candleholders fluted or crimped in the fashion of the tin pie-plates of later days. How the light from twelve candles set in a single fixture must have dazzled the eyes of the simple folk accustomed to the light given by the unstable wick of a fat-lamp, or the decorative pattern of dots of light scattered by the tallow-dip set in the decorative but dim lantern!

All early settlers got along with a minimum of light, content if the candle lighted the tiny area in which they were working or fell on the pages of a book. The undependable light from the fireplace helped a bit, and by its flickering glow mechanical tasks such as spinning were carried on. But most country people solved the problem of illumination by going to bed "with the chickens" and getting up at dawn in order to use the first rays of light. This "daylight saving" method had the complete endorsement of Benjamin Franklin, for he, inventive as he was, had not figured out any better illumination than that of every-day candles. These, though manufactured at home out of a waste product, the farm's tallow, took much tedious work to make; they required constant attention when lit, as they both smoked and dripped, and unless they were snuffed with care they left a horrid odor linger-ing in the air. After the introduction of kerosene, tinsmiths made various lamps out of tinplate. By this time, they were no longer decorated, for the impulse to do so was no longer alive in the artisans.

Another article both decorative and surprisingly useful was the pie-cupboard, created by the joint work of tinsmith and carpenter, to fill the need for a ventilated closet which would protect the weekly mass production of pie and cake from predatory creatures, yet allow a flow of air to pass over them in order to prevent mold. Wooden pie-cupboards or "safes" vary in size and may have single or double doors—a simple framework of wood filled in with panels of tin. Such panels were handsomely ornamented in characteristic fash-ion with perforations of different sizes and shapes, for even in this detail the craftsmen managed to be both practical and decorative. The larger oval slits contrasted nicely with the ordinary circular punctures, and together they created a considerable variety of designs, the makers using the identical technique by which they punched the holes in the early lanthorns. It is quite probable that the larger perforations used on the cupboards allowed investigating insects an entry, but modern squeamishness about insects was not an indul-gence which the old-time farmer folk could allow themselves.

Another one of the local articles which was made in pleasing shapes and patterns was the colander in which cottage-cheese was drained. Tin colanders came in various forms with heart-shaped ones in preponderance. This is not surprising, for the heart is a simple contour which turns out of molds satisfactorily. The creamy "schmier-case" as cottage-cheese is called in the "Pennsylvania Dutch" regions is the mildest kind of cheese, formed by setting a pan of milk in a warm place until it becomes quite sour and the curds separate from the whey. After it had been thoroughly drained in the colander, the curds were com-pactly pressed until they assumed the shape of the container and could be turned out on a plate.

When the pierced tin colander became outmoded, or if it rusted and was not replaced, the country housewife no longer had forms in which to shape the cheese. She then pro-duced it in a picturesque manner reminiscent of the methods of European peasants. Pouring the sour milk into a cheesecloth bag, she hung it in the shade on the branch of a tree near the kitchen door. This dripping bag was a familiar sight in the countryside. When it had drained sufficiently, the contents were put into an earthen bowl, and, enriched with yellow cream, became a favorite dish at the "supper table" of the country people, often accompanied by the equally well liked apple butter, in the making of which they were renowned.

We now take the observance of Christmas, New Year's Day, and Easter for granted, but the popularization of these holidays in Pennsylvania can be credited to the settlers of Germanic origin. In the early days, the Quakers were outstandingly against any such festivities, but the Germans, though the beliefs of some of their sects approached that of the Quakers in simplicity, never prohibited the celebration of Christmas. The Pennsylvania German custom of recognizing the advent of the holiday with an orgy of baking gingerbread figures and cookie-making is a far older one than the hanging of stockings and the decoration of the tree, ceremonies of comparatively recent introduction. Never forgetting the honey cakes, the marzipan, the gingerbread figures of their homeland, they transplanted the tradition, a very old one which is general to Continental Europe, to this new land, where it still flourishes. In Europe the molds in which these cakes were formed were made of wood, carved in intaglio, often by master artisans of the craft. Some of them are exquisite bits of miniature sculpture in bas-relief. Known as *springerle* or *marzipan* molds, they were used to impose their patterns on a cake dough stiffened with enough flour to take an impression clearly, or on a paste made of ground almonds, sugar, and eggs. Certain much simplified molds were used here, and cakes formed with them were hung as decorations on the Christmas trees of past generations, to be supplanted eventually by all the shiny balls and glistening metal ornaments of the present day. While the tradition arrived here unchanged as to substance, it underwent alteration as to the material used to shape the cakes, for the majority of cake bakers here used tin cutters instead of the wooden molds; a change probably brought about by economic conditions in this new country. Very few skilled artisans could devote the time to such a minor job as carving in hard wood the elaborate forms used by the bakers in their homeland.

To meet the demand, however, the whitesmith devised cutters of tin as a substitute. Horse or deer or bird or man, these delightful articles of the rural tinsmith's craft were turned out by him in infinite variations, as even a cursory examination of their rusted and sometimes battered shapes evidences. To the modern designer they ought to be an interesting source of playful forms. Though tin is a ductile material and capable of being bent into complicated outlines, the whitesmith understood the need of keeping the basic form simple. If it became too complicated, alterations in the shape of the cookie after its trip to the bake oven or the kitchen stove would so distort its outline that it would no longer gladden the eye of the consumer. Half of the enjoyment of the connoisseur of Christmas cakes lay in their shapes; the other half in their quality. To assure these dual pleasures the tinsmith devised many quaint and evocative forms.

A gingerbread baker of emigrant German stock was one of the remarkable and out-standingly picturesque figures in the Revolutionary war. He was Christopher Ludwig (anglicized into Ludwick), son of a baker in the Rhineland to whose trade he was apprenticed. At seventeen he became a soldier in the German army, later was a baker on a ship in the English service. In that capacity, in 1753 he made a visit to Philadelphia, which appealed to him as a place where he might practise his trade as "gingerbread baker," for apparently those delightful, picturesque cakes were unknown to the children of Quaker Philadelphia. With his mind filled with the business opportunity a bakery shop offered, he returned to Europe, where he furnished himself with the ornamental carved molds on which the eye-appeal of the cakes he planned to bake was to be based.

In Letitia Court, the little street in which was located the first cottage built for William Penn (which Penn later deeded to his daughter Letitia in 1701), Ludwick set up as a baker. The cake lovers of that day patronized him so generously that in twenty years he was a well-to-do property owner, with title to nine houses and a farm, and with savings of £3500. No one took up the American cause more ardently than he, and on it he staked all of his property and his savings. When General Mifflin, in order to furnish arms for the war, proposed to raise £50,000 by private subscription and there were protests against such a method, Ludwick shamed them all by saying he was only a poor gingerbread baker but they could put him down for £200. Congress appointed him Baker-General in the Army of the United States, and the bread that he furnished the soldiers was good honest bread, as honest as himself. His originality, wit, bluntness, and accent made him welcome in every camp. George Washington so appreciated his worth that he gave him a certificate in his own writing which Ludwick treasured as a diploma, proudly showing it to all visitors when they entered his parlor.

The profession of gingerbread baker seems to have been a general one, for there was a succession of them who made their living in Lancaster and other good-sized towns. One, nicknamed "Toodler," who was listed as "Ginger Horse Decorator," was said to have died from eating too much of his damaged stock. This was, indeed, a trade which produced many "seconds," for owing to the fragile nature of the cakes, the breaking off of bits was unavoidable, and a gingerbread horse minus a tail or leg had no charm for the child purchaser.

Though every housewife had her own set of cutters, she practised a system of exchange with her neighbors to add an even greater variety of shapes to her own assortment. Birds were exchanged for horses, light ones for those of darker hue; a quantity of common stars and hearts may have been the exchange medium for a few of a rare and desired form shaped by a treasured cutter which remained jealously guarded by its owner.

To this day cakes and cookies are baked in enormous quantities by women who are steeped in the tradition. Both in city and country they function under its compulsion.

Unlike their predecessors, who had large kitchens, much storage space, and many hands to help in the various operations, they awkwardly carry on the practice in tiny, modern, apartment kitchens, often with the very cookie-cutters which have been passed down from generation to generation. Their recipes, though copied off from old handwritten cookbooks, set up in modern card-index files, and baked in electric ovens, are those handed on to them by their feminine forebears. Even the names of some of the cookies have come down without change to the present day.

One common in Pennsylvania German regions is called the "Apee," a pale-tinted rich cookie, whose curious name, passed on from mother to daughter, is accepted without any questioning of its etymology. Though one no longer hears of it in Philadelphia, there is a tradition which credits its origin to that city. "Philadelphia has long enjoyed the reputation of a peculiar cake called the 'apee.' Those who partake of them have no conception of the origin of their name. Ann Page, lately living under another name and business, first made them many years ago, under the common name of cakes. The aged [this was being written in 1840 or thereabouts] may remember her small frame house in Second Street, two doors north of Carter's alley. On her cakes, she impressed the letters *A.P.*, the letters of her name, and from this cause, ever since the initials have been disused on them, the cakes have continued to be called *apees*."*

For lovers of tradition among contemporary cookie-bakers who may wish to mull over the ingredients of this local delicacy, I am giving the recipe just as it was given me by an ancient country woman of Lehigh County. It cannot be followed exactly, for one of the ingredients, "A" sugar—a mass of soft, damp, delectable lumps adored by children—is no longer obtainable, and the other, cream of tartar, has been supplanted by baking-powder. In any modern recipe there would be a reduction in such a lavish use of butter *and* cream, a matter to which no Pennsylvania German housewife was obliged to give any thought.

But even though you commit these sacrileges, if you will but refrain from marking them with your own initials and will astutely cut them with the correct cutter, the ghost of Ann Page is not likely to haunt you. The cutter, circular in shape, its edge formed in small scallops, was reserved by tradition for the "apee." To the knowing, this modest outline identified the tidbit, even though overshadowed by the great selection of impressive if less rich cookies offered, accompanied by apples and cider, to all visitors at the Christmas season.

"APEES" (Emily H's)

¾ lb. Butter	3½ cups Flour
1 lb. "A" sugar	1 cup sour Cream
3 Eggs, beaten separately	½ tsp. Cream of Tartar

To roll out, you must flour baking-board and rolling-pin well and add more flour to cut out, with cake cutter with scallops.

* John F. Watson, *Annals of Philadelphia*.

Tulip and Urn motif. From coffeepot made by M. Eubele, Berks County.

Motif from Coffeepot. Heavy repoussé.

Above, left. Punched tin coffeepot, with elaborately worked spout. Victorian touches combined with traditional symbols.

Above, right. Coffeepot, made by J. Ketterer, Berks County. The initials S. B. and B. B. appear over crossed sprays of leaves.

When Pennsylvania German tinsmiths began to turn out coffeepots, they enriched the surface with their favored motifs, the branching tulips in the usual urns, the peacock, the barn symbols and birds, worked out in repoussé dots, called "punched work." Planned for coffee rather than tea, their shape differed from that of the eighteenth-century English tole-ware teapot. The form is reminiscent of earthenware coffeepots, the lower inward slope of which was devised to hold back the grounds.

Coffeepots of punched tin are often marked on the handle with the maker's stamp. J. Shade, D. Gilbert, J. Ketterer, M. Eubele, and E. Angstad have been noted. When executing orders, the client's name and date were often added, in the tiny protruding dots of this technique. Made from about the 1830's to the 1850's, they were usually about 11" in height, topped off with a brass finial.

All illustrations, courtesy, National Gallery of Art, Index of American Design.

158

Left. Punched tin coffeepot. Made for Mary Weisner by John Shade of Upper Swamp Creek, Berks County, Pa. *c.* 1835.

Shade adhered in the main to this design, which is duplicated on the other side. Sometimes he rearranged the elements.

Courtesy, National Gallery of Art, Index of American Design.

Swiss and Rhineland folk were familiar with pewter, chased in a style called *"flecheln";* in English the term "wriggled" describes this type of engraving. To execute a wriggled line, a loosely held tool was tapped with a hammer. Under the tappings it moved forward, marking its progress with a series of short zigzag strokes. This technique, used on seventeenth- and eighteenth-century European pewter, was occasionally employed by local artisans in the ornamentation of tinware. The coffeepot on the right is an example, its heraldic banner and bird worked out in lines of close, zigzag strokes.

Courtesy, National Gallery of Art, Index of American Design.

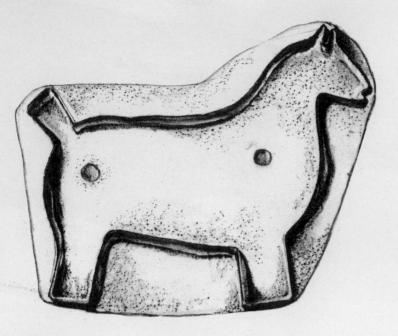

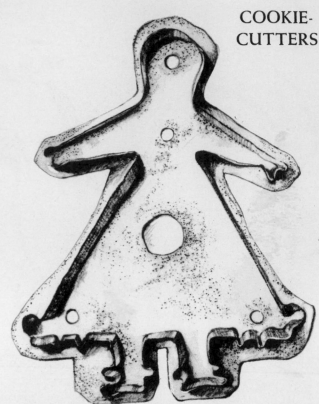

Early cookies were large affairs. The pantaletted child is 8¼" high; the sturdy horse, 6½" wide.

The designer of cookie-cutters understood their function perfectly. To really enjoy eating a cookie, it should have numerous little projections on which to nibble. Old-time children were skilled in this exploratory technique, which prolonged the gustatory delights of Christmas cookies.

All cutters, courtesy, Chester County Historical Society, West Chester, Pa.

At Christmas no Pennsylvania German housewife felt satisfied until she had made at least a bushel or more of cookies, cut out in decorative shapes. There were sugar cakes which were light in color, and molasses ones which were dark. Crude icing ornaments were added to enhance their ornamental shaping. Along with apples and cider, they were offered to each holiday visitor.

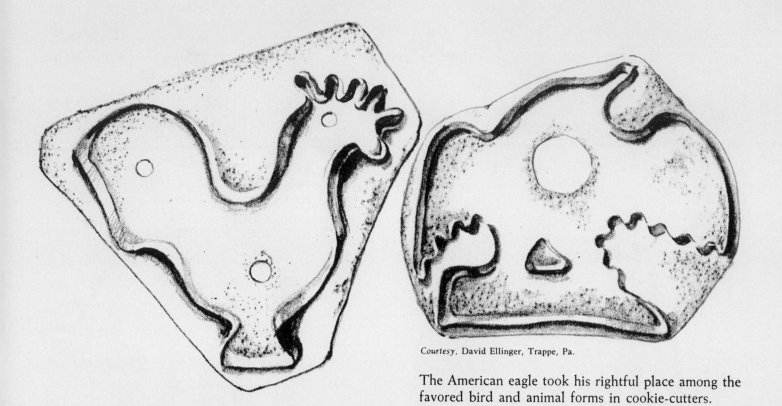

Courtesy, David Ellinger, Trappe, Pa.

The American eagle took his rightful place among the favored bird and animal forms in cookie-cutters.

COOKIE-CUTTERS

Before the days of the public-school system, "barring out the teacher" was a custom much in vogue. On that day the larger scholars took possession of the schoolhouse and prevented the schoolmaster from entering. When he redeemed his position by offering the demanded ransom—a general treat of cookies and ginger horses, ginger rabbits and some of the quaintly named candies of the day—he was allowed to enter his domain. Stubborn men resisted the blackmail as long as possible. Wise ones went away, leaving the barricade unstormed, the defenders at a loss.

The mounted nobleman or soldier, beautifully carved in wood, was a favorite design for cake molds in the eighteenth-century Palatinate. The tin cookie-cutters (to the left and on the following page), crudely shaped on more democratic lines, carry on the Old-World tradition.

Courtesy, Landis Valley Museum, Landis Valley, Pa.

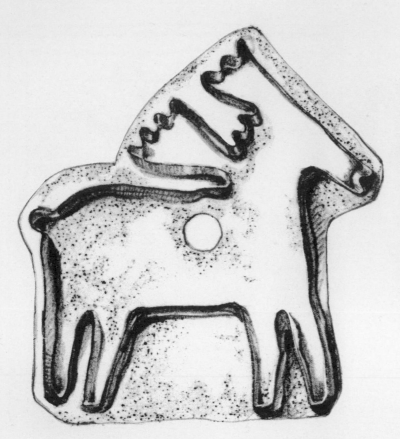

COOKIE-CUTTERS

Santa Claus is a comparatively modern symbol of Christmas among the Pennsylvania Germans. Up to the middle of the last century, a much rougher gentleman, called "the Belznickel", was the bringer of cookies, candies, and toys to the local young fry. Belznickel was played by the neighborhood wag, who went from house to house with stick in hand, dressed in a fearsome combination of old clothes, mask, and animal pelts. Children had been warned that he dealt out punishment as well as gifts; so they feared him as he laid about him with his stick, even though he distributed apples, cakes, nuts, and candy.

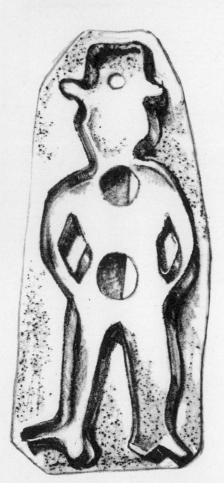

Above, courtesy, Chester County Historical Society, West Chester, Pa. *Right.* Philadelphia Museum of Art.

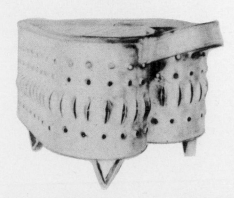

Courtesy, National Gallery of Art, Index of American Design.

Cottage Cheese Colander.

Before the days of refrigeration, sour milk was an ever-present commodity. But it was never wasted. Instead it was transformed into cottage cheese or "Schmiercase," a favorite article of food, accompanied by apple butter. Drained through perforated tin colanders, the resultant mild product was turned out in decorative shapes.

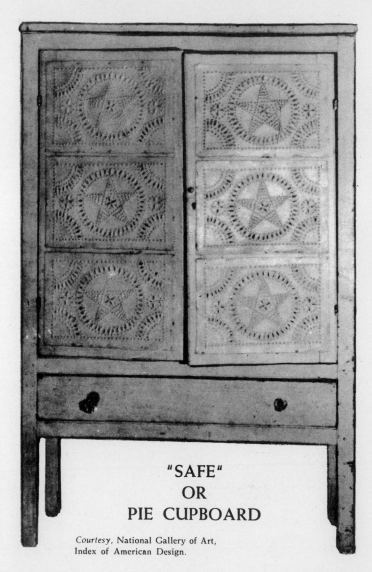

"SAFE" OR PIE CUPBOARD

Courtesy, National Gallery of Art, Index of American Design.

Pennsylvania Germans were renowned not only as bakers but as consumers of their own products. At every meal, a choice of three or four pies was offered. To house the products of the weekly baking orgy, they devised the "safe," an ingeniously ventilated cupboard of wood with doors filled with perforated panels of tin.

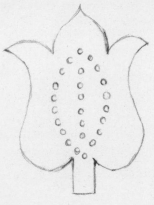

Right. An ingenious tin form, with a removable bottom (shown above), and a handled cover, which, when pressure was applied, molded the cottage cheese into the admired tulip shape.

Courtesy, David Ellinger, Trappe, Pa.

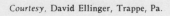

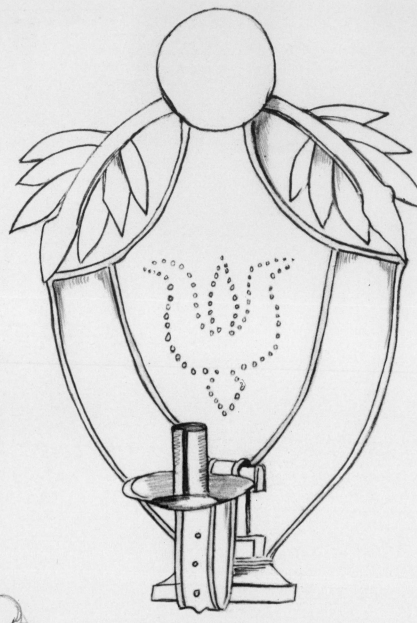

Courtesy, National Gallery of Art, Index of American Design.

Tin Sconce, from country church.

Combining classic laurel sprays of cut tin leaves, with tulip in punched work. Height 16".

In making lighting fixtures, local artisans experimented with the decorative possibilities of tin. It could be shaped over forms, cut with shears, fluted, crimped, or decorated with punched work in repoussé. As its highly polished surface served as a reflector, many types of candle sconces were evolved to utilize this characteristic.

Tin Sconce, from country church.

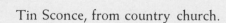

Courtesy, Pennsylvania Historical and Museum Commission, Harrisburg, Pa.

LIGHTING
FIXTURES

Almost all the possibilities of tin were exploited in this handsome lantern; which housed a simple, two-wicked fat-lamp.

Courtesy, Paul M. Auman, Millheim, Centre County, Pa.

The maker's name, bold tulip, and quaintly stylized trees. From a punched tin coffeepot.

Below. The technique of "wriggled" engraving on tin permitted more elaborate detailing than did that of "punched work". "Wriggled" tulips sprouting from a tree-like form. From a coffeepot.

Courtesy, Metropolitan Museum of Art.

Courtesy, Philadelphia Museum of Art.

THE SALVAGE ARTS—FRAGMENTS INTO QUILTS

"So we quilted and rolled, talked and laughed, got one quilt done and put in another. The work was not fine: we laid it out by chalking around a small plate. Aunt Sally's desire was rather to get her quilting finished on this great occasion, than for us to put in a quantity of needlework."
—Phebe Earle Gibbons—*Pennsylvania Dutch and Other Essays*

IN the early days, particularly in regions remote from the seaports, practically every piece of textile the settlers possessed resulted from their own infinite labor. Whether of flax or of wool, the fibres had first to be grown, then spun; after which, under the skilled hands of the weaver, the yarn went through the loom, to become a piece of linen or woolen cloth. Whether she was conscious of it or not, the user of such a piece of fabric never quite forgot the enormous amount of labor implicit in its production. Women treated every scrap of material with a respect almost impossible for us of recent generations to realize, surrounded as we are by unlimited amounts of every type of machine-made textile.

If, instead of being the work of her own hands, the piece of fabric, the bright chintz or sprigged calico from across the seas was one that had been purchased on one of the rare trips to town, it was valued even more highly because of the expenditure of money. Imported fabrics were costly, but the colonies were forced to depend on England for those textiles they could not themselves manufacture. On the small cargoes carried in tiny sailing vessels, which took several months to make the trip, freight and insurance charges were necessarily high. These boosted prices for the colonists; so that a piece of imported cotton became a precious possession—not only because of the outlay it represented, but because of its entrancing difference from the fabrics the woman colonist herself produced. Hers were pretty much alike, for no matter how fine a thread she spun, the resultant textiles always turned out much the same—plain, striped or chequered. To print the tiny, bright, sprigged designs so popular in the eighteenth century was a task far beyond the capabilities of home industry.

Always conscious of its cost, the housewife made use of even the tiniest fragment. An examination of any early piece of home needlework will show how general was this regard for fabric. During recent generations, the piecing and patching of fragments has been considered a sign of thriftiness in which there was more than a tinge of miserliness, but the colonial housewife, limited to her scanty supply of fabrics and quite honestly concerned about it, frankly used bits of material often no larger than an inch in diameter, to eke out a section of a garment or a quilt patch in order that it could be made entire and therefore useful.

With this innate respect for the value of material, women unconsciously developed into artists in salvage. Nothing was ever wasted, and out of bits of textiles, sometimes new, sometimes worn, which to less inventive minds would seem useless, they fashioned objects not only of use, but often of great charm and beauty.

Necessity demanded that the construction of bedding take primary place, and the fabrication of it was accepted by everyone as a household task, an inevitable part of every woman's life. Into its contriving went all spare moments and all the scraps of cloth saved from the making of garments. The instinct of thrift not only made use of bits of new material, but flourished equally well when faced by the challenge of fabrics no longer new. After the better sections had been set aside to be used in bedding schemes, portions of garments that showed so much wear that their life could no longer be prolonged even by the most ingenious mending were not discarded. Cut up in strips, they were eventually turned by skilled fingers or by the loom into useful and decorative floor coverings.

Waste was not only unthinkable, it was sinful. The Pennsylvania German housewife saved and sorted bits of material as easily as she breathed. Her whole life was an exercise in thriftiness. She had a definite plan for every scrap of fabric. When a linen garment was so worn and ragged that even the most cautiously appraising eye could see no further use for it as an article of clothing, she set it aside. It had a recognized value outside her own household economy. The world of paper manufacturing was dependent on this attribute of hers, as linen and cotton rags were the basic necessity of the early paper industry.

While the salvage of rags destined for the paper mill was the last in a woman's series of uses for waste bits of material, her first and chief plan for all pieces of fabric was the making of quilts for bed coverings. These quilts were thrown over the great tickings filled with goose feathers, which kept all the German settlers warm in the winter time. The custom of sleeping between feather "decks" (as they were called) was general only in regions where its advantages had been noted and adopted from the Germanic settlers. To finicky New Englanders and other Anglo-Saxon travellers through the Pennsylvania countryside, it seems to have been a novelty, for they frequently comment on it, usually disparagingly. Elkanah Watson of New England, used to blankets, perhaps was abroad too early in the autumn to relish so warm a bedcovering, when he stayed in an inn at Reamstown, Lancaster County, Pennsylvania, in October of 1777. He was moved to protest in his diary: "I was placed between two beds, without sheets or pillows. This, I was told, was the prevailing custom, but which, as far as my experience goes, tends little to promote sleep or comfort of a stranger."

Though today no one has a higher standard of neatness and cleanliness than the Pennsylvania Germans, in the early days the standards of the innkeepers in the State left much to be desired, if further accounts of the travellers through the rural districts are to be believed. The inns run by the Germans never lacked patronage, for they were known to furnish the best food and accommodations; nevertheless, year in, year out, their city-bred clients carried on a petty war with the proprietors over the subject of bed linen. A traveller either carried his own sheets and pillow cases, or, if he dared to question the cleanliness of those supplied by the landlord, he took his destined part in this war and invariably was worsted. In 1771 Elizabeth Drinker, a Quaker lady of Philadelphia, took a trip through the Pennsylvania German regions, accompanied by her city standards of cleanliness. The account in her voluminous diary records her defeat in this perennial battle between the Pennsylvania German innkeeper and the travelling gentry of British or European extraction.

"August 29. This evening our landlady, a dirty old Dutch woman, refused changing very dirty for clean sheets. Then, after much entreaty, she pretended to comply, but we found to our mortification she had taken the same sheets, sprinkled them and then ironed and hung them by the fire, and placed them again on the bed, so that we were all necessitated to use our cloaks, etc., and this night slept without sheets . . . August 30. H.S. and self each folded a dirty sheet nutmeg fashion and left them covered up in ye beds for the old woman to tug and scold at. May it be the means to mend her manners; her husband is a rich farmer."

Four decades later, we find the traveller and the innkeeper still in the same antagonism. In this case the traveller is a flighty New England girl, who, passing through the State in 1810, describes in her journal her accommodations in a Berks County inn: "Our bed to sleep on was straw & then a feather bed for covering—The pillows contain'd nearly a single handful of feathers, & were cover'd with the most curious & dirty patchwork, I ever saw—We had one bed quilt & one sheet." This mention of the patchwork quilt, no matter how lacking in cleanliness, indicates that needlework, wherever noted, was a matter of supreme interest to all classes of women in this country. And because this traveller calls it "most curious," its decorative interest must have differed vastly from the New England quilt patterns with which she was familiar.

After the urgent necessity for providing adequate bed coverings had passed, the making of quilts for display evolved into a really artistic outlet for women, whose ingenious minds and clever fingers created many striking designs. But "crazy quilts," the earliest type made, could not have been dignified by the term "designs," for they were only "constructions," the product of the compulsion upon every woman to make some use of everything. In the earliest days, when a housewife felt she had accumulated enough fabric in her piece-bag (an integral part of her household economy) to complete the top for a quilt, she seamed the bits together, mosaic fashion. The resultant "crazy quilt" while undeniably useful was completely lacking in æsthetic values; yet its fabrication brought a great sense of satisfaction to every thrifty woman who ever made one.

Though the Pennsylvania German woman manufactured innumerable "crazy quilts," the recollection of other colorful and beautiful bed spreads could not be downed, for these women had behind them a long tradition of handsome bed coverings. In every country peasants had always devised bed-clothing out of scraps of fabric, and the feminine Palatine settler here awaited only the opportunity and the money (or its equivalent) in order to carry on the custom of her mother and her grandmothers. If she could influence her husband into exchanging, at the country trading-post, a part of his surplus farm products, such as flax or flour, for a few yards of some bright imported chintz or calico, she was happy for she then had the means with which to create the brilliant bed coverings she craved. Never content with her stock, she was continually preoccupied with the planning of new and better quilts. The need to provide a dowry of such stuffs for each marriageable daughter and son and to pile up a store of quilts for the future use of the family remaining under the home roof-tree kept her fingers perennially busy. Countless quilt tops which, while complete in themselves, have never been carried through the final stages of work which would turn them into finished examples of bed covering, are telling witnesses to the devotion with which old-time women applied themselves to this type of folk art. Pathetic piles of faded patchwork blocks, not yet sewn together, and so old that their fabrics often show signs of disintegration, appear at country sales, as additional evidence of this passion for thrift and for needlework which drove each woman to make far more bedding than she had need of. Passed down from generation to generation in their uncompleted state, their survival to the present day is a touching demonstration of the hopefulness of all the women through whose hands they passed, every one of whom expected to put these blocks together to make the quilts for which they were originally destined.

But though much uncompleted work was tucked away in attic storage chests, other dower and blanket chests were equally well filled with finished specimens of the housewife's skill, all proclaiming the emotional satisfaction their maker derived from working out various designs, for nothing was more exciting to the woman of early days than a quilt pattern new to her. If uncreative, she docilely followed the patterns that were handed around from friend to friend, finding her means of personal expression in the colors she selected to work out the pattern. If inventive, she could run riotously through the spectrum in her choice of color, and her selection of form was limited only by her ingenuity. Her patience in setting the tiny stitches needed to sew down the elaborate shapes she devised was unlimited.

Before a woman began the needlework on a quilt, she chose the pattern, so that she might set to work with its demands for fabric clearly visualized. If she had only small scraps of material available, she selected a pattern which could be "cut according to her cloth," for a woman often commenced patterns before all the material had been assembled. If the motifs demanded portions in which larger and more wasteful sweeps were necessary, she waited philosophically for the time when she had either amassed such a collection of pieces or could afford to buy the needed materials. Most quilt patterns were devised for ease in handling, so that they could be worked in small sections or in repeating units. In spare half hours she took up a bit of the pretty work, which not only delighted her eye but gave her a moment of genuine relaxation.

The exchange of bits of fabric among friends and neighbors was an accepted social custom. Women and girls brought out their piece-bags and went over them amiably, passing from hand to hand small rolls of fabrics from their carefully gathered hoards, in order that each might add some new color variation to the quilt piecings they had under way.

The quilts created by the Pennsylvania German women were outstandingly individual. Favorite motifs used elsewhere in their folk arts are again employed with peasant-like directness in both conception and execution. This gives them a character peculiarly their own. Because of the faithful adherence of the Pennsylvania Germans to their own cultural standards and their flouting of those of their neighbors, these peasant characteristics, evident even in design, make the provenance of their quilts the easiest to identify.

We of the present day are much more appreciative of these qualities of naïveté and individuality than were preceding generations, and we prize the results as artistic expressions of the folk who created them. The gaudy hues which grated on the nerves of Victorian and Edwardian women, reared in surroundings of refined and muted color that automatically excluded anything as insistent as a Pennsylvania German quilt, women of today accept unperturbed. Color schemes, often of clashing violence, recall those of the original Russian Ballet which played so great a part in educating modern women to value the art work of the folk, hitherto unnoticed except to be derided. In the workaday lives of the women who assembled the quilts (they thought nothing of bringing together magenta and scarlet, green and lemon yellow), these brilliant aggregations certainly satisfied some deep-seated need.

The needlework of local quilts is amazing. Pennsylvania women attempted and surmounted difficulties inherent in the piecing together of intricately shaped patches, which equally industrious but less determined women in other localities rarely essayed because of the uncertainty of the results and the excessive tediousness of the work.

While the making of quilts was only a leisure occupation for the busy housewife, elderly women in the family, if relegated to sedentary tasks, spent much time in "piecing." Instruction was also their function. Small girls often learned the first steps in the use of the needle at the grandmother's knee. All Pennsylvania German children were trained from their earliest days to find their excitement in work, and little maidens would sit uncomplainingly for hours in low chairs, learning how to sew together the small square patches cut out for them by the grandmother. Painstakingly they labored over the back-stitch, which held the patches together more firmly than the simple running stitch. Under the supervising eyes of the elderly women, who were occupied in assembling something far more elaborate than the simple rectangles on which the infant pupils practised, each child submitted without protest to the necessary discipline of the needle and thimble.

Thus, very early in life a young girl acquired the adequate skill to begin to piece together some of the quilts for her dowry. No girl ever thought of marrying before she had prepared an ample supply of bedding for the home not yet realized. And part of the entertainment provided for the feminine guests at her wedding was the display of the quilts and coverlets she had made, the visible proof of her accomplishments as a needlewoman. But the bridegroom also brought to the new establishment a certain amount of similar gear as the contribution of his own family. Though perhaps somewhat lacking in fancy and in the intricate stitchery of twin hearts which the bride-to-be dreamily lavished on her best quilts, the dowry gift of quilts and coverlets furnished by the bridegroom's mother represented a tradition which was likewise never ignored. They too were always exhibited before the appraising eyes of the feminine wedding guests, equally expert needlewomen.

Quilts intended for everyday use were made in simple designs of squares, diamonds, or narrow strips, for these practical women wasted no unnecessary stitchery on objects destined to be impermanent. If, however, they were meant for keepsakes or were planned as an outlet for love of color and a release for nervous energy, then the work expended on them became a pure labor of love. Sometimes all the spare time of several years was occupied in piecing or in appliquéing one set of quilt blocks.

There are only two techniques used in quilt making, that of the pieced quilt and that of the appliquéd variety. Both techniques can be combined on the same article. In addition there is the stitchery called "quilting" which was a component part of all quilts. To make a pieced quilt, bits of fabric are cut out to predetermined shapes and seamed together to form more or less elaborate geometrical patterns. Skillfully contrasted color is used in order to define the patterns. An appliquéd quilt is made by cutting out patches of colored material to the shape desired and hemming them down on a plain background. Freed from the rigid limitations which geometry imposed on the pieced quilt, the technique of appliqué allowed for infinite variety in design; in fact, its possibilities were limited only by the degree of patience and skill resident in the designer and maker. Appliqué was thus a method capable of expressing the individuality of the maker, and we find it a favorite of the Pennsylvania Germans for their show pieces. So carefully were these cherished that many more appliquéd quilts than pieced quilts have come down to the present day. The latter were worn out long ago by daily use, while the former, stored away in a chest, were brought out only when a guest was to be impressed. Then, spread over the high feather-bed, the appliquéd quilt was a mute but often overwhelming testimonial to the housewife's ability.

"Quilting" is a term applied to the sewing of a running stitch along a line previously marked out, in order to unite the several layers of cloth of which every quilt was composed—the ornamental top, the filling, and the material chosen for the under side of the quilt. The designs used in quilting ranged from straight lines to elaborate scrollings and conventionalized floral and leaf forms. The knack of quilting was difficult to acquire, and many women skilled at piecing and appliquéing never became really proficient in the technique of running the needle nimbly along the marked lines, leaving the trail of tiny white stitches which, when ably done, made the reverse side of a quilt a thing of beauty and of almost equal interest with the top.

Before this skilled needlework could be performed, the patterns for quilting had to be marked out completely on the finished top. Then, with its filling and backing, it was put in the quilting frame, which was made from strips of wood and was constructed like the modern curtain-stretcher. These could be adjusted to the size of the quilt, either by pegs fitted into holes bored in the corners, or by clamps which held them together. The quilt was basted or pinned to a strip of heavy cloth already tacked to each bar. Every kitchen had, as an essential part of its furnishing, a set of low-backed wooden chairs which came in handy when the quilting was to be done, for their low backs were just the right height to hold the frames.

Quilting patterns were first marked around with the tracing wheel, a tool resembling a tiny, long-handled spur, and the resulting line of dots was then strengthened with chalk or a sharpened piece of lead. Straight lines were run along yardsticks or were put on with a string coated with colored chalk and held by two persons, one of whom snapped the tautly stretched cord in the hope that a line of color would be deposited on the quilt, an intention which not infrequently failed, for the technique, while speedy, produced an uncertain mark.

No woman was ever at a loss for quilting patterns. If she lacked ones of known elegance, she pressed into service all kinds of household utensils and used them ingeniously. Saucers and plates and handleless teacups gave her a series of circles in graded sizes, and cookie cutters provided more elaborate forms. The patterns for floral and scrolled devices found in the quilting designs on show pieces were often cut out of old letters, for paper was hard to come by. Sometimes quilting patterns were made of thin metal or of a stiffened, open-mesh, pliable material called mill-net.

Quilting was an occupation usually saved for the winter months, when the daily farm work made fewer demands on the housewife. All the preparations for providing the winter's food were now behind her—the garnering of foodstuffs whose preserving had taken up so much of her time. Out came the quilting frames to be set up in a warm corner of the house. If it was an everyday quilt, there were no needlework flourishes to eat up extra hours. In the spare time of one or two days, a woman finished a simple quilt and got the bulky frames out of the way, for they took up considerable space when in use.

But no woman quilted alone if she could help it. In the old days when there were few social outlets and women rarely had a chance to get together, the quilting-bee was a favorite excuse for party-giving. Taking the place that a game of bridge does today, it was a form of entertainment in which the hostess, in exchange for one or two lavish meals, received on the quilting frames the pooled needlework of a group of her friends. Women found a quilting-bee an unsurpassed form of entertainment. With their hands occupied, their hearts filled with a sense of virtue—for were they not helping out a friend?—their nostrils sniffing the scents of the food to come, they took the chance, sanctified by custom, to revel in all the neighborhood's gossip and scandal and to exchange recipes and patterns. A good speedy quilter, one whose fingers kept pace with her nimble tongue, made the most desirable guest, for every hostess hoped that the work in her frames would be completed before the guests departed.

So highly prized were fine specimens of quilting and quilts that exhibitions of these household arts were always a part of even the earliest annual county fairs, that delightful American institution which flourishes to the present day. Since the toil of women as well as men helped to develop this country, it was only just that they should share in the recognition which these exhibitions afforded. The naturally conservative Pennsylvania Germans were far from the first to organize agricultural societies, but when they finally adopted the idea, they too, like other well-established societies in other sections of the country, gave prizes for the work of women. At its first fair, in 1852, the Lehigh County Agricultural Society offered a premium of $1.00 for the best quilt, $.50 for the second best, the uniform standard of prizes for various types of women's entries. While this was low in comparison with some of the rewards for male achievements (the best plower won $4.00), the matter seems unimportant until the offer of $2.00 "for the best ham, prepared by the exhibitor" brings sharply before the reader of the old premium-list the relative importance of ham and of needlework in the minds of the men who planned this form of recognition. How must Miss Hewson of Coopersburg have felt, whose "elegant quilt, made of 14,000 pieces" received only an honorable mention, when some other woman received all of $2.00 for a ham, to which her personal contribution in labor was of practically no consequence, since it represented only her selection from a whole smoke-house full of them! By 1944 the scale of values has slightly altered, as the premium on certain types of quilts has advanced to $1.50, exactly what was offered for homecured ham!

In 1847 a country hotel was the scene of the first county fair held in Montgomery County. To this women were invited; they were given space to show both their handiwork and objects of folk art abstracted from the almost sacred "spare rooms." So fearful were the housewives at the first public appearance of their precious household goods, that they as well as their blushing and modest daughters stood watch every moment over their rare possessions, here consecrated to new uses.

Today, along with the earlier quilts, other curious, outmoded arts and crafts which are the handwork of women of a generation or two ago still make their annual appearance at the fairs, to compete for premiums established years ago when interest in them was at its height. There is work in shells, in seeds, and in leather; there are conventional laces of European origin—Honiton, Battenberg, Hardanger, and Cluny, their very names almost forgotten. These are no longer salvage arts, nor do they represent any personal, artistic impulse on the part of the women who made them—the daughters and granddaughters of the creators of the highly individual quilts. Rather are they the result of a movement started in the mid-nineteenth century by *Godey's Lady's Book*. By furnishing designs and patterns in arts and crafts, weighted with the authority it carried, the periodical brought a horrid uniformity to household decoration and unintentionally became the means of destroying the.creative impulse in most women. With one accord, women felt ashamed to be found working on a purely homemade article; they hastened to spend money to learn those fashionable arts and crafts for which manufacturers and even publishers so willingly provided not only the materials but even the stamped patterns.

After the Civil War a general decline in taste was evident in all branches of the decorative arts. The machine, the world's newest toy, with its ability to multiply forms, was played to the utmost; the cheapness of its product destroyed the craftsman's pride in the work of his hands. This wave of bad taste filled the house with machine-made gimcracks and moved the spinning wheel into the parlor along with the gilded coal shovel, the equally gilded and beribboned rolling-pins, and the hand-painted banners of plush and of velvet, but eventually it toppled over by the weight of its own hideousness. Victorian curlicues were supplanted by the functional severity of the Mission period, and later by the more graceful era of Colonial furniture. The use of this latter type of furnishing (both as antiques and as reproductions) fostered the needlework appropriate to it, so that the interest in the very old craft of quilt-making was considerably revived. Many modern women can reproduce the old patterns, or if they find themselves incapable of doing the kind of work their grandmothers did, modern industry will do it for them. Patches cut by machine with far more accuracy than the hand could possibly manage are furnished to them, together with patterns for their assembly, and if a woman can follow the printed word and hold a needle she can achieve a presentable imitation of the beautiful handwork of her grandmother.

Cradle Quilt, 1832.
Berks County, Pa.

Pennsylvania German women, not controlled in their quilt making by standards of taste current outside their communities, contrived pleasing though unorthodox arrangements of their familiar motifs, the tulip and the geometrical form. While not at all conventional in its spotting, the composition of this quilt is very satisfying.

Courtesy, Pennsylvania Historical and Museum Commission, Harrisburg, Pa.

Appliqué Quilt. *c.* 1850, York, Pa.

Artistic self-expression is evidenced in this striking quilt, appliquéd in red, yellow, green, and blue calicoes, enriched with embroidered stitchings. Blocks are put together with bands of color, a regional preference.

Courtesy, National Gallery of Art, Index of American Design.

APPLIQUÉ DESIGNS

Six blocks from a quilt of 42 different patches, all the work of the same needlewoman. Her bold, original designs have an authentic folk touch. Fruit and flowers are stylizations, difficult to name, but in addition to those pictured, it is possible to identify a man with a dog on a leash, pheasants, ducks, and various trees on other blocks not pictured here.

Pillow Sham.

Additional accessory for dressing up a bed.

Courtesy Landis Valley Museum, Landis Valley, Pa.

Courtesy. Landis Valley Museum, Landis Valley, Pa.

APPLIQUÉ QUILT

To amuse themselves, children of past generations folded squares of paper into eighths, cut pieces at random from the folded edges, and were enchanted, when the papers were unfolded, by the designs disclosed, seemingly as if by magic. Using the same method, their practical mothers and grandmothers evolved innumerable patterns for appliqué quilts. The simple "oak-leaf" pattern, of red on white, a great favorite in the 1820's and the 1830's, was easily made by this method.

But sometimes a more ambitious woman who possessed infinite patience and deftness attempted a piece of appliqué as difficult to handle as the one shown here. Family tradition has it that, on request, a visitor tore out the design from a piece of soft wrapping paper, using only his fingers for tools. The oddly repetitive, curving lines of the large motifs tend to support the story. Strikingly colored, in henna-brown and bright yellow.

Crib Quilt. Tree of Life, *c.* 1875.

That always ornamental motif, the Tree of Life, supposed to be rooted in Paradise, has been an inspiration to many peoples. It was the frequent choice of ancient potters, of oriental rug makers, and in recent times it flourished just as luxuriously on the very best quilts of Colonial needlewomen.

The details of this Pennsylvania German presentation of a motif of such ancient lineage are worth close study, for they are worked out with the means at hand. Birds perch naturally on the branches, and there many kinds of flowers blossom, their botanical relationships cheerfully ignored. Actual ivy and oak leaves, their forms easily identified, serve as the pattern for the ones cut of cotton, not only for the shape but for the correctly observed veinings, executed in tiny quilting stitches. Small circles, later to be lined up as graceful sprays of berries, were marked around a thimble.

APPLIQUÉ "SHOW" TOWEL

Although most "show" towels were traditionally embroidered in cross-stitch, in later days other types of needlework appeared. The towel on the left represents one of these departures in technique. Its bold Trees of Life are worked out in appliqués of plain and figured calicoes. It was probably made by a local maiden to match a quilt; the set would be destined for her "Haus-Steier" (outfit), without which no one was expected to marry. From the author's notebook.

Facing page. Garden of Eden Quilt. The idea for this novel and lovely quilt, narrates its maker, an elderly Pennsylvania German woman, came to her in a dream. With scissors and needle she worked it out, this dream of Adam and Eve in their flowery Paradise. On the quilt, a cluster of three snakes dives through the boughs of a neatly branched apple tree. One of these snakes, bearing an apple, tempts a pale Eve, who is flanked by a fox whose interest is centred on a fleeing hen. Adam sits on the sidelines, quietly watching the tempter.

Opposite this group are another Adam and Eve, followed by another fox, with still another snake leering from behind a flowering spray. Butterflies, hovering over long-stalked tulips, add a note of innocent gayety.

In the upper half of the quilt, a fully clothed Adam leaning on a spade fills in a space to the left of a well designed tree-like motif, and, rake in hand, an equally well covered Eve takes her place to the right. This group is surrounded by a frame of flamboyant flowers and leaves. From Somerset County, Pa.

GARDEN OF EDEN QUILT.

Nineteenth Century.

THE SALVAGE ARTS—RAGS & REMNANTS INTO RUGS

"No trade or profession in Pennsylvania is bound by guilds; every one may carry on whatever business he will or can. . . . It is a surprising fact that young people who were born in this new land, are very clever, docile and skillful; for many a one looks at a work of skill or art only a few times, and imitates it immediately, while in Germany many a one has to learn for years to do the same thing perfectly. But here many a one is able to produce the most artful things in a short time."
—Mittelberger's *Journey to Pennsylvania in the year* 1750

A FIRST trip through the rural districts in the unchanged farming sections of the State might lead a stranger to believe that all the householders and their families were away from home. The shades at the parlor windows are closely drawn, the windows tightly shut. But to the initiate this blank appearance is only conclusive evidence of the local respect given to the "best things," among which the store carpets on the parlor floor take high rank.

For a long time after the early settlers had acquired a few comforts in life, floors remained bare or were covered with a homemade product. When a good carpet was finally purchased, it was treated with honor. The darkened windows of rooms opened only for the most solemn family gatherings kept any ray of light from striking the parlor "Brussels" carpet. Thus all the original brilliance of its bouquets of monotonously repeated roses was preserved unaltered. This veneration given the machine-manufactured article in early days was general. The good housekeeper who darkened her parlors was neither dead nor ill. As a Pennsylvania German woman emancipated from such traditional *mores* succinctly put it: "Those women just suffer from a bad case of 'parlor carpet'."

Elsewhere in the house, homemade floor coverings covered the bare boards—so frequently scrubbed that the grain of the wood stood out in relief—and took the hard wear of daily use. But even homemade floor coverings were not produced until the housewife began to accumulate such a superfluity of materials that she could afford to employ it for such purposes. When a textile became so ragged that it had passed even the hand-me-down or cut-me-down stage, then and then only was it considered proper to cut it up for carpets. Papa's discarded pants, grandma's ancient woolen petticoat, the battered everyday school clothes of the children, all were grist to this thrift-mill run by busy hands which turned useless garments into the material out of which floor coverings were made. By such salvaging, a long life of further usefulness was given to these apparently exhausted textiles.

Floor coverings made from worn materials fall into three general classifications: rag carpets woven on looms by professional weavers from material prepared in the home, braided rugs, the making of which was entirely a homecraft, and hooked rugs. The Pennsylvania German women never turned to the making of hooked rugs with the eagerness and concentration of the women of New England, whose rugs, designed with elegance and refinement, made them fitting companions for the mahogany furniture of the Colonial period. Perhaps the shorter winters in Pennsylvania, which gave women less time for indoor tasks, the far greater preoccupation with the preparation of food, both for sale and for home use, the many outdoor tasks in which they engaged on their large farms, all these may have been factors responsible for the small amount of time they devoted to the making of hooked rugs. Their preferred floor covering was rag carpet, the only thing available to most colonists, for in the early days any kind of marketable carpet was extremely rare, even among well-to-do city dwellers. To country folk it was absolutely unknown; even if they had been able to possess it, its care would have been merely an added burden under the rough conditions of pioneer life.

Preparing and sewing carpet rags was an occupation which took up many a winter evening. Discarded garments were brought out, cut or torn into strips about half an inch wide, and sewn together, to be rolled later into balls. Children submissively helped to roll these rags into balls of uniform sizes, but privately considered it rather a chore.

After a woman had accumulated enough balls of rags to make the carpet she had planned—for she knew in advance how many pounds were needed to produce the desired yardage—she discussed its production with the neighborhood carpet-weaver, an artisan whose trade was a common one at that time. The color and width of the longitudinal borders came under immediate discussion. As these rainbow-hued bands were the only area in which individuality of choice could be expressed, the selection of colors for these warp yarns was a serious matter. While she wanted them to be attractive, she was equally concerned lest they duplicate her neighbor's. Such rainbow stripes were always woven of wool, and, for the main body of the carpet, the best artisans used a linen instead of a cotton warp, in order to insure for it as long a life as possible. The old-time carpet-weaver, like many other artisans, was often a man of two trades. Weaving was the one at which he worked in the cold weather, and his shop, a small wooden outbuilding on his grounds, was often an informal gathering place for his feminine clients, meeting there to discuss the colors and patterns for their future orders.

When old garments were being cut up, material was also selected to be set aside for braided rugs, which were great favorites. In comparison, much more material went into their construction than into a rag carpet, but as they could be turned out entirely at home, the making of them furnished another spare-time occupation for thrifty women. It was not easy to sew braided strips of fabric into oval or circular shapes guaranteed to lie flat. Until the knack was acquired, beginners were frequently discouraged when they found that all their efforts had produced an object whose form was more akin to a bowl than to a rug. But after they had acquired the skill to produce a rug, women of a creative bent, not content to go on turning out simple ovals and circles, devised variations of the basic idea. On a loosely woven textile base, they arranged braided rondels in patterns. These were combined with hooked-in sections, creating a new type of hand-made rug. From the very nature of the materials of which they were composed, braided rugs were usually artistic and harmonious in tone.

Salvaging of material went even further than the cutting of rags for rag carpets and braided rugs. Scraps too short to be useful in either of the above types were the material out of which hooked rugs were made. The technique of rug hooking made slight demands on material; it was planned to use long or short pieces equally well. Among the various salvage floor coverings, hooked rugs presented the outstanding opportunity to use color and personal ingenuity. With them in mind, thrifty women dyed their rags for rugs at the same time that more important dyeing projects were under way. And real artists in thrift saved the brilliant dyes left over from dyeing eggs at Easter time for the same purpose.

The life of the contemporary hooked rug is a short one, for its endurance depends upon the strength of the base through which the strands are pulled. Burlap, made of jute, generally used today as a foundation, is not a long-wearing material. Antique hooked rugs, which have survived to the present day, were hooked into a base of linen or hempen sacking, a far stronger fabric. This was stretched on a wooden frame and the pattern to be worked was marked out on the sacking with ink or charcoal. Pennsylvania German women, long isolated from outside decorative influences, used their familiar motifs, selecting those which could be worked out easily. Crude in coloring and often naïve in conception, their hooked rugs stand, as do all their other arts, in striking contrast to those in other parts of the country, which came in contact with French and English influences and produced rugs inevitably affected by them. The hooked rug of Pennsylvania is apt to be small in size, and of considerable informality in execution. When not working with traditional motifs, the designer frequently chose motifs to be found on the farm—dogs, cats, horses and houses. These bold and primitive conceptions often are very appealing.

But these individual interpretations of motifs on hooked rugs have gone the way of all the other folk arts once carried on in the State. Some years ago the demand for hooked rugs to accompany furnishings of the Colonial period became so great that commercial interests undertook to supply it. Mass production tends to debase all design, for it rules out the individuality which is a result of genuine creativeness or personal whimsy. Formerly, women lacking any inventiveness could usually rely on a talented neighbor whose ability as a designer enabled her to "draw off" her own patterns for her less gifted friends. Today, because of the ease with which she as well as her friends can purchase a commercially designed, stamped pattern on burlap, not even the gifted woman produces her own quaint designs or her own adaptations of familiar motifs. And what is sad to contemplate: she is quite content to work out these blatant commercial stampings, replicas of which can be found wherever the insidious manufactured designs have penetrated. No longer is it necessary for her even to salvage the material with which to work, for mills are glad to sell her their waste clippings. The use of such material further reduces her work to an inescapable level of mediocrity. But since present-day fabrics no longer have the interminable wearing qualities of those of early days, the compelling need to make use of every scrap has passed, and the day of strong, long-lasting rag carpets and soft-toned rugs is about over, taking with it still another traditional craft.

And so it was gratifying to come across, as I recently did, the evidence of the survival of the frugal traits which were once the very life-blood of the rug-making crafts. The background for them was a very old, tiny house set in rolling country, formerly good farming land but now reverted to wooded hills, its original state when the house was first built. Only a short distance from a main artery of travel, the absence of a good road leading to its wooded seclusion had set the locality back in time several generations.

Though commerce had entered the dwelling, for the head of the house was a country antique dealer, the family life was carried on in a tradition but slightly altered since the days when the tiny house was first built. No modern convenience had been allowed to enter it. The old smoke-house was still its close companion, its interior blackened, its fireplace intact. Almost touching the front porch was the great iron kettle, swung from a bar set between two poles, still used as in the earliest days to heat water for washing or for large-scale cooking operations. On the day of my visit it had been used for soap making, and sixty-five creamy bars of soap were laid out to dry on the porch floor. The Government—for it was then war-time—might plaster the country with appeals for waste fats, and city housewives who had no further use for them would dutifully respond with their savings; these old-fashioned folk turned a deaf ear and converted their fats into laundry soap, as they had always done.

Behind the line of irregularly cut bars of drying soap on the immaculately scrubbed porch, three elderly people, neatly dressed, sat primly in their chairs amid a jumble of old garments. One was cutting them into rags for rag carpet; the second was sewing these cut rags into a continuous strip, which she passed to the third, a very ancient woman, almost a centenarian. The latter, with very few faculties left to her, was still able to perform the few motions necessary to roll the rags into compact balls, a task learned in her earliest youth and one which she was carrying on mechanically, knowing instinctively that work was good and waste an evil thing. The rags the three old people so neatly prepared probably were never woven into carpet, but the compulsion to salvage them was a pathetic survival of the very frugality which had enabled them and their forebears to survive in the backwater section in which they persisted in living.

186

Pennsylvania German women made comparatively few hooked rugs, but those they fabricated were quaint and whimsical, both in design and execution.

Above. Horses, birds, trees, stars, and crescent moons are mingled in a manner surprisingly modern.

Below. Susan Clayman signed her rug, in local fashion, to express her pride in this work of her hands, obviously destined for her "Haus-Steier" or "outfit," for it bears twin hearts and two sets of initials, hers *to be*, and his. It is a sampler of traditional motifs: the urn with flowers, the tulips, the eight-pointed star of the Medes, and the swastika, or good-luck symbol, as it was then regarded.

Hooked Rug. Eight-segmented rosette dominates the field.

Courtesy, National Gallery of Art, Index of American Design.

Embroidered Rug of homespun wools, in brown, gray, russet, purple, and pink. 35″ x 43″. Bold and untraditional stitchery employed to depict decorative cocks and strong floral forms.

From the author's notebook.

Hooked Rug. A virile example of folk art and folk color. Red birds with orange wings on ochre field are bordered with bands of vermilion, purple, orange, yellow-green and magenta. Stars of pure cobalt.

Modern Hooked Rug, made by a Mennonite woman, picturing historic buildings and the famous Conestoga wagon.

Many pairs of turtle doves, and twin hearts shyly introduced among the profusion of details, identify this rug as part of a bride's "outfit." The motifs used are identical with those worked out painstakingly on childish samplers; an unusual example of needlework, turning to account ability and motifs acquired early in life. Probably made by a Mennonite girl, for in the border she introduced a device favored by Mennonite needlewomen for "show" towels and samplers: a curious symbol of a crowned heart, surrounded by lilies. See page 56. Length 58½". Width 32¼".

THE SALVAGE ARTS—RAGS INTO PAPER

"A Paper-Mill near German-Town doth stand.
So that the Flax, which first springs from the Land,
First Flax, then Yarn, and then they must begin
To weave the same, which they took pains to spin.
Also, when on our backs it is well worn,
Some of the same remains Ragged and Torn;
Then of the Rags our Paper it is made,
Which in process of time dost waste and fade;
So, what comes from the Earth, appeareth plain,
The same in Time, returns to Earth again."
—Richard Frame—1692

WHEN, in going through her pile of mending, the forehanded and thorough-going Pennsylvania German housewife came across a shirt or shift of her own spinning now too badly worn for even her skilled needle to repair, she regretfully laid it aside to await the visit of the rag peddler. In her preoccupation with her daily affairs, she probably saw no connection between the rag collector who took her wornout clothing and the colorful and beautifully ornamented paper documents she noted on her walls, which recorded for her the really important events in her life—her marriage and her children's birth and baptismal dates. But without her energy and her unending watchfulness, the very paper of these cherished family documents (one of the outstanding artistic achievements of the Pennsylvania Germans) would not have been possible, for the paper industry depended entirely on the linen rags salvaged by her and by all other women of her ilk.

The slogan "Save Rags" was as popular in the eighteenth century as its successor, "Save Paper," was in the war years, and for the same reason: the lack of raw material. With one noteworthy exception, the profession of rag collector was a humble, an unsung calling. That exception was Benjamin Franklin. Franklin's lively, practical interest in rag-collecting was based on his concern with paper, for in addition to his printing. shop, he ran a stationery business, importing considerable stock from Europe. Unless he was assured of a steady supply from one source or another, he could not stay in business.

The first printing press in the entire colonies was established in Pennsylvania only four years after the founding of the colony, and the first mill to produce paper was set up four years later. Virginia, it is to be noted, waited over a century to have its first paper mill, and fifty years after the founding of that colony one of its governors remarked that he hoped the press would not be set up for another hundred years as "it encouraged sedition and libels on the church and the King."

191

The establishment of paper mills in the colonies was one of Franklin's many interests. When, eventually, William Parks wished to build a mill in Williamsburg, Virginia, the first one to be started south of Philadelphia, Franklin sent the proprietor of a mill near Philadelphia, a German named Conrad Scheetz, along with two carpenters to erect it. After Parks had his mill, the essential raw material, old rags, proved to be lacking in Williamsburg, for its elegant inhabitants found many occupations more amusing and diverting than the sorting out of wornout clothing and linen for the paper industry. Franklin undertook to supply the need. With his usual common sense, he advertised in his own paper that he would pay one cent a pound for rags delivered at his printing office. Since it was made financially worth-while for housewives to part with material for which they otherwise might have found further use in their household economy, Franklin was instrumental in collecting in a few years over 300,000 pounds of rags, which he sold to various members of the infant industry.

The first paper mill in the colonies has already been mentioned. It was established by a German Mennonite colonist, William Rittenhouse, in Germantown in 1690. Coming as he did from a line of paper-makers it was quite natural that in the new country he should engage in a trade with which he was familiar. While his neighbors were busy in establishing their new settlement, he formed a company and set up the mill, which furnished paper for the use of the local printery. As the demands of the printing business could not rely on the uncertain arrival of shipments from overseas, many other small mills sprang up near Philadelphia. These mills, manned by German workmen who were excellent paper-makers, supplied the paper needs of the colonies. So important was the business considered to be that during the Revolution, when the Government began conscripting men for the army, the paper-makers petitioned the authorities not to take their workmen away or the mills would close of necessity, cutting off the supply of printing paper for the Government itself. The paper business was adjudged essential, and it carried on.

From the contemporary world, in which the supply of paper normally seems superabundant, it is hard to take oneself back to a time when paper was not only scarce but expensive. There was only one way to make it, and that was by hand, from linen or cotton rags. These were purchased at large from the general public by country merchants, peddlers, and curiously enough, retail booksellers.

To transform a pair of linen pants or a shift into a piece of fair paper was a slow process, a matter of several months. It began by disintegrating the rags. Fermentation was depended on for help in this stage and took place after the rags had been piled in mounds and kept moist. In several months disintegration was complete. The rags were then macerated between two millstones and immersed in troughs of water. After being cleaned, they were triturated into pulp by a series of large wooden hammers called stampers. These, operating in a trough through which clear water constantly flowed, rubbed and further frayed the material without too greatly lacerating the fibres. A homogeneous mass resulted from these operations; when added to water it was called pulp, the base of paper-making.

Handmade paper is made in a mold, which consists of a wooden frame the size of the proposed sheet, covered with a screen of copper wires set about 1/16 inch apart. This is close enough to prevent the fibres of the pulp from sifting through and yet open enough to allow the water to drain away quickly. These wires are held together by lines at right angles spaced about an inch or so apart. Fastened to the upper side of the screen is a device of wire twisted into a design. This makes an impression in the paper called a watermark, thus identifying the mill and its proprietor.

To make a sheet of paper, the operator holds a removable frame called a deckle (*deckel* means "cover" in German) over the top side of the mold, thus forming a shallow tray. This he dips into a vat of frequently stirred pulp, brings it out in a level position, and shakes it so that the fibrous particles are evenly deposited to form a sheet as the water drains through. Then he hands it to another workman who carefully removes the deckle and lays a woolen "felt" over the damp fibres, which adhere to the felt, so that the sheet can be handled by means of the felt backing. When six quires or 144 sheets are complete the stack is pressed and then hung up on lines to dry, later to be sized and surfaced.

The watermarks used by the first paper-makers in the State followed a tradition of symbolic design. As almost all the paper mills were owned and operated by German colonists and immigrants, it is natural to expect to see familiar motifs used in their watermarks. A search for them is gratifying, for it reveals not only the expected tulip but also the other characteristic devices for which they evinced a preference. Some are curious and imaginative; later on, when the New World began to erase some of the Old-World memories, the watermarks underwent a change. They were replaced by patriotic symbols, by the maker's name, or by his simple initials—another loss to local decorative arts.

If it were not for the strength and excellent quality of the paper made in these early mills, the examples of one of the leading folk arts of the Pennsylvania Germans, the beautifully illuminated hand-lettered texts called "fractur writing" would never have lasted to the present day. The homemade ink in which they were written was so corrosive that it often ate neat holes through the manuscript, but where it was not touched by this powerful combination of oak galls, copperas, gum arabic and vinegar the paper holds together as well as ever. As "fractur writings" were highly valued as family records, sentiment as well as the sturdiness of the paper contributed to their preservation.

Fractur manuscripts made here were the local flowering of a European tradition transplanted without substantial change to this new country. They were used by the ultra-conservative until the universal spread of the printing press wiped out all need for the records illuminated by hand and the last practioner of the art of the mediæval scribes no longer found it worth while to practise his ancient craft. In Germany the law demanded that a record of vital statistics be preserved; it followed that trained scriveners were always available to provide the necessary documents. Because of this need, in any plan for the immigration of colonists to Penn's lands, a schoolmaster or minister was always included in the group. These "educated" men, in addition to their ability to read and write, were expected to be proficient in the art of "fractur writing" in order that they might supply the new settlers with the documents custom demanded. In strange new surroundings they kept up the old traditions, and being set free from the limiting artistic conventions of their homeland, in the Pennsylvania German counties they developed fractur writing into something lively, original, and even more decorative.

"Fractur-schriften," as it is called in German, is a decorative calligraphy named after a sixteenth-century German type face called "fraktur," which was itself an imitation of the work of the manuscript writers of the day. It was considerably less rigid in outline than its predecessor, the early German Gothic or black-letter. Another source of inspiration was provided by a type face called "Schwabacher" which featured an even rounder, more cursive letter. With these type faces as a springboard, the Pennsylvania German scribes evolved a personal style of calligraphy which varied from the extremely professional to the extremely naïve, the result of a lack of thorough training.

The persistent practice of the European mediæval art of manuscript illumination for considerably over a century in a new and different environment would indeed be strange if we did not recall that, when only one copy of a document is needed, the art of "engrossing," as it is called today, still has its place. With all its facileness the printing press has not quite wiped out the last trace of the mediæval calligrapher, still relied on when needed to produce an impressive piece of lettering.

It has been pointed out that in the early days in Pennsylvania, the scribe's craft was joined to that of the country schoolmaster or clergyman. This representative of learning was expected to be a very versatile man, and was called on to give advice in many fields. As scribe, he prepared legal papers and wrote letters for the analphabetic; as carpenter he kept the school building in repair. If the settlement lacked a minister or the minister was absent, the schoolmaster took his place. When necessary, he acted as janitor, church clerk, choir leader, and organist. Despite the variety of his occupations his income was pitifully small. To add to it, he and his sons worked for his neighbors on their farms. From the labor of his daughters, whom he hired out to spin, he wrung a few extra pence. As there was always a steady demand among his neighbors for handwritten documents certifying important family events, such as births, baptisms, and weddings, the schoolmaster or clergyman further added to his income by specializing in the production of these rustic papers.

School teaching in the eighteenth century was a desultory affair. Children of the rural districts were taught to read in order that the precepts of the Bible and hymn book could be imparted and take root. Writing and ciphering completed this elementary education, which was considered quite adequate for farm children. Since some teachers were hired by the members of a community and others by Lutheran or Reformed congregations, the administering of the curriculum was free of any taint of standardization. Schoolmasters kept school if guaranteed enough pupils and opened and closed the term at a time convenient to all concerned. School might open in late September and again it might be postponed until mid-November. The overhead charged in 1789 for tuition by a man who was a teacher of long standing was "7 shillings a quarter" to which charge he added the stern injunction: "and the firewood you must bring to the school house."

To teach writing and at the same time to demonstrate his skill, the country schoolmaster prepared a beautifully handwritten manuscript called the *"Vorschrift"* which was the individualistic forerunner of the familiar, more formal copybook of the nineteenth century. From it children learned how to form the numerals and the capitals and small letters both in German script and in fractur writing. When they had learned to read, the pious maxim which headed the paper and on which the schoolmaster lavished his greatest flourishes and most elegantly ornamental capitals carried to them its specific injunction to lead a godly life. A *Vorschrift* was often presented to a pupil as a reward of merit and as a token of the instructor's regard. As evidence of this personal intention, the maker frequently signed his name, a naïve testimony to his own admiration of the flourishes he was able to produce with his fluent craftsmanship.

A quaint and charming custom of the more kind-hearted among the schoolmasters was to present a drawing of a bird or a flower as a prize for diligence and good conduct. These little gifts were carefully saved from generation to generation. Today they bear witness to the artistic skill of their makers. While the form of the *Vorschrift* was governed by usage and varied but slightly, the greatest variety of decoration and artistic conception in fractur is found in the birth and baptismal certificates, called *"Taufscheine,"* which the schoolmasters also executed in order to earn a little extra money. The early *Taufscheine* were entirely hand-drawn and hand-colored, but were somewhat supplanted towards the end of the eighteenth century by the pushing product of the printing press. This at first supplied only the text, leaving the surrounding decoration to the inventiveness of the fractur writer, who added it and filled in the information in the blank spaces left in the text. Later on, the entire certificate, decoration as well as lettering, was printed from woodblocks and type, leaving the coloring to the scribe who provided it when he supplied the vital statistics. Eventually, except for the filling in of names and dates, the printing presses took over the entire job, resorting to woodblocks to furnish the colors once painted in by hand.

The decorations on *Taufscheine* and other related manuscripts cover a wide range of subject matter. Floral motifs, which predominate, are almost invariably pure conventionalizations, with the exception of the tulip, whose stylized form is still close enough to the botanical one to be so identified. The fractur writer picked up his inspirations from many sources. Lions, crowns, and unicorns are obviously taken from the symbols used in heraldry. Quite innocently, in employing heraldic devices on their simple rustic documents they transplanted the trappings of a class from whose domination they had freed themselves when they emigrated. There is irony in their use in this country by men who, when forced by many wars and the persecution of petty princes to leave their homeland, had deliberately left behind their respect for armorial bearings and had arrived imbued with a fierce dislike of king-craft.

Highly decorative birds are one of the favorite motifs. While the greatest number are sheer stylizations, a few are identifiable as parrots, peacocks, eagles, and doves. Pomegranates, plucked from traditional textile designs, disclose their Persian inspiration. Ingenuously drawn angels, worldly human figures, and an occasional mermaid are quaintly delineated. Heart shapes are very common, with symbolic religious connotations. Pictorial representations of actual objects taken from nature or landscapes are infrequently encountered, but geometrical forms are often seen. The use of architectural forms and constructions seem of nineteenth-century inspiration.

Besides producing *Taufscheine*, the fractur writer illuminated family records in Bibles, drew and painted the frontispieces in song-books, made charming bookplates, and lettered the *"Haus-segen"* or house blessing—a prayer invoking the blessing of God on the family and its dwelling.

Each fractur writer seems to have adhered closely to his original choice of motifs, introducing slight variations in arrangements to avoid monotony, but nevertheless retaining his own decorative idiom over a period of many years. As a practical workman, he saw no good reason to change an already satisfactory design, perfectly acceptable to his undemanding clientele. As a schoolmaster, if he occasionally discovered a gifted pupil he expected the pupil to copy the fractur set before him. The student, perhaps planning to set out as a schoolmaster himself, drew and colored as faithfully as his ability permitted, but as he was even further removed than his master from the original European source of inspiration, the pupil's work almost always shows an artistic deterioration—unless he was specially gifted. Occasionally, by an infusion of fresh ideas offered by more highly skilled penmen newly come from overseas, the degenerative processes resulting from copying were temporarily halted.

Many persons who were not creative artists nevertheless had a lively urge to draw and paint. At a time when all other amusement was rigidly limited, an indulgence in drawing and painting was sometimes permitted on Sunday afternoons. Beautifully executed religious texts and precepts in fractur were set before young persons as models. These they laboriously copied, deriving both pleasure and, it was hoped, spiritual profit from the quiet task. Customs changed slowly, successive generations occupied themselves in the same fashion as their parents, and so motifs passed on from parent to child. One of these transmitted fractur designs unconsciously records the history of the paper-making industry, from the original on handmade rag paper, through one on a machine-made stock, to the final copy, which is drawn just as painstakingly on a wood-pulp, blue-ruled paper of the type used by children in school.

But children were not the only perpetuators of tradition. The professional fractur writers themselves repeated the same design over and over. Some seem totally unaware of the social changes taking place about them. At the time of the Civil War, they are still tracing off ladies dressed in a costume fashionable in the Revolution, a motif which the fractur writer must have acquired from a distant predecessor in the art.

Beautiful fractur writing is sometimes found in the account books kept by artisans and craftsmen other than calligraphers. In these old ledgers, pages or borders of fine ornament are interspersed with matter-of-fact records of customers' names and charges for labor. It must have been a lively love of decoration that found an outlet for itself in this fashion. If, as sometimes happened, several generations thriftily used the same account book, the life of the fractur tradition was prolonged, for each generation conscientiously adorned their own pages with the colorful work, tracing line for line the motifs their ancestors had drawn.

When the State system of free public schools replaced the privately supported schools which had been kept up by the Pennsylvania Germans ever since their arrival, the country schoolmaster, often none too well trained, sometimes lost his job. If he was a specialist in fractur writing, as so many of his kind were, his secondary occupation would still bring him a modest living. Among those custom-loving folk, the Pennsylvania Germans, despite the widening activities of the printing presses, there were many who continued to demand for their family records the gaily painted fractur writings which made such bright, decorative spots on the walls. And so, along with other itinerant craftsmen who made their rural rounds on the dusty roads of the nineteenth century, there went an occasional fractur writer. In horse-and-buggy or on foot, he joined this dwindling company of die-hard artisans, all of whose old-time crafts were so soon to be wiped out by the modern age.

As recently as the beginning of the twentieth century, an elderly man carrying an umbrella and a case containing the tools of his craft could be seen trudging the dusty roads of the most Pennsylvania German of the eastern counties, following his graceful craft. Like any other travelling salesman, the old calligrapher made the rounds of his territory annually, calling on his regular clients. Families who were traditionalists to the core anticipated his coming, saving until his arrival the data that they wished preserved. He was always a welcome visitor. Seated at the center table, he brought the Bible records up to date and gossiped a bit about family histories, for his profession of fractur writer to the neighborhood necessarily acquainted him with its family affairs. In his favorite color, red, he carefully lettered and illuminated the *Taufscheine* his clients ordered. A visit to the local pastor furnished him

197

with the names of the newly baptized and the recently confirmed. Forearmed with this information, he called on their families to acquire new customers.

This old gentleman, a veteran of the Civil War, was one August Bauman, a German-speaking Hungarian emigrant. Though his nationality was Hungarian, his German name, his use of the tongue, and his profession as itinerant fractur writer in Pennsylvania all tend to suggest that he may have come from any of a few locales in Hungary whose customs were so like those of the Pennsylvania Germans that it was necessary for him to make only slight adjustments in order to feel at home. For in Hungary, embedded there like the proverbial fly in amber, are certain villages which maintain a Germanic culture in the midst of the surrounding Magyar one. Set up in the late eighteenth century as a resettlement project, these villages were peopled, as was much of southeastern Pennsylvania, by folk from the Palatinate.

Like the Pennsylvania Germans, these transplanted Palatines were dominated by a passion for scrubbing and housekeeping. Like them, they were governed by the same superstitions and talismanic gestures. Annually, since these folk were faithful to their *mores*, the skilled penman made his calls on his clients to prepare the records they considered essential to the maintenance of their cultural traditions.

A man from such a village, stubbornly determined to follow an outmoded profession, could still have found a field for it among the Pennsylvania Germans even in the late nineteenth century. Because of their fondness for traditional ways, August Bauman, probably the last of the itinerant fractur writers, was able to carry on, past the turn of the century, the profession he loved, the ancient art of manuscript writing.

Fractur Writing in Gothic text, executed by Christian Peters in 1777. Pious, rhymed injunction. Intricately worked initial reflects the last glimmer of the tradition of illumination which, reaching its height in the seventh-century Book of Kells, the famous example of Celtic art, was never surpassed.

Alphabet from *Vorschrift* (writing lesson). Late eighteenth century. Using homemade ink and goose-quill pen, schoolmasters made their own writing lessons. No special system of penmanship was used. Lacking such a standard, the scribe, to show his skill and impress his audience, occasionally shaped letters that were more decorative than legible.

Vorschrift. 1796. The gift of a *Vorschrift* served as a complete writing lesson, a keepsake from teacher to pupil, and an injunction to a godly life.

Elaborately Illuminated Psalm. 1802. Work of the Reverend George Geistweite, Centre County, Pa. (For details, see pages 262-263.)

The carefully differentiated birds and the spotted wildcat are evidence that the maker of this fractur was not only a master of the craft but somewhat of a naturalist as well. The birds are lovingly set down, even to the accurately drawn claws and tongues. The native "bob-cat" seems somewhat abashed by the exotic display into which he wandered.

Birds, Flowers, and Urn.

A red and yellow striped vase is the support for an evenly balanced arrangement of birds and sprays disposed around a curiously constructed central flower. Tiny birds interknit in the design are reminiscent of the work produced on the Ephrata cloisters, shown on pages 206 and 207. Red, yellow, blue, and green define this elaborate conception, drawn on a slightly smaller scale than shown here.

Illuminated Text.

"Roudolph Landes's hand and Quill" set down this graceful spacing of tulips, leafy sprays, and quaint angels, whose crowns levitate as easily as they themselves. The work of a skilled penman who filled in the pious inscription (here omitted) after the decoration was fully drawn. The colors are vermilion, brown, blue, and yellow, painted in the previously quill-outlined motifs. Additional penstrokes of red and yellow were used to enrich certain areas. The text was "written the 6th of February in the year 1816."

Birth and Baptismal Certificates by Martin Brechall.

Martin Brechall, a Hessian, was both an excellent penman and a stern teacher. When not executing birth certificates such as these, he held school in Northampton County, Pa., sometimes in farm kitchens. That he was a prolific worker during the early nineteenth century is evidenced by the many pieces from his hand. These are characteristic.

Illuminated Title Pages from Manuscript Songbooks.

Written in German. Penwork in red, yellow, and the brownish-black of homemade ink. The upper one was made for Barbara Gross in 1812; the lower, for Abraham Oberholtzer in 1814.

THE EPHRATA CLOISTERS

In the Lancaster County wilderness of the early eighteenth century, Conrad Beissel, a dominating religious fanatic, separated himself from a separatist sect, the Dunkers, and founded a celibate community, calling it "Ephrata." His entranced followers adopted new names, gave themselves up to poverty, hard work, noble living, celibacy, and odd mystical beliefs. At its height, in 1757, the colony had three hundred members. Besides being self-sustaining, the members practiced all the monastic arts, illuminating manuscript songbooks, singing together beautifully in chorales, and turning out not only the paper but some of the best bookmaking in the colonies.

In addition to their press, the Ephrata cloisters ran a writing school which copied off by hand the many books needed by the colony. Large sheets of handsome, bold fractur carrying religious texts covered the walls in their buildings. One of their handmade books, "The Christian ABC Book", made by Anastasia and Iphigenia, is a style book for fractur writing. Finished in 1750, this large volume, 12 x 15 inches, contains a series of alphabets of various sizes, the largest being 12 inches high. The capitals, supposed to have been drawn by Beissel, are constructed with a series of swinging, voluptuous curves, all interstices of the letters filled with additional scrollings and floral forms. A passionate devotion to the work caused the individual calligrapher to further elaborate all possible areas with minute stipplings and dottings, in the manner of steel engraving. Significant symbolistic motifs also entered into the enrichment of the capitals.

Decorations on this and the opposite page are typical of minor but delightful fragments used to fill out the unused portions of the staffs remaining after the termination of the music notes in the songbooks.

Courtesy, Historical Society of Pennsylvania, Philadelphia.

206

Cut Paper Art from *"Zum Andenken an Schwester Martha"* (Ephrata manuscript).

Above, right. Page Ornament. Note heart, crown, doves, and tulip incorporated in foliage. Actual size. Drawn around a pattern made from folded and cut paper. Background in fine stippling.

If the ability to draw was lacking, an eighteenth-century Protestant nun of the Ephrata Colony, when asked to contribute a page to an illuminated songbook planned as a gift for a member of the community, was not at a loss. She cut a pattern out of paper, drew around it, and then filled in the background with minute pen stipplings. Thus she held her own among all the beautiful hand-drawn decorations found in the manuscript book of psalm tunes, called *"Zum Andenken an Schwester Martha,"* a combined contribution of the art of the sisters, who labored in loving, mediæval fashion to produce this memorial.

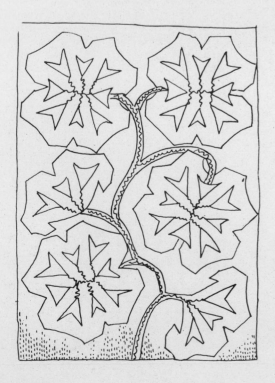

Left. Motif cut out of paper, shifted in various positions to make the design. Slightly reduced.

The human figure is frequently used in the manuscript books. Both men and women wore hooded white robes and wooden sandals.

Birth and Baptismal Record of Elizabetha Bechtel, 1802, Berks County.

Although many such certificates have survived between the pages of old Bibles, some were interred with their owners.

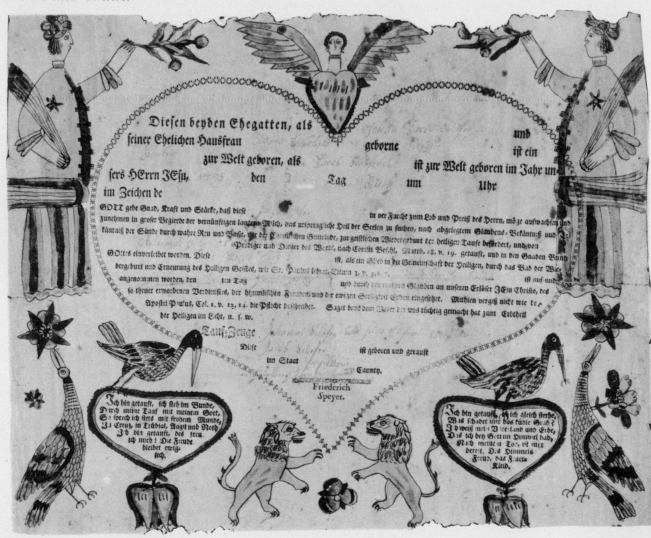

Record of Birth and Baptism.

Early printed form of certificate with hand-drawn decorations of extreme naïveté. The angels are "girdled by the wind." Printed by Friederich Speyer, 1798, in Reading, Pa.

Baptismal Certificate of Elizabetha Schlosser, 1808.

Simple and well-balanced arrangement of tulips surrounding a central heart. Another example of this artist's work is on page 246.

Certificate in Fractur, 1779.

Birth Certificate, the work of a prolific fractur writer of Northampton County. Red, yellow, and the faded brown of old ink define the blowsy female angels hovering over flamboyant flowers and foliage.

Ornamental Drawing on Paper.

Elaborately worked tulips, hummingbirds, barn symbols, and large, unidentified birds create an intricate pattern on this very early piece.

THE WORLD OF FASHION

Birth and baptismal record of Salme (Salome?) Wannemacher, 1809, of North-emton (Northampton) County. Figures from the world of fashion and tulips from the world of the folk fraternize agreeably.

Courtesy, David Ellinger, Trappe, Pa.

Courtesy, Charles Sessler, Philadelphia.

Decorative Drawing.

The inspiration for this fractur drawing comes from sources outside the tradition. Inscription (not shown), translated, reads:

She: "Ah my love, have mercy. Come and kiss me."
He: "I have no time for love. I must practice soldiery."

The Reverend Daniel Schumacher, who wrote this certificate in his own hand (*m p p - mano proprio*) for Christian Kaupp was an active organizer of Lutheran congregations in the early days. His graceful, knowing calligraphy conveys an effect of eighteenth-century daintiness.

In 1822, the birth of Maria Eva Freylinghaus of Jonestown, Lebanon County, was indicated on this record. The fractur motifs served as inspiration for the lower certificate on the facing page.

212

Birth and Baptismal Certificate, 1787.

Although the artist is unknown, his motifs indicate he looked both wisely and well at the work of the Reverend Daniel Schumacher, the upper illustration on the facing page.

Crude, naturalistic portrayal of houses, fences, and trees makes the birth record of Jacob Blanck, born in Lebanon County in 1827, very unusual.

Left. Motif from birth record.

Right. Offhand decoration in red, green, and yellow

Pennsylvania German Watermark, 1776. Actual size, 4″ x 5″.

Excellent paper made by early Pennsylvania mills was sometimes watermarked with curious devices such as this.

Ornamental Drawing. Six birds, five tulips, three hearts, and three urns arranged in a balanced decoration. 12″ x 16″.

214

Verse from Psalm. Made for M. Schwartz, 1836.

Hearts bordered with scallops, together with grotesque, heavy-beaked birds, were the preferred motifs of a fractur writer who signed himself "A.W." He worked in York County in the early nineteenth century.

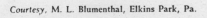

The well-behaved child received, for good behavior, a picture of an animated bird, poised on a floral spray, drawn by teacher's own hand.

Left and above. Characteristic birds taken from other fractur drawings by "A.W."

THE WORK OF
HEINRICH OTTO

Heinrich Otto, of Lancaster County, was an all-round decorator. In the last quarter of the eighteenth century he produced not only fractur paintings drawn by hand but also printed ones, executed from blocks he carved himself. These were later hand-colored and inscribed with the necessary vital statistics. Decorated chests from his hand show much refinement.

Above. Woodblock from which certificates were printed. These motifs, obviously Otto's, were taken over, in part, by the scribe whose work is shown on page 209, lower illustration.

Left. Decoration by Otto. Found pasted inside the lid of a dower chest, a choice and safe place to preserve birth certificates.

Hand-drawn and hand-illuminated fractur by Heinrich Otto. 1782.

216

Wall Motto. Typical motifs used as frame for religious text. Adam and Eve block added to this type of printed sheet. Hand-colored.

Detail from Decorated Chest. Elaborate forms and soft color distinguish the work of Otto on chest made for Jacob Rickert. 1782.

Printed Fractur. Characteristic Heinrich Otto fractur printed from woodblocks in 1784. Calligraphy by Jacob Otto. Units of the design were often juggled about for variety. The cherub's head is a familiar eighteenth-century typographic ornament.

Right. Birth Certificate of Sara Hachenburg, by Francis Portzline. 1819.

Courtesy, National Gallery of Art, Index of American Design.

Watermark of Henry Katz. 1798.

THE WORK OF FRANCIS PORTZLINE

Right. Birth Certificate of Johan Georg Hackmeister, Union Co., Pa. 1800.

Courtesy, Philadelphia Museum of Art.

Watermark, Evergreen tree. 1776.

All watermarks, courtesy, James Francis Magee, Jr., Philadelphia.

Birth and Baptismal Certificate of Benjamin Portzline. 1838.

Though Francis Portzline of Union County signed his work (shown on this and the facing page), even without his signature it is easily identifiable. For he developed a basic scheme and vigorous line to which he generally adhered, although from time to time he added new elements of interest. His drawings of birds approach studies from nature.

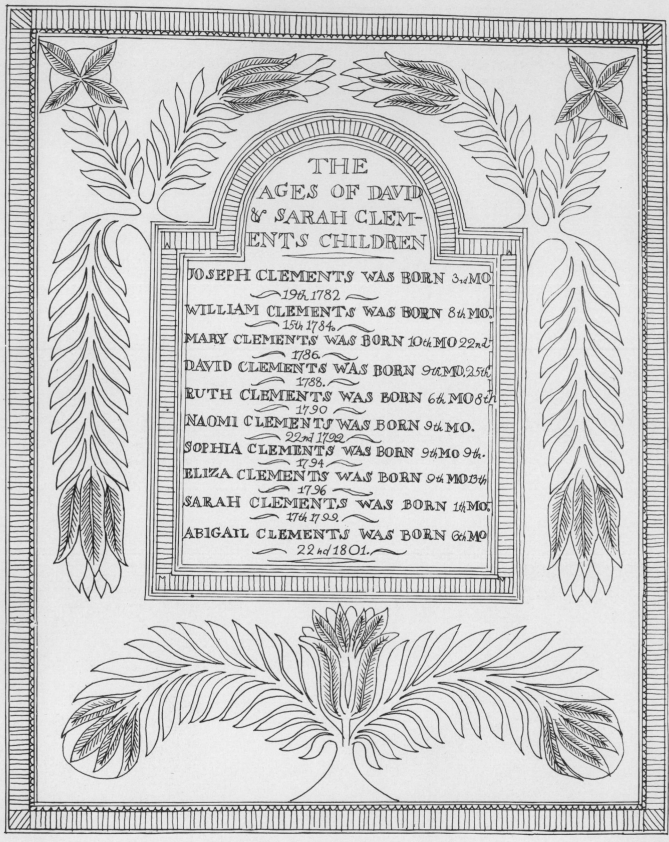

THE
AGES OF DAVID
& SARAH CLEM-
ENTS CHILDREN

JOSEPH CLEMENTS WAS BORN 3rd MO
19th 1782
WILLIAM CLEMENTS WAS BORN 8th MO.
15th 1784.
MARY CLEMENTS WAS BORN 10th MO 22nd
1786.
DAVID CLEMENTS WAS BORN 9th MO. 25th
1788.
RUTH CLEMENTS WAS BORN 6th MO 8th
1790
NAOMI CLEMENTS WAS BORN 9th MO.
22nd 1792
SOPHIA CLEMENTS WAS BORN 9th MO 9th.
1794
ELIZA CLEMENTS WAS BORN 9th MO 13th
1796
SARAH CLEMENTS WAS BORN 1th MO.
17th 1799.
ABIGAIL CLEMENTS WAS BORN 6th MO
22nd 1801.

Birth Record of the Clements Children.

Birth records were occasionally used by the English colonists, who took over the idea of *fractur* and developed a personal interpretation of it. This consists of a simple decorative declaration of the name and date of a child's birth and the name of its parents. But the Clements family waited until the family roster of ten was complete before committing its members' names to paper. Set in a modest Georgian panel, the vital statistics are excellently lettered. The decoration framing it results from a curious marriage of the then fashionable English tradition and the Pennsylvania German tradition, but so deftly has it been accomplished that it cannot be termed a *mésalliance*.

Birth and Baptismal Record of Susanna Kreb. 1838.

By the second quarter of the nineteenth century outside influences have visibly altered the character of fractur. Folk motifs are replaced by the backwash of the much earlier classic revival. In this design, common to Centre County, itself a region far removed from the original settlements, statuesque but démodé ladies pose before a naïve entablature.

Left. Birth record on facing page has unusual black ground, embellished with red and white.

Right. Watercolor made for "Miss Frances Taylor 1831," a drawing which found a ready sale over a long period. As fashions changed, so did the costume. As social attitudes altered, so did its details; the wine glass becomes a bouquet; the decanter, a vase.

Courtesy, Mrs. Norman A. Anders, Towamencin Township, Montgomery Co., Pa.

Above. Cacti, a precious novelty in the 1840's were the pride of the farm wife who brought one on to bloom. In her bold treatment of the scarlet *phyllocactus*, set in its scalloped blue-green leaves, Maria records that family pride.

By the 1840's, even the most rural districts were relinquishing their traditional points of view, a change which can be deduced from the nature of the studies in the painting book of Maria Heebner, a young Schwenkfelder girl of Montgomery County, Pa.

Although Maria sometimes painted the time-honored motif of a bird on a flowering spray, and copied pictures of rabbits and dreamy little boys, she also carefully observed the potted plants in her home, the flowers in the garden, the fruits and vegetables on the farm. These she drew with a love of the flower itself, a sure feeling for decoration, and an inherent delight in color.

In her painting book are the red and yellow columbine, the daffodil and cowslip, the perky johnny-jump-up, a pink rose in a pot, and a yellow rose, complete with thorns and prickles. She tried several times to paint an intense blue iris, flanked with butterfly. With rose-colored hyacinths, a difficult subject, she was quite successful. The tulip appears but once, unquestionably drawn from nature; in the one subject where one could have expected folk memory to dominate, it is completely absent. After putting down strawberries, fruit in baskets, a few birds on twigs, her interest flagged. It is said a concerned stepmother saw to it that she made the best of her talent; so after a long interval (for there are no summer flowers shown), she again began painting, carrying on with the unusual red tigridia, a spray of purple grapes, the red oleander, and a hickory nut on its branch, certainly an unusual selection.

Even the humble cucumber with its yellow flower was not ignored. Maria set it down conscientiously to its last tendril and bristle.

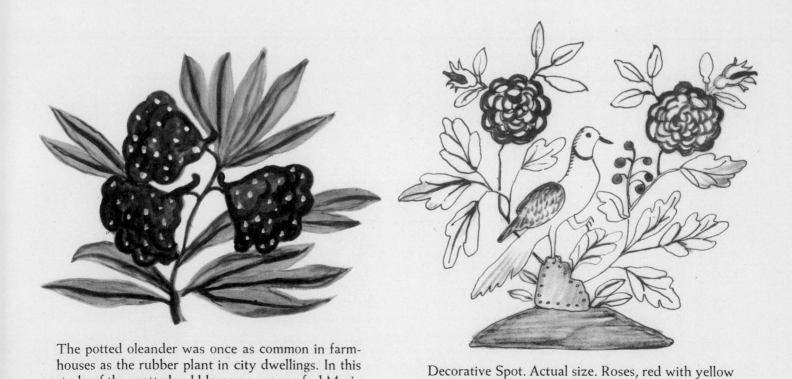

The potted oleander was once as common in farmhouses as the rubber plant in city dwellings. In this study of the spotted red blossoms, we can feel Maria Heebner's affection for it.

Decorative Spot. Actual size. Roses, red with yellow centers. Birds, yellow with black spots. Leaves and base, green. Berries, blue.

THE LOVE OF COLOR

"The barns are built of stone, very large, and have, in the lower part, the stables, with eight or twelve doors and windows, and over this is the barn, properly so called. At the end of the building there is a passage where the wagons stand under cover; the windows, doors and roof are frequently painted of a reddish brown color; cattle of all kinds surround these farms."
—Maximilian, Prince of Wied,
Travels in the Interior of North America 1832-1834

THE farm landscape in eastern Pennsylvania is a colorful one. On the warm red of the soil, the diverse crop plantings impose a varicolored pattern of vegetation, a pattern bordered with an edging of distant bright blue hills and accented here and there with the red of barns. And as if this were not enough, the folk who dwell in these regions resort to cans of paint in diverse colors to add their own suggestions for heightening an already brightly pigmented scene.

Both men and women are passionately good housekeepers. The neatness of the farm buildings, the care of the fences and hedgerows, the love of fresh paint noted everywhere, are but extensions of the housekeeping instinct which finds its outlet in constant improvement of every section of the property, whether it be expended all over a farm or confined to the limited space around a village house. In addition to being kept beautifully tidy, a property will be made as colorful as its owner's ingenuity can devise, for the love of strong color is still a dominant passion in the Pennsylvania Germans. Though the æsthetic value of the results, as demonstrated by examples one sees everywhere, may well be disputed, there is no gainsaying this love of color. It stems from a long folk tradition behind these people, a rustic tradition in which bright hues furnished their forebears a cheap and satisfying substitute for bourgeois elegancies in matters of surface and texture. In their use of color there is no restraint or repression.

The eye of a Pennsylvania German would be starved by the white, black, and green of New England, and the grey and white of the lovely stone houses of the English settlers in the State were as little to his taste. When a farmhouse of this type came into his possession, he enlivened its Quaker coloring by any means at hand, for in its original state he thought it cold and repellent.

Perhaps it was this very greyness of the local stone which led the Pennsylvania Germans into such a lavish use of red in flowers and paint, for of all colors it is their favorite. Apart from its predominance on the farm buildings—a subject that will be dealt with more fully later on—red is a color which holds them entirely under its sway. Not for these rural folk are the subtle shades, those to be found in floral hybrids—the delicate mauves, off-

225

yellows, faint pinks and lilacs, for they consider them "washed-out," a term they would apply to fabrics of the same hues. With a can of red paint, an active and energetic Pennsylvania farm woman will create novel and even startling effects. After she has attended to the whitewashing of all the fences, the lower parts of the trunks of the fruit trees on the lawn, and even mountain boulders if she is settled in a region where they crop out in the grass, she adds decorative notes. The chairs on the porch will sing out in a well-considered scarlet, and discarded iron kettles, once so important in the fireplace, now used no longer, are given a coat of the same color, are supported on three sticks, and then are set out under the trees on the lawn, to hold a cherished house plant. A discarded kitchen boiler is irresistible; to use it in another capacity appeals to her sense of thrift. An equally thrifty male member of her family saws it in half lengthwise; then it too is covered with scarlet, filled with pink and purple petunias, and set out as a pair of handsome flower boxes.

The flower gardens of the present-day country women are just as indicative of their color preferences. Out of the great variety of hues offered in the floral catalogues, pure reds, purples, and pinks are still the favorites, with yellow and white much less in evidence. Plants of a neat habit of growth exert a special appeal, particularly if they turn red some time in their life cycle. *Kochia*, or fire-bush, is a favorite in country gardens, for its neat, green, unimaginative, oval forms, turning a dismal red in the autumn, make it a popular border plant, often used to surround a central planting of vermilion cannas and purple petunias. Scarlet sage has a perennial appeal, and as if by predestined affinity, is almost invariably seen in juxtaposition to red brick. This same building material is frequently the background for barberries, which can always be relied on to turn to a cheery autumnal warmth, and for red Japanese maples, which state their position as to color with their first young leaves.

Brick itself is rarely left to weather in order to soften its natural hue. Instead it is often treated to a fresh coat of strong red paint. As it is both expensive and troublesome to have the lines of the pointing repainted, the red expanse usually blares forth unbroken by any line of white. The city of Reading (pronounced Redding) has always seemed to me to be most aptly named. Viewed from a height, the older portion of it presents the effect of a solid red mass, set off only by the green of foliage. Not only did its worthy citizens follow the prevailing fashion of painting the bricks a relentless, heavy red, unmitigated by any tinge of brown, but they gave the house roofs a coat of the same color. This accounts for the curious effect, noticeable in lesser degree, in other old Pennsylvania German towns. The prevailing redness is taken for granted by the dwellers in the towns, who accept it without question as the color assigned by tradition to brick buildings. Even though a present-day tavern keeper, to attract attention, may paint his pre-Revolutionary brick building a modern white, he sees to it that all the architectural details, even the rainspouts, are picked out in a lovely scarlet.

While this love of red is rarely departed from except for an occasional flier in orange on porch furniture, I recently noted a very old country bar-room and hotel which had swung over to the cooler end of the spectrum for its color scheme, with results quite as dazzling. Against a background of plain grey stucco, its porches and tiers of highly ornamental, cast-iron balconies, which by long tradition are usually painted black, are now accented with two tones of the most intense blue the painter could supply. Blue also defines all the wooden trim on the building and makes a fine contrast to the red and yellow of the beer advertising posters.

The fondness for strong color brought in by the Germanic colonists had at first little outlet. Intense preoccupation with mere survival took up all their waking hours. The first log house with its crude dull brown surfaces was soon made even more sombre by layers of soot and smoke. Later on, as lime was available for the purpose, its interior darkness was mitigated by whitewash. While this certainly made for a lighter if not gayer interior, the opportunity for bright color was not presented until furniture began to be built of something more than crude sections of logs.

Now, confronted by smooth surfaces, the temptation to spread color was irresistible —and Venetian red, a red oxide of iron (the pigment known as barn red), was painted on everything that would take it—a gaudy practice which set the Pennsylvania Germans apart from their neighbors, who evidently left their furniture in the browns of nature. It was not a practice which elicited general admiration; rather it tended to bring forth disparaging comments such as one made by Dr. Johann David Schoepf, a highly educated, scientifically minded gentleman, himself a German but hailing from another region of the homeland. Travelling here in 1783-1784, he became rather petulant about the natives' lack of zeal in improving themselves socially, and thought they lived, in the country particularly, not only thriftily but badly, with every action controlled by their dominant passion, the acquisition of more land. He notes, "The economy of the German farmer is precisely the same as that customary in Germany, even though his neighbor sets him a better example. A great four-cornered stove, a table in the corner with benches fastened to the wall, *everything daubed with red.*"

Besides appealing to his color sense, the use of red oxide of iron appealed to the farmer's sense of thrift, for it was not expensive. Even the linseed oil, the medium in which it was mixed, was something he himself produced, for it was pressed from his flax-seed, carefully saved at his annual flax harvesting. But though the eminent Doctor Schoepf was distressed by his fellow countryman's peasant-like manner of housing himself, in common with every other traveller he gave unstinted admiration to the great barns, whose enormous surfaces incidentally provided the largest area on which to use red paint. No matter how inconspicuous the family lodging place, these barns were flaunting advertisements of good management and successful farming. Even the most superficial and frivolous passerby (and there were some who travelled the same roads as the profoundest professors) could not fail to note these imposing buildings, three and four stories high, with their stone ends and thatched roofs.

Although the desire to own land may have seemed a puerile ambition to the eminent Dr. Schoepf, it was that very desire that made the German the outstanding farmer he undoubtedly was, for he not only respected but husbanded the soil. By practising rotation of crops and returning fertilizing elements to the soil (a method at first ignored by his English neighbors), he set a new pattern for farming. The German settlers were the first to give the barn its position of prime importance in their scheme of agricultural planning, a place it still holds.

These barns are known as Swiss bank-barns. They are often very large, and in early days were built of squared logs, thatch-roofed. Today they are built of stone and wood, or of brick with a wooden superstructure. They face south, so that sunlight falls in the barnyard, with the great doors leading to the upper story, the entrance to the haylofts, on the north side. Wherever possible the barn is built into a rise of ground in order that the hay wagon may be driven directly into the upper story. If the surrounding ground is flat, it is necessary to build a stone-walled ramp to make entrance at the upper level possible. The walls of a barn built of stone are often of a fortress-like thickness. In barns with the end-wall construction of brick, ventilation is provided for by leaving openings between the bricks, arranged in nicely spaced, decorative patterns which furnish an unexpected touch of ornamentation.

On both stone and brick barns, the side overlooking the barnyard is made of wood which juts out over the lower foundation of stone for about six feet, affording, underneath, a sheltered walk the whole length of the building. Under this "overshoot" is a series of doors, each divided in half, horizontally; these open on to the stalls of the stock. The great, flat wall above them, sometimes 100 feet long, whose plane is unbroken except by necessary doors and windows, offered a wonderful surface for decoration. The settlers, particularly those of Swiss descent, with a long tradition of decorated buildings behind them, hitherto had lacked the place and opportunity for this type of colorful expression, for in this country the rough stone of the dwellings they built presented a surface that posed a problem. The decorative tradition was maintained, however, and the difficulty of surface overcome, by transplanting the idea from the house to the face of the barn, on the wooden surface of which it was easy to paint.

While decorated barns are no longer found in all the regions settled by the Palatine immigrants, they continue plentiful in a few of the eastern counties, particularly Berks, Montgomery and Lehigh. Here heavy "barn red" still furnishes the background for colorful geometrical motifs, often five and six feet across. These are arranged in as balanced a fashion as possible, in spite of restrictions imposed by doors and windows, whose positions are dictated by necessity and are not controlled by strict architectural canons. There is a great variety of pattern in the geometrically divided circles, a variety which seems to be limited only by the decorator's patience and by his ingenuity in wielding the large wooden compass with which he chalks out the designs on the wooden wall. When freshly painted, the colors used are apt to be brilliant yellows, blues, reds, and greens, which, together with white, are defined with vigor against the red ground. Time softens them to a pleasant unity with their background.

The number of the circular decorations used on the barn varies: on the main face there may be only two or as many as seven, for their number is governed by the number of blank spaces available between the openings, a number which changes with each barn, there being no exact pattern for the placement of doors and windows. When they are painted as a pair, the same device is used. When more than two symbols are used, they may vary, and do, both in pattern and size, the central one being the largest. The gable ends of barns are equally well decorated, sometimes with the same devices that are used on the face, often with different ones. The structural lines of the barns are usually bordered with broad white bands, a treatment also used to define the door and window trims. In addition, supplementary false arches are painted over the doors and windows, occasionally interlacing in a Moorish manner. These bands create an additional space-filling feature.

In certain districts the lower edge of the barn face, instead of being defined with the straight white band, has the upper rim of this band carefully marked out in scallops, which stand out against the red background like an old-fashioned white cambric petticoat ruffle against one of red flannel. In addition to painted lines defining non-existent arches, the four corners of the face are sometimes filled with quarter circles, subdivided into fan-like segments, which further enliven the general effect.

In horse-and-buggy days the decorator of barns seems to have limited his output to an area which he could reach conveniently in his leisurely vehicle, for in any given neighborhood there will be found a great similarity in the motifs. Neither the country painter or his client strove for originality. After the decorator, a practical man, planned a pattern, he used it on the barns of all his clients, introducing variations only when the spaces on the barn compelled it. Drive on a few miles beyond the periphery of a certain decorator's art and your eye will be caught by another demonstration of what can be done with a geometrically divided circle. The device most frequently met is based on six divisions, for obviously that is the easiest to make with a compass. Symbols planned with four and eight segments are next in frequency. In certain sections the barns will be taken over by someone who was adept at working on a basis of sixteen divisions. Within these fine subdivisions the decorator created patterns which in their intricacy sometimes roughly suggest rose windows.

Before the era arrived in which primitively drawn horses and cows began to be painted freehand in the spaces formerly occupied by the geometrical symbols, a compass and a straight edge were the only tools necessary in order to work out even the most elaborate

229

patterns. At first glance it might seem surprising that the most generally used motif, the tulip, is never in evidence on the barns. But as these designs were painted on the barns at a considerable height from the ground, it is obvious that a free-hand design could never be tackled with any assurance that it would turn out as planned; whereas a rigid, un-emotional tool like the compass could be depended upon absolutely to produce the same satisfactory result each time. Even the device of the heart, frequently seen, is constructed geometrically on a base of tangent circles.

These symbols are generally believed to be "hex signs," a term disliked by present-day rural Pennsylvanians. Their purpose supposedly was to protect the barn from lightning, and the livestock from harm resulting from the machinations of witches. Though there is probably reason to think that some such superstition once accounted for the practice, it is evident that it is no longer the controlling motive. The lightning rod salesman has been far more persuasive than the belief in ancient magic, for most of the decorated barns, though dazzling with motifs, are equally well equipped with lightning rods. At the present day, when a farmer renews the decorations on his barn every time the barn is repainted, it is probable that he does it because it appeals to his sense of decoration and enhances the appearance of the farm.

But this striking tradition is slowly being wiped out. Nowadays one sees far too many barns whose symbols have been painted over, as the faint traces of their outlines seen through coats of paint rather sadly bear witness. In some areas, modern many-windowed barns, in grey, white and yellow, built without the distinctive overhang of the Swiss bank-barn (which, while undeniably picturesque, kept sunlight from lighting the dark interior), are gradually replacing the decorated red barns. Severe and sanitary, they demonstrate the triumph of modern scientific farming over old folk ways. Because barns of this later type no longer invite the colorful decorations once so generally used by a folk deeply attached to their own traditions, their adoption is removing the last traces of a unique manner of exterior ornamentation.

Still the love of strong color persists, to find its outlet elsewhere. While the refined world shudders at the color magenta, and ladies of the garden-club level consider it a sign of original sin if it crops up uninvited in their borders, the Pennsylvania Germans not only harbor it in their gardens but introduce it on their tables. They delight in magenta-colored, pickled, hard-boiled eggs, which, when cut in half, display their greenish-yellow yolks, a color combination which makes the sensitive shudder. To prepare this gaudy comestible, a commonplace article of food among Pennsylvanians and without which no country picnic would be complete, the eggs are submerged in a mixture of beet juice and vinegar, which can always be relied on to produce a strong purple-pink. Farm women heighten the color of other articles of food. Cabbage salad or cole-slaw is made a bright greenish yellow by the addition of turmeric, a spice that enhances both the flavor and the hue.

Noodles for soup and pot-pie (a boiled dough cooked with chicken) are colored yellow with saffron. While it has lost its position as a desirable flavoring in the western world, except in Levantine regions and in countries where the Moors once penetrated, nothing gives more evidence of the great conservatism of the Pennsylvania Germans than to find saffron still in use in the country, at least until very recently. As a medicine it has a most ancient history, so it is not surprising to find it formerly used by old-fashioned country folk as a tea to "bring out the spots in measles," or to learn that its strong yellow color was considered magically effective for jaundice. Until the introduction of aniline coloring matter, saffron had a very definite place in the kitchen, for it was used to give a better color to butter. The country folk value it very highly, and when the imported saffron was unprocurable they found a substitute in the stigmas of the spring crocus, the sight of whose purple, yellow, and white blossoms is so welcome after a long winter. A careful observer driving along the country roads when the crocus was in bloom might note a patch of purple flower petals lying on the grass outside the whitewashed fence which surrounded the dooryards of the farms. To the initiate this was a sign that the housewife had finished gathering the tiny stigmas of the crocus blossoms in order to acquire her yearly supply of saffron—the purple patch consisted of the discarded petals.

The Easter tradition of dyeing eggs in bright colors and patterns and the use of the rabbit as a symbol of the season were introduced into this country by the early German immigrants, and spread from them to the English-speaking regions. The custom of egg-hunting outdoors is an equally old German fashion brought over unchanged—the practice much more general in times when eggs were a less esteemed and less expensive article of food. Brightly colored eggs were hidden in the garden and in the house, in places accessible to small children, who, basket in hand, were delighted to hunt for these gay objects. Sometimes they found not only the many-colored ovals but the Easter rabbit himself, whom they believed to have placed them in the shrubbery, in the crotches of the fruit trees, or underneath the delicate new leaves of the plants.

Before the days of commercial egg-dyes, the housewife evolved various ways of coloring the eggs, methods brought from overseas and used here in the manner of her forebears. If eggs were boiled in water in which onion skins were placed, the shells took on a variety of pleasing shades of a rich reddish brown, depending on the strength of the infusion. Extra ornamentation was obtained by scratching designs on this color. Scraps of calico were saved from year to year to provide bright colors and patterns which could be transferred to the eggs. When the egg was tied up in a scrap of calico and then boiled, the pattern and color were transferred from the printed cotton to the receptive surface, with incidental blurrings.

One of the really curious folk objects, representing another transplanted Germanic custom, was produced for the Easter celebrations by the local bakers. From the same dough with which they made their loaves, the bakers fashioned the Easter Rabbit which supposedly laid the eggs. On this bread sculpture they placed a raisin for the eye, and, in what is definitely a peasant-like conception, they inserted a dyed, hard-boiled egg in a position which furnished convincing proof to the child consumer that the rabbit was the source of the egg. The location for the egg was set by tradition. Though it was immodestly placed directly beneath the tail, the position was accepted unquestionably by all small children. But Anglo-Saxon delicacy winced when it noted the peasant directness of the placement, and the bakers, to mollify these American customers of theirs put the bright egg in the abdominal region. Even this was a little too strongly suggestive for the ultra-refined, who again registered their protests. Now certain chastened bakers, when they make the Easter rabbit for their clients, omit the egg, as a sacrifice to American prudery, leaving the rabbit with no visible evidence of his procreative ability to support the weight of the entire tradition.

What a sojourn in the oven did to this form modelled out of bread-dough was startling, and apt to depress anyone sensitive to form. But to those folk, devoted to ancestral customs, these baked rabbits with their highly colored eggs were an essential part of any celebration of Easter.

Though there are comparatively few outlets left for the personal expression of a love for color and pattern, the Pennsylvania German woman has artlessly supplied herself with one which not only gratifies her eye but is satisfactory to her creative sense. While she cares for her houseplants, with which she fills every available window in the winter time, she can revel daily in the clash of scarlet against magenta, lemon, and purple, of green against orange and pink. For these startling color schemes—so recently taken up by modern designers and labelled Brazilian, Ecuadorian, or nondescript "peasant"—have always been acceptable to the country woman, for she saw them daily in her collections of handsome and brilliant houseplants. The Pennsylvania country women in particular have always had great "luck" with plants. Despite the dicta of garden clubs, which prefer that leaves appear in their usual green, patterned and multicolored foliage have a particular appeal for them; so the richly colored, variegated coleus and figured-leaved geraniums will be featured in the assortment of plants, once housed by an earlier generation in old tomato cans but now flourishing equally well in contemporary containers.

Slips of a cherished plant will pass as gifts between friends. Women take an enormous but quiet pride in the fine condition in which they keep their plants, and like to share that pride with the passerby. Once, in a small neat town, I saw an extraordinary specimen of an African Violet, with the pot tilted in such a fashion that its purple perfection could not fail to catch the eye of everyone. The owner, having taken superb care of it, felt that she had a creative share in producing its intense color and innumerable blossoms. In the identical spirit that makes an artist exhibit his paintings, she was demonstrating with this charming display her own artistry, in her own gallery, the parlor window.

These colorful galleries of the Pennsylvania Germans are so outstanding that a glance at the windows will furnish a clue to the ancestral background of the inhabitants of any house. Travel any main road out of Philadelphia, and when every window you see is crowded with a collection of superbly healthy plants, instead of a few specimens, you will know you have arrived in a "Pennsylvania Dutch" section.

Another plant which must have been grown for the pleasure it gave the eye as well as for its value in folk medicine is the "balsam apple," (*momordica balsamina*), a climbing vine once very common in regions settled by Germanic folk. There is nothing else in the vegetable world quite like its knobby, gourd-like fruits, which, after ripening to a brilliant orange, burst open in three or four sections to disclose a remarkable crimson interior, filled with crimson seeds. They look for all the world like fleshy, pendant lilies, morbid blossoms far removed from the earthy uses to which they were once put. For these startling fruits, steeped in bottles of oil, once provided the traditional European household remedy for cuts and bruises, burns and chapped hands, a remedy used without alteration by all Palatines. Though the balsam apple certainly delighted the eye of the housewife when her glance fell on its tropical brilliance brightening the trellis around her kitchen porch, she had other than æsthetic plans for it, since it was destined to be submerged in alcohol as well, to transform it into what was then considered an infallible cure for rheumatism. Still seen occasionally today, it is probably cultivated only because of its striking form and irresistible color, for even the most conservative folk are aware that in the modern world there are many remedies far less painful in their application than the stinging poultice of the balsam apple.

Although it was comparatively easy during the growing season to have plenty of color outdoors, and in the winter time the windows were gay with plants, women used to resort to ingenious homemade methods to introduce color elsewhere. In the bedrooms it was not difficult to achieve, for any of the work of their own hands, the strongly patterned and brilliantly colored quilts and coverlets, furnished a focal center. In earlier days, cotton textiles seem to have been the chief source of brilliant color. Only a few out of the great range of rainbow-hued pigments available nowadays to every woman who has an urge to brighten walls or furniture were then obtainable. And they had to be purchased, a matter of considerable importance to the farm wife in earlier days, for she had little or nothing to expend on such frivolities.

Women who longed for something gayer than the cold, utilitarian, unattractive white-wash which covered the walls of their houses solved their problem in various ways. Those who were easily satisfied tinted the whitewash a light blue, for that coloring was at hand— a dash of the same bluing used in the weekly laundry. Those who craved a warmer color or even dreamed of wallpaper, when there was no money to spend on it, were put to more trouble. Nevertheless, ingenious women worked out methods which both accomplished their ends and gratified their sense of thrift, a dominant consideration. A woman could start with whitewash and end up, after considerable hard work, with a patterned, dull-rose wall, quite as satisfying in her eyes as the unattainable wallpaper. Begging her husband for some of the Venetian red, the basis of barn paint, she mixed it with the whitewash. This combination produced a dull pink, the intensity of which was easily varied by the addition of more or less whitewash. To keep it from rubbing off, skim milk, a product always available on a farm, was added as a binder. If the dull pink on the wall still did not suggest the wished-for wallpaper, she did not renounce the beauty she had visualized. Cutting a large potato in half crosswise, she whittled a geometrical design in it. This primitive printing block, dipped in uncolored whitewash and pressed on the wall, left a satisfactory white pattern on the dull rose ground.

But even the lack of common Venetian red as a tinting agent did not hinder a woman determined to have a more colorful wall. Recently I heard of an elderly country woman who took great pride in her newly tinted kitchen walls, of a rose-beige hue, a color she herself created and applied. This aristocratic tint was obtained by the simplest, most peasant-like means. Living in a neighborhood where there were many outcroppings of the rock known as red shale, this doughty female took herself to a likely spot, where the wheels of many wagons passing over the shale had crushed it to a dull reddish dust. This dust, passed through a very fine sieve, provided her with a dull red coloring matter, which, when added to kitchen whitewash, gave it a soft tone of the utmost refinement.

Touching attempts such as these in decorating walls are all that remained of the European tradition of interior wall ornamentation, an art practised on various cultural levels in every country. In the Old World, country as well as city churches had elaborately patterned walls, executed by the local decorators, whose product, even if not artistically well-conceived, nevertheless satisfied the rural clientele. Though mass migration and the difficulties inherent in making a new settlement in this country interrupted the immediate transplanting of this tradition, it is heartening to find that when the new settlers planned the building of a permanent church edifice, the colorful tradition of the homeland, and not the plain and austere traditions of the new country, still had its influence on the decoration of the interior. This is evidenced by the description of a country church built in 1762 by a Reformed congregation in Worcester Township, Montgomery County, Pennsylvania, which was the seat of some of the earliest settlements. Some sixty years ago, a county historian, indulging in reminiscence in the fortunately leisurely fashion possible not only to that day but to that profession, described it as "having been painted on the inside with strong colors and highly ornamented with a number of inscriptions on the walls, as is still remembered by many of the older persons. . . . The few highly colored pieces of wood, found underneath the woodwork of the recently demolished church, still indicate the remarkable character of the painting."

Today, as a result of the insistent influences of the changing taste of successive generations, there is left no trace of the peasant tradition of decorating, either in public buildings or private dwellings. Personal expression is now satisfied by working with cans of paint bought at the store and applied with great abandon wherever the wielder of the brush fancies.

As evidence of what can be done in a small space to give vent to this persistent passion for color, something which no fetters of fashion can restrain, I shall describe a farmhouse which I noted in one of the Pennsylvania counties. It was small, square, and white, firmly rooted at the intersection of two country roads. On its simple and pleasing form, doors, window trim and shutters seem to offer the only opportunities for a contrast of color, since it lacked other architectural features which might be picked out in paint. The brown and yellow applied to these features was inoffensive and did nothing to detract from the modesty of the little house. But it was evident that this was not sufficient for its owners; they felt that it lacked vitality, and they remedied that lack with a dose of strong color elsewhere on the grounds. With paint perhaps left over from a scheme of decoration used in the interior of the house, the ordinary galvanized iron mail-box, usually left its inconspicuous grey, was given a coat of intense bright blue. The post on which it stood was enlivened with a violent green. The over-sized, departmentalized "outhouse" was painted a handsome scarlet, bordered on all edges with the brilliant green. Over the whole gay ensemble loomed the heavy, dull red of the barn, which, while restrained by comparison, added its variations to the colorful scheme, which at the time I saw it, was made even more startling by a drift of purple larkspur growing lustily beside the earthen ramp leading to the hayloft.

All this was not the accidental result of an accretion of earlier decorative attempts; each of the colors was fresh, indicating that the paint had been recently applied. It was obviously an expression of the owners' love of color, and as such was put there to be admired.

To this day, in the regions settled by the Pennsylvania Germans, barns bear great circles of ornament. These two and four others, each five feet in diameter, decorate the face of a Lehigh County barn.

Courtesy, Mrs. Naaman Keyser, Jr., Plymouth Meeting, Pa.

Contemporary Barn Symbols from Berks, Montgomery, and Lehigh Counties.

Experiments with the compass resulted in star-shaped or petalled forms. With this tool all possible combinations of entwined curves and straight lines were explored.

Decorated barns are gay affairs. Lines defining non-existent arches were painted over doors and windows. Scalloped bands sometimes edged the face.

From the author's notebook.

Barns were once painted uniformly red. Today they can be seen in white, gray, yellow or green. The ornamental decorations are disappearing.

From the author's notebook.

INDEX

241

244

Urn and Flower Decorations from Early Birth and Baptismal Certificates

This urn was drawn to the right and left of a circle containing the information relating to the birth in 1804 of Henrich Geiger, Heidelberg Township, Northampton County.

The inspiration for this odd plant growth must have been the "crown imperial" (*fritillaria imperialis*), beloved of Colonial gardeners. From a certificate made for Michael Schmidt, 1787, Rey Township, Cumberland County. Woodblocked outline filled in by hand in color. Printed by Johann Valentin Schuller.

245

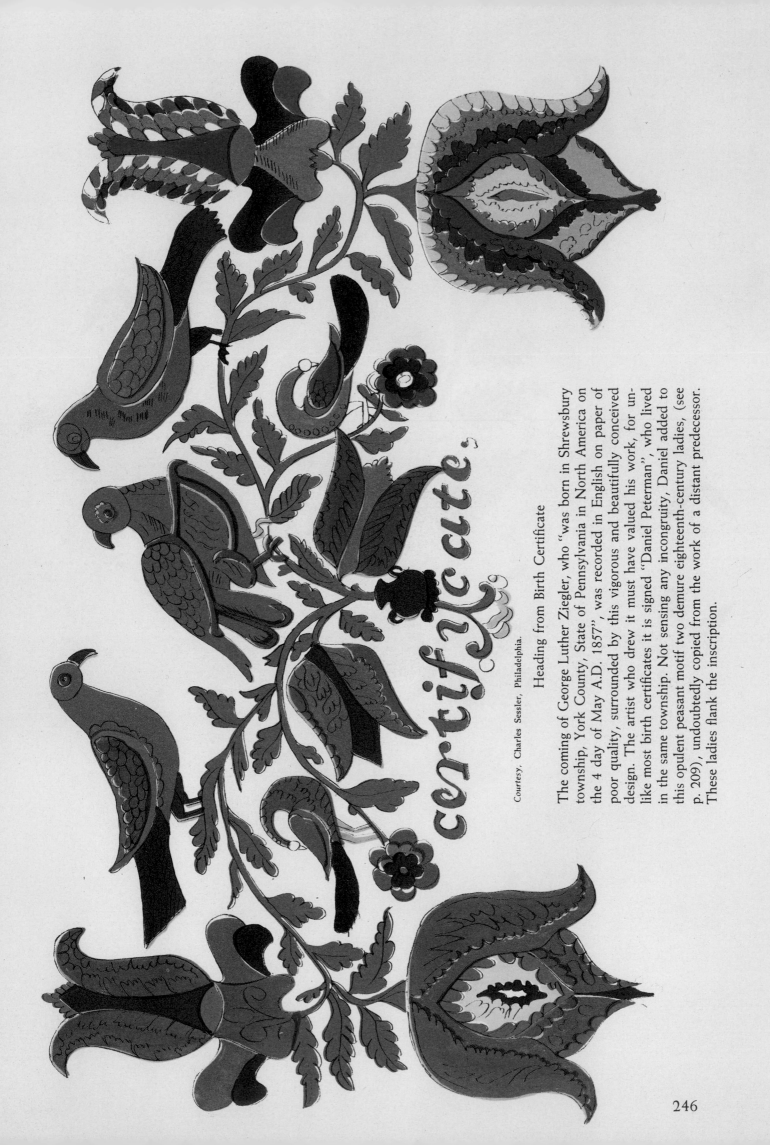

certificate

Courtesy, Charles Sessler, Philadelphia.

Heading from Birth Certificate

The coming of George Luther Ziegler, who "was born in Shrewsbury township, York County, State of Pennsylvania in North America on the 4 day of May A.D. 1857", was recorded in English on paper of poor quality, surrounded by this vigorous and beautifully conceived design. The artist who drew it must have valued his work, for unlike most birth certificates it is signed "Daniel Peterman", who lived in the same township. Not sensing any incongruity, Daniel added to this opulent peasant motif two demure eighteenth-century ladies, (see p. 209), undoubtedly copied from the work of a distant predecessor. These ladies flank the inscription.

246

Stencilled Border

Hand-stencilled design on cotton fabric, only 11½″ wide. This narrowness suggests that it may have been used as a bed valance. In the first four decades of the nineteenth century, stencils were used as a time-saving device by craftsmen, in the decoration of tinware, walls and furniture. As one of the genteel arts, stencilling was also taught to young ladies exposed to the boarding-school education of the period.

Section of Chest Front

Though the artist who decorated this and other notable chests limited himself to his few basic motifs diversely arranged, he never failed to achieve a richly patterned surface. Chests from his hand, with their light-hued panels set against dark gray, green, or mottled grounds are the most elaborate extant. Other examples of his work are shown on pages 92 and 93.

Panel from Chest

One of a pair, painted on unfinished wood. The bold, dark background sets off not only the tulips and pomegranates harmoniously distributed against its rich blue, but it also sets the decoration apart from most others of its ilk, which are usually painted on very light-hued grounds. Another piece by the same decorator is shown on page 106, upper example.

Rhythmic Tulips from a Sgraffito Plate.

From birth certificate.

No matter how quaint the presentation, the lion's tail maintains its traditional heraldic position.

From *fractur* drawing.

Unusual sinister bird, horned and heavily clawed.

From dower chest. The unicorn of fable appears unchanged.

Certain creatures of heraldry were transplanted from the armorial bearings of Old-World families to the birth certificates of Pennsylvania German children, or to the dower chests of young maidens. There they pose proudly amidst incongruous floral embellishments.

Left. From birth certificate.

251

Fragment of Embroidery

In colored silks on fine cotton cloth. This may well have been taken from a baptismal cloth, for in the eighteenth century such cloths were embroidered in a similar fashion.

Chriſtian Graf

1790

Fractur Drawing
Original is 12½" x 15½".

Corner of Appliqué Quilt

The countrywoman's habit of using her appliqué quilts as counterpanes, and then only on high occasions, has fortunately preserved many of them to the present day. Constant service depleted the stock of pieced quilts, though they were made in far greater numbers. As necessary bed coverings, pieced quilts had a long, honorable life; when no longer employable in that capacity, they were demoted to many lowly uses. When they were very old, mounds of them sometimes travelled about in moving vans, serving as covering for equally ancient and humble pieces of furniture, now rising in the world to their new status of "antiques."

For ease in handling, quilts were fashioned in blocks. Pennsylvania women were fond of putting quilt blocks together with contrasting bands, a method which enabled them to introduce additional color, (often to the detriment of the scheme). Nevertheless, this treatment gave their work a feeling of peasant strength and crudity and makes it easily identifiable.

So brilliant are the hues of the quilt shown here (a brilliance which the printing inks used here cannot approach), that they must have been completely satisfying to their user's love of color. The blocks are set together without contrasting bands. On the original, magenta (named after a forgotten Italo-Austrian conflict in 1859, and a color which sets up its own battles), an intense green, and a scarlet are appliquéd on the sharpest of yellow. These bold hues, combined with somewhat familiar design elements, result in a striking motif. In contrast to the strident color, the quilting is most modest: closely spaced, diagonally crossed lines.

Four Quilt Blocks

Selected from a group of motifs, no two alike, unquestionably the personal expression of a Pennsylvania German woman. A primitive and excellent designer, nothing daunted her as subject matter for her conceits; even the Tower of Babel flanked by two palm trees appears in appliqué in the collection.

In making these designs, the needlewoman's approach was strikingly different. She envisaged the quilting not as something superimposed or used to fill blank spaces, but as an integral part of the design.

Courtesy, M. L. Blumenthal, Elkins Park, Pa.

Fractur Drawing, 1797.

Unlike most of his fellow craftsmen, who drew outlines in brownish-black ink, brushing in the color masses, the maker of this *fractur* created an effect of unusual refinement by adding pen-drawn outlines in vermilion and tinting the flower forms with the same linear method.

These delicately patterned areas are set in opposition to strong swirls of color painted in with a brush.

Taufschein of Daniel Dubs

Born in Centre County, Pa., Sept. 22, 1813.

Tulips with chequered bases spraying out from hearts or cartouches are the hallmarks of this *fractur* writer, whose work seems localized in Centre and Union Counties.

Courtesy, Paul M. Auman, Millheim, Pa.

Right. Woodblock.

From printed birth certificate. Carlisle, Pa., 1828.

Courtesy, Philadelphia Museum of Art.

Courtesy, Metropolitan Museum of Art.

Late eighteenth century. From Dauphin County birth certificate.

Left. **From Lancaster County certificate of birth, made for Anna Margaretha Knauer, born in 1766.**

Courtesy, Miss Edna Albert, Gardners, Adams County, Pa.

BIRDS, STYLIZED AND NATURALISTIC

Decoration c. 1850.

This flowing design enhances the pages of an old Lancaster County account book. Three generations used the same ledger; three generations faithfully copied the same motif, the last with colors taken from a child's paint box. Length 12½". Width 7".

Decoration on Chest

One of two panels on dark green chest, balancing a central cartouche lettered "Eva Catharina Geigerin. 1790". Moorish finials on the columns are an oddity. Height of chest 26". Width 50".

Panel from chest made for
Susana Ackerman in 1792.
Body of chest is green;
moldings, red; feet, brown.
The owner's name is en-
closed in a heart-shaped
cartouche.

Enlarged details taken from the *fractur* shown on Page 201, made by a minister of the Reformed Church, the Reverend George Geistweite, who seems to have had both the soul and the patience of a mediæval monk. He, too, like his monastic precedessors, found exquisite pleasure in creating minute detail in his illuminations, filling in every area with loving care, scamping nothing. Every flower petal is tipped with another color; the tiniest bird has claws; the fine checks in the borders are 1/16″ blocks of red, yellow, blue, and green.

Like the mediæval scribes, he loved to draw birds and animals, featuring some as corner decorations and entwining others in elaborate floriated scrolls. On this *fractur* are to be found peacock, deer, unicorn, and lion; horse, bear, dog, cock, and hen; the double-headed eagle, the pelican, and various other carefully drawn but unidentified birds.

Not only was the Rev. Geistweite the circuit-riding minister in Centre County, Pa., from 1794 to 1804 but he was also the schoolmaster of the first school in the county located at Wolf's Chapel, near Aaronsburg, Pa.

Left. Two panels, enlarged from the original size of 1½″ x 4½″. On the margin of the manuscript drawing is written a series of explanatory captions. The upper drawing is titled, "Wait not solitary where an angry unicorn (can approach you)."

These decorations form a frame for quotations from the Thirty-fourth Psalm, 1-4, 13, 14. "I will bless the Lord at all times: His praise shall continually be in my mouth," etc. The *fractur* is marked on the reverse, "Henry Bower (picter February 20th, 1802)".

Motifs on Chest of Drawers c. 1830.

Four-drawer chest, from the Mahantongo Valley, has its dark green body decorated with different motifs, scaled to fit the varying sizes of the drawers. The motifs shown are taken from drawers #2 and #3. Other examples of the work of this region are shown on page 104.

Courtesy, Philadelphia Museum of Art.

Though awkward in appearance, the correctly sloped back and saddle-shaped seats of poplar made plank-bottomed chairs distinctly comfortable. The rounds and spindles of maple or hickory were spoke-shaved or turned on the lathe. The chairs were given three coats of paint and one of varnish before they reached the "ornamenter." Then, with stencil patterns, bronzing powders, raw cotton, camel's hair brushes, and transparent oil stains, he produced the roses, fruit and birds so popular everywhere in the mid-nineteenth century.

Victorian rosebuds, almost unrecognizable in their red and yellow translation, are oddly coupled by a country furniture-decorator with a circle filled with waving vertical lines. Chair painted a brownish black and enlivened with dashes of red, flung with fine abandon on rungs, spindles, and seat.

Courtesy, Carl Schurz Foundation, Philadelphia.

The simplest of all barn symbols, effectively used on the end of a Berks County barn. Scores of variations based on the elementary six divisions of the radius into the circumference show that the untutored mind, charmed with this principle, had lots of "fun with the compasses."

From the author's notebook.

On this barn, tradition and modernity meet. Green asphalt shingles cover all but a panel of the original red wooden surface on which two bold symbols are displayed.

Symbols based on four divisions are easily achieved and, therefore, common. Those based on five points require a knowledge of geometry—so are less frequently seen.

From the author's notebook.

Lid of Trinket Box

Anna Margareda Alberd (Albert), formerly Anna Margaretha Knauer, a fragment of whose birth certificate is shown on page 258, kept her trinkets in an unpainted wooden box, 9½" wide, 20" long. Its sliding cover was decorated with this well-spaced grouping of both familiar and novel conventionalizations, and the empty spaces filled in with an insouciant arrangement of her name and the date, 1793.

Courtesy, Miss Edna Albert, Gardners, Adams County, Pa.

Panel from Dower Chest

Boldness and simplicity are the features of this panel used on the ends of the elaborate chest shown on page 92, lower illustration.

Fractur Painting in Two Colors. 1800.

An unusual restraint in color distinguishes this freely stated decoration. Original is slightly smaller.

Portion of a Book Plate. 1808.

Greatly enlarged from hand-drawn frontispiece of song-book belonging to Anna Hoch.

BIRDS AND PARROTS

The appearance of exotic parrots among every-day Pennsylvania German motifs seems strange until one realizes that the Carolina Parroquet, the only parrot of eastern North America, once flaunted its red and yellow head and green body in Pennsylvania fields. Farmers, enraged at their nibbling of young corn shoots, killed them in great quantities. They are no longer seen.

Detail from birth certificate, York Co., 1801.

Motif from Sgraffito Plate

The designer of this plate must have loved intricate patterns, for he outlined all the main constructions with small strokes and dottings. That he abhorred blank spaces is evident, for he filled every one with an ill-judged application of green blotches (here purposely omitted), which practically obscured his really original treatment of a circular area. The birds are strangely abstract.

Right. Drawn in Bucks County, Pa. "Oct. the 12th, 1820" for Margareth Heller.

Below. From birth certificate belonging to Carl Dietz, born "19 ten May, in Jahr 1818" Lehigh County, Pa.

19th Century Variations in Tulips

From Birth and Baptismal Certificates

The tulip was once made the excuse for a gambling splurge of exactly the same type as modern stock-market speculation. This odd financial jamboree reached its greatest height in the Netherlands from 1634 to 1637. During the "Tulipomania," as the period was dubbed, speculators paid out and received large sums of money for bulbs they never possessed or wished to own. Both high- and low-priced bulbs made it possible for rich and poor to engage in the traffic.

Though the "bubble" collapsed, a genuine love of the flower persisted in real gardeners, who willingly paid comparatively high prices for rare bulbs. Tulips blossoming in many forms and colors not only create one of the garden's high moments but furnish an easily drawn form, which local craftsmen followed until the impulse to decorate completely disappeared.

Panel from Chest

Drawn in full on page 97, upper example. Tulips and urn, quite individualized in form. Languidly but decoratively executed.

Decoration. Birds and Flowers.

Striking, well-contrived design of formal birds and stylized radiating petals, seemingly based on the sunflower. A decoction of the gum which exudes from cherry trees was the *fractur* writer's rural substitute for exotic shellac, and was laid over the colors to heighten and preserve their brilliance. Slightly enlarged from original, which is 6½″ x 7½″. *c.* 1830.

276